JOURNEY OF A LIFETIME: THE FIRST 100 YEARS

The Memoirs of Ilja Buz

July 27, 1920 – July 27, 2020

TATJANA BUZ PITTS

DORRANCE
PUBLISHING CO
EST. 1920
PITTSBURGH, PENNSYLVANIA 15238

Dorrance Publishing Co
585 Alpha Drive
Pittsburgh, PA 15238
Visit our website at *www.dorrancebookstore.com*

ISBN: 978-1-6853-7295-8
eISBN: 978-1-6853-7831-8

JOURNEY OF A LIFETIME: THE FIRST 100 YEARS

The Memoirs of Ilja Buz

July 27, 1920 – July 27, 2020

Dedication
This labor of love is dedicated
to my father, Ilja,
whose stories entertained and enthralled those of us
who were privileged to hear them
to my siblings and their families,
to enjoy and share the rich legacy our father left us,
and to my husband, Duncan,
for his loving encouragement to complete this project.

Introduction

Our father, Ilja Buz, passed away on November 29th, 2020, four months after celebrating his 100th birthday. He left us in the midst of the COVID crisis (although he did not die from COVID), which made attending his funeral to say goodbye impossible for some of us. But he left us with memories of who he was and perhaps that is most important.

He was gentle, hardworking, wise, and caring. He put providing for his family above everything else. In spite of the hardships he experienced or because of them, he would help anyone who needed assistance and was always ready to listen to the problems of others and share valuable insight. He was an amicable man who never met a stranger.

Our father was the consummate storyteller. He enjoyed sharing his experiences with anyone who would listen. And he had a lot of stories to tell. About ten years ago, he was encouraged to write his memoirs so he started putting his stories to paper. He first wrote them in Russian, his first language. A few years later, he translated them into English.

In 2016, the local newspaper did an interview with our father about World War II from his perspective as a Russian soldier. It was also videotaped and has been viewed by more than 68,000 people on YouTube (you can find it by typing in Ilja Buz).

When I retired, I volunteered to edit the English version, to make the stories flow a little smoother. Sadly, the effort took longer than it should but finally, here it is. As I have been rereading and fine tuning each story it reminds me of those times I would come to visit as an adult. Dad and I would sit at the dining room table for hours at a time and I would hear those wonderful stories of his youth, of wartime, of life after the war, immigrating to Canada and so much more. Some of the stories I heard more than once but each retelling revealed another nugget of detail and made the story even richer.

They are stories of hardship and endurance, of struggle and triumph, of desperation and deliverance, of survival and faith. The stories are intertwined with humorous anecdotes and written in such detail that allows readers to see through his eyes. These are the stories of Ilja Buz.

Dad, thank you for your love, wisdom, guidance, and all those wonderful life stories. We love you and miss you. Till we meet again in heaven.

Table of Contents

CHAPTER I

Before I was Born

All the days ordained for me
were written in your book
before one of them came to be.
(Psalm 139:16)

My father's family tree begins with Grandfather Anton. He was married to a village girl named Avdotja. They had five sons and one daughter, who died at an early age. The oldest son, Gerasim, was born in 1880, Piotor in 1883, Alexei (my dad) in 1885, Ivan in 1887 and Pavel in 1889. Grandfather could have been born around 1845–50. Grandfather died around 1894, around the age of fifty, when my father was nine years old. Grandfather had at least one brother, Michael. I don't remember hearing stories from my father about his childhood or what kind of a father he had.

Serfdom was abolished during Father's childhood but a large part of the arable land still remained in the possession of landlords. A household without a horse couldn't cultivate the land and was forced to work solely for a landlord. Those who had a horse were able to rent the land on a fifty-fifty basis, giving half of the harvest to the landowner. Regardless of his large family Anton was better off than other peasants. When he died, Grandmother was left with two horses and two milking cows. With the help of her young sons, she managed to maintain the material wellbeing of the family. I remember Grandmother carrying me in her arms. That would bring her age close to eighty.

The population was mostly illiterate at that time and sending children to school was frowned upon as being a waste of time. Grandmother had a different mindset. Her sons attended parochial school, located eight kilometers away from the village. After four years of schooling her oldest son, Gerasim, stayed home to manage the household. Her second son, Piotor, was able to continue his education and became a teacher when he was seventeen years old. The story was told as follows:

After graduating from parochial school with honors, Piotor was sent for further education forty kilometers away from home. In spite of the disapproval of the villagers, Grandmother loaded two sacks of flour and a live ram on a horse cart and brought Piotor to boarding school. They were met by the principal in an empty class room with desks piled up against one wall. After listening to grandmother's plea, he handed Piotor a sheet of paper and told him to write a short composition. There was not enough light in the room and it was also very cold. Piotor pulled one of the benches close to the window to use as a desk and kneeled beside it as he wrote. His fingers got too cold to hold the pen and he had to stop writing to warm up his fingers by blowing on them and rubbing his hands together.

In those days penmanship was one of the main subjects. I remember Uncle Piotor's handwriting being equally as skilled as the writing on the bank notes of Imperial Russia. A bundle of those out-of-circulation bank notes was kept in the chicken coop and I often admired the writings on them. My father told me that when I grew up, I would own an accordion with the bellows made from imperial bank notes, but it remained an unfulfilled dream.

The boarding school was run like a homestead and grew everything for its own use. Working in the field and looking after domestic animals was a part of the school's program. Graduates became skilled with every facet of village life. They learned how to sow and harvest crops, milk cows, and butcher pigs. They were carpenters and blacksmiths, singers, and chorus conductors. Among the peasants a teacher was the most respected person next to the priest.

As the head of household, Uncle Gerasim was exempt from the draft for regular duty in the armed forces, but after WWI started he was mobilized with the rest and was killed and buried in Austrian territory, leaving behind a wife and daughter. I don't know about Uncle Piotor's service in the army but he returned as a Major-in-reserve.

Alexei, my father, served for four years in an artillery regiment in the Far East, in a Siberian city called Khabarovsk, located on the east bank of the Amur River. Upon completion of service, selected soldiers were offered a trip to the United States for two years. Those who managed to establish themselves during that time could remain there as immigrants or they could return home at government expense. It was an attractive offer, but Father declined the offer, feeling he would be too homesick. In 1929, when the Soviet government started collectivization of the villages, he regretted his decision but it was too late.

Father was commissioned as a supply officer for the trainloads of soldiers returning home. His duties were to feed them and pay them their daily allowance until they reached their destination. I heard this story several times; how proud he was to be trusted with so much money and have an armed guard standing at the door of his compartment. Another story my father told about those times was when he was approached by a bearded man in one of the railroad station's mess halls. This stranger knew where my father was from and named every member of his family. He concluded by predicting my father would live to be eighty-five years old. After two near-death experiences he believed the old man's prediction and practically lived by it. My father died on December 9th, 1969, four months short of his eighty-fifth birthday.

The bedtime stories my father told me were about his life as a soldier. I liked to lie on his bare belly and fall asleep listening to his booming voice.

One story was about how they were fed on Sundays after church. Dinner was a thick soup with a chunk of meat in it and porridge smothered in butter. It sounded so delicious I could almost taste it and it made my saliva run. Sunday's ration also included six walnuts and one hundred grams of vodka. My father said he put on so much weight that his ears became "invisible." For a little boy, who never saw a walnut, those stories were out of this world.

Then there was the story about one strong soldier who was able to lift a cannon by one wheel. Every time he demonstrated his strength his trousers would split on the seam revealing a bare behind. I found it very funny and laughed until my belly ached.

One scary story was about a soldier who was dragged away by a Siberian tiger while on guard duty. It was winter time and the soldier was in a heavy overcoat made from sheep skin. As he was leaning against a wall he dozed off and was grabbed by the tiger. He managed to fall out of the heavy coat and survive. The next day a small patrol followed the tiger's tracks and came upon the remnants of the coat. Not finding his prey in the bundle the angry tiger shredded the coat into small pieces.

Another soldier lost his arm to a tiger but survived. The tiger was shot and its frozen carcass was displayed in the city square. The soldier's soup utensil was placed in the tiger's jaw where passersby would place money for the injured soldier. There were many other such stories but my memory can't recall all of them.

In 1912, long before meeting my mother, Father returned home and married a girl from the village, Stary Sondyr, four kilometers away from ours. Her name was Alexandra and she was tall and slim women like my mother. I remember seeing the faded picture of the newlywed couple hanging on the wall for a long time. A year after the wedding they had a son named Gennady.

In those days it was the custom that the oldest boy in a family would marry first and move out from his father's house. It was also a custom that the whole village would help young couples get started by building them a one-room house. Using only crosscut saws and axes, the men of the village would cut logs and haul them to a building site where carpenters would erect the log hut, fitting every log to each other. The hut would then be disassembled, carried to its permanent location log by log, and re-assembled.

Grandma donated a cow and a couple of sheep to help them get started. Her horses were available for them to use all the time. In a short time, Father was reasonably well established. He was a hard worker and ready to build a good life for his family but there was a calamity brewing unknown by the simple people.

While rumors about an approaching war were going around in the cities the news was slow in reaching the rural areas. The Morse Telegraph was barely thirty years old and the Trans-Siberian Railway was built even later. Living 1,400 kilometers from Moscow and thirty-five kilometers from the nearest railroad station these people were not concerned with world affairs. To be content with life all they needed was a good harvest. They tilled the ground, sowed seeds, and harvested crops. It was during that long-awaited harvest time when the news about war reached the village. I don't recall when I heard the story the first time, but still remember how scared I was. I spent many long winter nights lying awake and thinking, "What would I do if a similar calamity occurred in my lifetime?"

This is how I can describe it now: It was a typical hot day in August. It was harvest time, when people are in the field before daylight trying to get as much done as possible before the sun comes up. By midday, when the temperature was the hottest, people would find a cool spot under the horse buggies away from the sun's heat and try to get some rest. This was the quiet hour of the day interrupted only by the occasional neighing of a hobbled horse nearby, or a meadow lark singing high in the sky. Through the shimmering heat wave a church steeple could be seen in the distance. This is where the District Administrator's office was located.

Suddenly a cloud of dust appeared near the town, indicating the advance of a fast rider on the road. The rider passed by waving his arms and yelling; "War! Mobilization!" People were up and running toward the road under the increasing roar of women and children weeping. This is how villagers received the news about total mobilization. The country was at war with Germany. After a few days the village seemed empty. All the men from twenty to forty years of age were gone.

My father left with two older brothers. All three were married. Each had at least one child. My father left his wife with baby Gennady in her arms not to see them again. During the time he was away, Alexandra got her horse buggy stuck in the mud. While trying to lift it out she got a hernia, which was the cause of her death. Shortly after, the baby died as well; in his grandmother's arms. So, after four years, my father, a thirty-four-year-old soldier returned from the war to an empty hut.

Village people were very superstitious in those days and believed in witches and witchcraft. One such witch whose family was at odds with my father lived in our village. It probably began with something trivial between young people, but when Father returned home after the war the friction between them was serious. Village gossips blamed the witch's sons for Alexandra's death, saying they saw her in peril but instead of helping, deliberately ignored her.

Father returned home with an assortment of "war souvenirs," including an Austrian carbine and four hand grenades. With rifle in hand, he went to see the witch and threatened to shoot her sons. It is possible that the woman was really scared and begged him for mercy. He was temporarily appeased by the old woman's humiliation, but the hatred between them only increased and lasted their lifetime.

One winter he suffered from joint pains so bad that he couldn't stand on his feet after sitting in one place for half an hour. One Russian woman recommended a folk remedy to him; to boil an armful of ferns and sit in the hot brew for as long as he would be able to endure. The remedy cured the problem, but Father suspected the witch for his illness.

Several years later, Father was recovering from another near-death sickness. He came out by the gate to sit in the sunshine and saw a one-ruble bill in the mud. He took it as cursed and thrown there by the witch that brought his sickness. In the presence of his brother, he chopped up the bill with a spade, took it to the witch's gate and threw it in her yard. Shortly after, the witch's granddaughter died and she blamed my father for it. Hidden animosity probably dwelt among the families all their lives, nearly affecting me, but I will describe that later on.

Mother's Roots

My great grandfather Daniel spent several years in the army of Imperial Russia in Poland. In those days, military service was very long and soldiers were allowed to marry. Daniel returned home with a Polish wife. Her action should tell something about her character. It is hard to imagine a woman walking 2,000 kilometers to a strange land with a different language and different customs. What attracted her to Daniel remained a mystery. I think that he was either a very handsome man or a very good story teller (or both).

It was the time of serfdom in Russia, similar to slavery in America. Peasants were the property of their landowners. A master had all the rights and he could do whatever he pleased with his people. Each landowner was obligated to send a certain number of healthy, young men to serve the Tsar. Those who were selected had to reach the appointed place on foot. Walking was the only way to get from one place to the other. The fastest means of transportation was a horse and buggy, a luxury affordable only for the rich.

It is not known how many children they had but one of their sons was called Vladimir (my maternal grandfather). Vladimir was married to Ugas, a girl from his own village. They had three boys and six girls: The oldest was a boy Alexei followed by three girls Maria, Matrena, and Ulyana. Next was a boy named Nicolai followed by two more girls, Daria and Alexandra. They were followed by a boy, Igor, and the youngest, a girl, Vera.

According to local custom siblings were married or given away in marriage in turn, starting with the oldest. Matrena, the third oldest in the family, was married to a man from my father's village. The two villages were only three kilometers apart so it was not uncommon for unmarried siblings to pay casual visits to their newly married sister. During one such visit Daria, the sixth child of Vladimir's family, met my father.

Soon matchmakers were sent to Daria's parents to ask for permission to marry. It was customary not to expect an agreement on either the first or second visit. It was a very delicate diplomacy for the parents not to give in too soon or not scare away the groom by playing hard to get. But in this case my father's request was flatly refused without any explanation. He was hurt and angry especially with her father. They had similar characters and were both extremely proud men.

By local standards Vladimir was a wealthy and well-respected provider for his family. His house was three times larger than any other hut in the village and was surrounded by an apple orchard dotted with beehives under the fruit trees. He always had at least one team of good workhorses and a couple of foals instead of the customary one horse per homestead. He could afford to build a house and supply the primary needs for married sons, and provide a dowry (one cow) for each daughter. Mainly he was proud of his obedient and hardworking children. What was he looking for in a future son-in-law? A widower wasn't his first choice for a girl from a good family. Also, there were two older siblings to be married before Daria.

My father saw himself in different light. He was good looking man, who could read and write and spoke fluently in three languages. He was a mature man who had spent eight years in the army and saw the world. That made him feel he had more to offer than any bachelor who had never been married. Deeply hurt by the refusal he decided to take the bull by the horns and show his future father-in-law with whom he was dealing.

Losing hope for her father's blessing Daria decided to elope. Eloping was frowned upon but often done, especially by girls from well-to-do families. So, plans were made with at least one sister's help. It was too risky to open the gate during the night without waking up the whole family so she decided to climb over the eight-foot wall. The step ladder was ready nearby and her sister would return it to its place after she was on the other side.

Daria's heart was pounding as she climbed the ladder with her belongings in the darkness of the night. Her future husband was waiting on the other side of the wall. Most likely his heart was pounding as furiously as hers. She threw her bundle of belongings to him to catch and jumped.

Hand-in-hand they took the shortcut across the ploughed field to her sister, Matrena's. They spent a few days there waiting and hoping that her father might change his mind and give his blessing. After all, it was better to let her get married than to be a subject for the local gossips. For a few days everything was quiet. Her sisters didn't dare visit and there was no other way to get news. Finally, they decided to get married without her parents' blessings but the parish priest refused to perform the wedding so they were wed in a church seven kilometers away from our village.

A few weeks after the wedding, my father went to visit his father-in-law to talk things over but found the gate locked from the inside. It was obvious my grandfather was not ready for reconciliation but my father didn't have the patience to wait forever. He decided to take the bull by the horns literally. He came back a second time carrying a length of rope. He climbed over the fence, tied Daria's "dowry" cow by the horns and led it out of the gate. He saw the curtain on one of the windows moving slightly. Someone was watching him from inside but no one came out to confront him. Gradually the rest of Daria's belongings were brought to her by her sisters.

The following year the central Volga region was hit by a drought, followed by a famine. This was the beginning of a long and difficult life for my parents.

I don't know how my mother's first encounter with her father went but clearly remember her carrying me often to see Grandma. I remember Grandfather's never-smiling face. For a long time, he ignored me. I did my best to get his attention by always being on my best behavior but without success. I felt guilty around him but didn't know why. Later his attitude changed. He took me to see the beehives located in a deep ravine in the forest. There was a log hut where I tasted honey, most likely for the first time in my life. My opinion of him didn't change. I remained timid and shy. His indifference towards me remained forever. That justifies the old saying, "There isn't a second chance to make a first impression."

Chapter 2
My Childhood

I heard the story about my birth from my paternal grandmother. She was the midwife who delivered me into this world. Her face faded from my memory a long time ago but memories of her remain clear as if it were yesterday. I remember seeing Grandmother every day. For the first couple years of my life, she was my baby sitter and it seemed she carried me everywhere. I remember her carrying me to the local policeman's house to get white porridge. I t seems she did that for a long time. Later I learned that I was born one year before the famine in the central Volga district. The Red Cross supplied millet for hungry children. People called it American porridge. She also used to carry me to see uncles and aunts.

I remember the foot path alongside a woven, wicker fence leading to the threshing floor behind the garden. It was summer and as she carried me in her arms, she pointed toward the horizon saying, "There is Daddy, working." In the far distance I could see two black dots, my father and the horse moving back and forth across the field, plowing the steaming earth. The smell of the earth tickled my nostrils. I also heard the buzzing sound made by "growing grass." I didn't know then that the buzzing sound was created not by growing grass but by the bees. Also, meadowlarks were singing as they flew in the air flapping their little wings. Grandmother explained how those birds would fly straight up to the sky and then fall towards the ground like a piece of earth and land safely. It may be then that I got the feeling that security came from heaven.

I remember hearing the story about how my parents "lost" me. It was harvest time and they were busy unloading sheaves of grain on the threshing floor. I was asleep in my baby carriage. I woke up and managed to get out of the carriage, crawled under the pole fence and walked out into a field of oats. My hair was the same color as ripe oats so it was difficult to see me from a distance. Calling my name didn't help, so Father climbed onto the barn roof. He saw me waddling along a couple hundred meters away.

I remember my parents' worried faces when grandma got very sick. During her illness I was left alone at home while they tended to her and didn't get to see her again even after she passed away. She must have been over eighty years old when she left this world, but in my memory, she remained a strong and cheerful woman.

I vaguely knew what it meant to be dead. On a certain day in the summer people went to the cemetery to visit dead relatives. I think my father probably took me there once or twice to visit his deceased son's grave. On several occasions he talked about how old Gennady would be had he survived. That may have been what prompted me to ask him a challenging question. Once when driving by a deep ravine in the horse buggy I asked him, "You wouldn't throw me down there, would you?" Father assured me he wouldn't do that.

After grandmother's death, Cousin Sophie came into the picture. She was the fourth child of my father's younger brother, Uncle Ivan. She was about ten years old when she started to babysit me. She used to come to our house with her younger brother, Ivan, and spend all day babysitting us. Once she climbed a pole fence with a couple of other girls, while holding me in her arms. Perched on the fence, they started to bounce on it. Suddenly the top pole snapped and everyone fell to the ground. As she fell, Sophie dropped me on the opposite side of the fence, onto a thick growth of stinging nettles. My bare bottom was on fire from contact with the nettles and watery blisters welled up with a terrible, burning sensation. Fortunately, the blisters didn't stay long. By the time I stopped sobbing they were gone.

Ivan's older brother, Nicolas, was my godfather. According to custom, on Easter Sunday I had to go to their house and sit on a pillow holding an Easter egg. The women believed that if a family member's godchild sat on the pillow for a reasonable length of time without moving, their hens would hatch many chicks. I spoiled everything on my first attempt. I couldn't sit still for even five minutes. Every time I got off the pillow someone grabbed me and put me back. After several attempts they gave up and the hens didn't hatch any chicks at all that summer. Ivan's mother wasn't happy and she consistently reminded me about it until I grew up and left the village.

Back to my beginning...I was told I took my first steps when I was about eight months old. Mother nursed me till I was a year old. It was summertime and people slept outside. Our bed was made up on the porch, where I slept between my parents. One day Mother was resting in bed when I climbed up to her to get my meal. Everything was as cozy and warm as usual but a big surprise waited for me. I took her breast in my mouth and let it go so fast that Mother gave a surprised look as if to say, "What is wrong?" It tasted so bad I never wanted it again. Years later I heard my mother tell the story of how easy it was to wean me from breast-feeding. She smeared her nipples with mustard just before I came to nurse.

After that my diet changed to a soft-boiled egg or porridge. In addition, every evening after milking the cow, my mother would bring me a full cup of warm milk to drink. It smelled like cow and I didn't like the taste of it. Initially, I tried to raise a fuss but quickly decided the consequences would not be worth my objections. There was a wide, leather belt hanging on the wall that my father used to hone his straight razor when he shaved. It was also probably used on my rear end at least once so I would know how it felt. All it took was my mother's glance toward the belt to make me down the cup without a fuss. In time, the amount of warm milk I was expected to drink increased. I remember drinking it from a copper cup that was made from a cannon shell. My father brought the shell home as one of his war souvenirs and it was always a point of conversation how he made it himself.

Our diet varied only slightly depending on the season but for the most part it was the same from one year to the next. In the summertime I drank lots of milk and often ate soft boiled eggs. Early summer greens were onions. People ate chopped, green onions mixed in buttermilk. Soup from nettles or chives was popular. Goosefoot (a weed) was another green that was sometimes used in soup but I didn't like it. Toward the fall the variety increased to include cabbage, and turnip and beet greens. Porridge made from barley, oats or millet was popular year around. In addition, an "instant" cereal was made from spelt that was eaten at harvest time, when time was a valuable commodity.

The process of making this cereal was simple. Spelt was first scalded in a large container of boiling water, and then dried in a hot oven until the grains became very hard and brittle. In the hulling mill the husks were removed and the remaining grain coarsely ground. The final product was a millet-like texture that, when mixed with boiling water, was ready to serve in five minutes. It was served in a deep bowl with a spoon full of melted butter in the center. I liked to dunk each spoonful of porridge into the butter before putting it in my mouth.

Tea was a regular after-meal drink and the main treat for visitors. Lots of tea was consumed during harvest time meals. Water was boiled in a samovar, which means self-cooker. Except for very poor households every family owned a samovar. It was central to Russian culture. The samovar was lit every time a visitor showed up.

Up until 1925, store shelves were pretty much empty. People would improvise by using raspberry leaves to make tea and would use dried, red beets and apples as a sweetener. When sugar became available in the stores, tea drinking became my hobby. I remember the first time my father returned from the market carrying a bluish-white cone of solid sugar. He had to use an axe break it to smaller pieces and a special side cutter to break it down even further. I would put a pea-sized piece of sugar in my mouth and it would last while I drank a whole cup of tea.

Salt was scarce during those times as well. Some people traveled hundreds of miles to the Caspian Sea just for sack of salt. And matches were in a category by themselves. The matches that could be purchased were of such poor quality that half of each box was wasted trying to light a fire.

They became a popular subject of jokes, such as, "It takes half an hour of rubbing, half an hour of hissing, and half an hour of stinking before you can get a fire lit." On the upside, using so many matches to light a fire left many empty boxes for me to play with.

All my toys were fashioned from available materials around the house. My mother sewed me a doll from old rags. My godfather fashioned toy animals from linden tree bark and dolls from straw. A good thing about those was that they were expendable so I didn't worry about broken or lost toys as they were easily replaced.

The days passed by slowly during the cold winter months when I had to stay inside. I passed the time playing with my toy animals. Father's old sheepskin overcoat became the pasture. I would fold it in different ways to change the landscape by making hills and valleys. And I often fell asleep on it while I was playing, squashing my animals.

Monotony and boredom became familiar companions very early during the winter months. I was happy to see any visitor, especially one of our relatives. On rare occasions cousins took me outside for a sleigh ride. Sometimes my father took me to his brother's place so I could play with my cousins. Once we visited a family with grown boys. The boys gave me a piece of beautiful, dark blue wrapping paper to play with. I was happy to have such a treasure, but the next day brought disappointment. As I played with the paper, the color came off and everything I touched turned blue, including my face. That was the end of my fun with the wrapping paper as my blue treasure was thrown into the oven.

The turbulent years of WW I followed by the civil war (known as the Bolshevik Revolution to westerners), created real havoc in the land. Everyone lived day-by-day trying to survive on a meager diet. Law and order could be found only in peasants' dreams. Bands of deserters roamed around robbing poor peasants. During the night horses were stolen from stables and lone travelers were robbed on the roads or killed. People continued fighting against each other; literally fathers against sons and brothers against brothers. White Guards fought to re-establish the monarchy and the Red Guards fought for self-government. Morale and discipline in both armies were low. The civilian population suffered more and more injustice, and peasants started to rebel against the governing body, which was called the Revolutionary Soviet.

In our region a rebellion, known as the Greatcoat Battle, was started by Tatars who lived in three large villages located side by side. Rebels murdered the district administrator and a female teacher. That day my father was on duty as a messenger in the District Office and he narrowly escaped the rebels. The local authorities called in an expeditionary force of Red Guards. The rebels disbanded and left the district to hide out. Soldiers surrounded all the men from the Tatar villages and executed them in a nearby forest.

One of the men miraculously survived the execution. The story of his recovery was retold every time he came to our village. Apparently, when he was shot, he fell into deep snow and got covered by the dead bodies of the other executed rebels. When he regained consciousness, he saw a single light in the distance and walked toward it until he came to a Russian village. He knocked on the window of the house with the light. The couple in the house let him in and cared for him till he regained his strength. Incredibly he recovered without medical help but was badly disabled, couldn't talk and his hands shook constantly. He lived out the remainder of his life by begging from house to house until his death.

One incident from that time period is especially etched in my mind. Mother had baked several loaves of hard bread and stored them on a shelf. She was holding me in her arms when several soldiers barged into the hut. They were hungry and wanted the bread. Mother begged them through her tears to leave the bread alone because that was all she had to feed her child. I felt very guilty for causing her to suffer. If she didn't have me, she wouldn't be crying.

A smallpox epidemic struck the country when I was two and a half years old. Friends and relatives stopped visiting each other. The days were long, lonely, and gloomy. I sat at the window hoping to see someone outside but I could see only houses with heavily draped windows across the street. Mother looked very sad and often cried. She also hung blankets on the windows and the house became gloomier. Darkness was supposed to ward off sickness or make it easier to endure but it was boring to sit in the dark.

Many children were sick and those who were not sick were waiting for sickness to hit. In those days preventive medicine didn't exist. Nobody knew about vaccinations or how to care for a sick child. Soon I fell sick and didn't remember much about the next three months. One can only imagine what a child afflicted with smallpox looks like; like a chunk of raw meat because not a spot of healthy skin remains on his or her entire body. It is very itchy. Scratching opens sores and leaves ugly scars. To prevent scratching my face, my hands were tied in tiny flannel pouches. It didn't help much. I remember rubbing my face and calling out to my mother that I was scratching myself. She tied my hands so I couldn't reach my face. Soon I wasn't able to move at all.

At the worst point of the sickness my father's veterinarian friend stopped by our place. Looking at me he told my parents, "He is not your son anymore: better get used to it before he is gone." But I survived the epidemic, unlike many boys my age. One boy lost sight in one eye and the other remained blind. Some parents lost two, even three children. It was a very sad year.

After two months scales of dry skin started to fall off my body. The soles of my feet separated like the sole of a worn-out shoe with the skin attached only on the heels and toes. Mother clipped the loose skin off with scissors. It was spring and I could see green leaves on the top branches of the birch trees as I sat in my crib and looked through the window. But I wanted to see green grass. When my mother stepped out, I succeeded in standing up on my shaky legs to look outside. I just managed to say, "Look at the green grass," when my head started to spin and I fell flat on my back. After that incident, I remained in bed another month.

It was around my birthday when my mother brought me outside for the first time since getting sick. I was sitting on the bottom step of the entrance to our house, propped up by an old coat. A hen with little chicks was pecking the bread crumbs at my feet. The fluffy, little bundles were so close to my feet I could catch them easily but as soon as I touched one of the chicks, the mother hen flew right at my face and I fell off the step. She kept jumping on me, beating me with her wings and scratching me with her talons. Hearing my screams, my mother came running and saved me from the vicious hen.

As soon as I was well enough, Cousin Ivan took me out to play with the other children but I soon realized how weak I was. Initially, I couldn't keep up with them as they ran and jumped over the narrow stream, which I couldn't cross. However, by the end of summer my strength returned to normal and I was able to keep up with the gang.

Chapter 3
My Dogs

The winter following my recovery from smallpox, Father's veterinarian friend came for a visit. He was wearing a bearskin overcoat and looked like a giant. He squatted down to look at me and said; "Look what I brought for you." He opened his coat to reveal a white puppy with black ears. It was a female puppy of a species common in our region that could endure the harsh climate. It was a real surprise for me and all I could say was, "Does it bite?" My suspicion was justified soon after, when she started to bite strangers without warning. Because we couldn't break her of this nasty habit, she was kept on a chain her entire life. She slept on the straw next to the horse stable and could run to the front gate and back. On the plus side, not one stranger was able to open the gate and walk in.

When she went into heat she used to whine and howl day and night until she was let loose. Then she would disappear for several days. One of her litters produced a black, borzoi-mix puppy. Generally, black fur was a disadvantage to a hunting dog because rabbits could see it from a distance and run away but this dog was a good hunter and was able to outrun the rabbits. Because that smart dog caught so many of them, my mother learned how to prepare rabbit and we enjoyed many delicious meals.

Nearly every year my dog had a litter of four puppies. They were given away or "disappeared" all at once. At first, I was worried and felt sorry for her, especially when I found out that the puppies were disposed of in a very cruel way, by drowning. The last time a litter of puppies disappeared she managed to free herself and bring them back. When Father saw the dog suckling her lost litter, he was surprised beyond belief. He had buried them alive far from home but the mother dog found them and brought them back. When Father saw the dog snarling at him with open fangs, he decided never again to dispose of the litters.

From that time on, we kept several grown dogs. Father halfway joked about raising five or six German Shepherds and making a winter coat from their skins but he gave up that idea too. My godfather made a harness for the dogs to pull a sled in winter. I had lots of fun riding the dog sled with my friends or hauling straw from the threshing floor to the stable.

The dog population was controlled by "dog catchers" who were licensed by the district Elder to dispose of any that did not seem to have a home. Every winter, the dog catchers would travel from village to village shooting free-running dogs on the street and loading their carcasses on a horse sled. If someone's dog was shot that was the end of it so people who wanted to keep their dog watched out for the dog catcher and ensured their dog stayed off the street when he passed through their village.

One winter when I was about four years' old wolves appeared in masses. They were so bold they walked on the street during daylight. The village people took it as a bad omen. That winter only a few dogs managed to survive. The rest were eaten by the wolves. The wolves would hunt in pairs. The male would come to the gate, leave his mark, and walk away. The unsuspecting dog would come out, barking only to be grabbed and dragged away by the wolf's mate.

I remember a few wolf stories told by older people. One of the most memorable is about a man with a crude nickname "Urinated." As the story goes, "Urinated" was walking home from a neighboring village when he saw pack of wolves coming his way. It was mating season and a pack of males was following a female. Being in an open field "Urinated" was totally helpless so he stretched out on the snow face down to await his fate. The female wolf approached him as he lay still on the ground, sniffed him, and squirted him with urine before walking away. One by one the pack of wolves repeated the female's action and continued to follow after her. "Urinated" made it home safely but made the mistake of bragging about his ordeal, hence earning him his nickname.

The other story had to do with my father. He was returning home one night by horse and buggy. It was late in the fall when nights are very dark. Travelling in the dark one had to depend on the horse's sense literally, because a horse knows the way home even in the dark. It was still five kilometers from the village when the horse was startled by an unusual noise. My father heard the panting sound of running creatures that seemed to be headed in his direction so he stopped the horse to listen more closely. Suspecting that they may be wolves, his hair stood on end. Suddenly he was surrounded by some of our dogs. They were whining and barking as they jumped on the buggy to lick his hands and face. Father often reflected on who was the happiest on that occasion, he or the dogs. How they knew where he was and who sent them while the rest stayed at home remained a mystery.

When I left home in 1936, to attend university, only the original, old dog remained. She was very happy to see me when I returned home after ten months. And she was still chained. Mother noticed the dog's agitated behavior two days before I returned so when I showed up it seemed to prove that there was an intuitive nature in dogs that humans lacked.

After seventeen years, when dogs usually die from old age, our oldest dog's life ended tragically. While running loose in the street one day, she was bitten by a stray, rabid dog and had to be disposed of before she became rabid herself and a danger to humans. In those days people believed that a rabid dog shouldn't be touched, so Father borrowed a shotgun to kill the dog. While he was walking back with the gun the dog was sitting in the middle of the street looking at him. He said a chill ran up and down his spine. He stopped and faced the dog, aimed at her forehead, and fired. The dog sat looking at him and licked the blood that was dripping from her nose. Father didn't know what to think because it was not usual for a dog to sit still after being shot. He left the dog where she sat in the middle of the road and went into the house. The next morning, Father found the dog in her usual spot on the straw next to the horse stable, frozen to death.

Chapter 4

My Home

Prior to 1917, our village was called Stepenovka, Stephan's Place. No one knew why. It may be that the first settler's name was Stephan. After the revolution, the village was renamed Pochinok-Bybyt, which, loosely translated, means Temporary Settlement. It stands on the northern slope of a rolling hill. When I was born the settlement consisted of about thirty families. Two rows of log huts with straw-covered roofs faced each other. Our hut had two tiny windows facing east and one window facing the south.

The front fence was made from long poles with a gate wide enough for a horse buggy to get through. Uncle Piotor's place was across the street from ours with exactly the same front gate. I don't ever remember using the gate to come in or go out, preferring to take a "short cut" by squeezing out between the poles. A proper gate that provided privacy was built when I was about nine years old. One morning I was on the top of the gate helping the carpenters. Suddenly, one of them raised his hand and pointing to the north, yelled: "Look! The house is on fire!" I jumped to the ground and ran to the burning house. Its straw roof burned down in no time. I was commended for saving the baby from the burning house but I don't remember doing it.

Behind the gardens ran a deep ravine that spanned the entire length of the village. On the lower end of the ravine, under a tall willow was a wooden bridge. I could see the bridge through our front windows as well as the road to my mother's village. On the opposite side of the ravine lay a cultivated field stretching upward about two kilometers, forming a slight curve on the horizon. Father told me that on Easter morning the rising sun would jump and roll, rejoicing for the risen Christ. One Easter morning I arose early to see the spectacle. I stared in amazement as the rising sun seemed to jump and roll. People in those days did not know about the harmful effects of staring at the sun but that one event did not seem to have a negative impact on me.

To the west a wide valley with a fast-running, shallow creek spread past the lower end of the village. The spring-fed waters were knee-deep the entire length of the valley. During the summertime, the one-meter-wide stream ran through the meadows. Lush grass grew up to our armpits along with several kinds of edible greens, and ripening wild strawberries on the slopes alongside the valley kept us busy for weeks. The meadows stretched six kilometers to the narrow river, Cubnya, where the Russian villages, Aleksandrovka and Lutsk, were located. Lutsk had a tiny church where I was baptized. Before the revolution the villages were owned by landowners. Forests interspersed with tall pine and spruce trees stretched to the horizon twelve kilometers away. All the building materials and firewood for the surrounding villages came from there. It was also the place where people gathered white mushrooms for pickling.

As I mentioned earlier, after recovering from smallpox I spent every day with Cousin Ivan. His friend, Grisha, a red head, had a brother, Vasily, who was the same age as me. One day Ivan and Grisha decided we should look for wild duck eggs. To get to the nests we had to walk through knee-deep spring runoff. We rolled up our pant legs and, holding hands, walked in carefully feeling the bottom with our feet. We didn't know about the hidden treacheries of strong streams and inadvertently stepped into a deep hole washed out by the spring waters. Before realizing what happened we were out on the opposite side of the stream coughing and screaming. After regaining our composure, we were warned to keep our mouths shut so nobody would know about our near mishap. After that experience, we were successful in gathering ducks' eggs and did so several times.

Eventually, fertile soil washed down by spring waters, turned the swamp into arable land. It was good soil for growing flax and hemp, which grew so tall it could hide a rider on horseback. Since hemp is the cousin of marijuana it might have made an interesting smoking substance but fortunately nobody knew about it although the pollen from male plants had enough potency to make heads spin. It may be that the girls who were weeding the male plants before harvest knew its secret and that's why they sang all day long.

Tokayevo was a large Tatar village located up the river to the west of us. The people in our village often talked about the dangerous road through Tokayevo, where a band of robbers lived. Their leader was a wealthy Tatar called Shakoor. Travelers were robbed in daylight just for the fun of it. Horses and cows were stolen from locked stables. People were afraid for their lives but didn't report robberies. There weren't enough police to enforce the law so people were left to fend for themselves, for the most part, to conduct their affairs and resolve any issues; but they were not sufficiently organized to withstand ruthless bandits.

In 1924, the government, under Lenin, introduced a so called "New Economic Policy," which gave peasants the freedom to conduct their businesses as they saw fit. It seemed to work well for everyone. Harvests were good and peasants were selling their products in the marketplace and buying factory-produced goods. Father and his brothers traveled to faraway places to sell grain and returned every time with new farm implements and rare treats not seen before. Shakoor, as a moderate landowner before the revolution, gained the rights to own the land next to our village. At harvest time he would bring his people to set up camp on our meadows. Nobody objected to them being there for fear of retaliation and realistically, the haymaking season was over and they couldn't cause any damage by camping there.

One day during harvest time, Shakoor rode to our gate in his horse and buggy and asked Father to fill a large wooden keg with fresh water from our well. He was smartly dressed in a black, satin shirt girded by a red waistband and baggy pants hanging over well-polished boots. After Father filled the barrel, Shakoor asked if it would be okay to return the next day for water. On his last visit, Shakoor asked Father if he had heard about a policeman, who was found dead under the bridge and who he thought the killer might be. After Father's vague response, Shakoor smiled and said, "Now you know," and drove away. It was common knowledge that Shakoor's man did it, but his boldness left my father dumbfounded. That wasn't the last time he saw Shakoor.

The following winter, Father and Uncle Pavel took two sled loads of grain to Alatyr, a city ninety kilometers away. On the return trip they had to pass through several Tatar villages and finally, the place where Shakoor lived. It was late at night and Shakoor's residence was all lit up. They were having a feast. Uncle Pavel, who was travelling ahead of Father, fell asleep and his horse took the wrong road. Father called out to Uncle Pavel hoping to wake him up. Suddenly, two men came running out of the shadows of Shakoor's porch. One of them grabbed my father's horse by the muzzle and the other grabbed my father by his sleeve. He was dragged inside and pushed down on a bench near the door.

Shakoor appeared through the door and looked straight into Father's eyes as he said to someone, "Pour him a large glass and let him go." After Father downed the full glass of vodka, Shakoor said, "This is payment for the water. Now we are even." When Father mounted the sled, the man holding the horse stepped back and his horse took off at a gallop. Uncle Pavel was still sleeping when Father caught up with him. He had to yell several times for Uncle Pavel to awaken, but once he was awake, he urged his horse to go faster and they galloped all the way to the village.

Every summer Father patrolled the meadows after dark. He wore a loose overcoat to keep his illegal Austrian carbine hidden in his sleeve while he was riding his horse. On one occasion he was surprised to find bandits feeding their horses on the meadows. He left his horse in the bushes and walked up the hill to get closer to the bandits so he could have some fun with them. He carefully aimed his carbine at their bonfire and pulled the trigger. A cloud of sparks flew from the fire and the bandits disappeared into the dark. For a while it was really quiet and then he heard a whistle and then another. Once the bandits felt they were safe they re-assembled in the dark and started walking toward Father's hiding place but he was long gone, having snuck from there in a hurry. That same summer the arm of the law caught up with Shakoor and his band. The whole band was ambushed and every member of the gang arrested, brought to trial, sentenced, and executed. That ended the legend about Shakoor the Untouchable.

My parents made lots of beer and moonshine. When they invited relatives for a feast or were invited by them, a lot of drinking went on. When a guest got drunk, I served them a glass of beer and they gave me money. I remember during one party I collected enough money to buy a horse. What I didn't like was when someone dumped a hand full of change into a full glass of beer and made me drink it to retrieve the money. I remember doing it several times and getting sick.

One time my father's trusted friend came for a visit. I was four or five years old at that time. He used to stop at our place casually to share secrets with Father. He would bring Father's rifle, which he hid at his place or pick it up from us, depending on the situation. After drinking some moonshine, they left the table with half-empty glasses and stepped outside. After they were gone, I decided to taste what they were drinking. I took a little sip from one of the glasses. It had a burnt smell and tasted slightly sweet. I kept sipping little by little and the rest was blank. Afterward, I learned that Mother found me under the table unconscious. That evening they were invited to a celebration with relatives but couldn't go because of me.

When I was six years old, Father told me that my mother was sick and I would have to stay with my grandmother. I was very scared. The next morning, he came to bring me home, and on the way back, he told me that during the night a stork brought a little sister, Vera, for me. I had seen the birth of lambs and puppies before that, but still believed the stork story. I remember the cradle hanging from the ceiling, suspended by a coil spring. It was a woven, oval basket made from tree bark. It was rocked by pulling a rope suspended from the bottom of the basket.

Mother was always busy and I had the chore of rocking the cradle when my sister cried. One time I was left alone with her. She wouldn't stop crying and rocking didn't help. I got really angry and pulled the rope really hard, then let go. Vera nearly bounced out of the cradle but at least she stopped crying. I kept doing that until Mother caught me red-handed and lectured me never to do it again. She didn't punish me but always threatened that she would tell Father. I don't remember being punished so probably she never told him.

For me a typical winter day started by waking up and seeing Mother at the stove. She would start the fire and put a cast-iron pot full of potatoes in the stove. When the potatoes were ready, she would remove some for breakfast and mash the rest for the pig. For breakfast potatoes were peeled and fried. Father liked his with sauerkraut. Through the winter that was the standard breakfast, eaten with bread and various milk products. Every household baked their own bread. Mother formed most of the bread dough into loves and let them rise. The remaining ball of dough was rolled flat and baked over burning embers in a cast iron pan. When its upper crust puffed up the soft bread was ready to eat. It was cut into four pieces and slathered with butter. It was very tasty.

After the baked loaves of bread were removed from the stove, a clay pot with soup ingredients was set in to cook on low heat for dinner. Leftover soup was eaten for supper and the next day for dinner. Everything, from meat to porridge to yogurt was cooked and baked in the stove. During the summer time the stove was used only for baking bread. Other cooking was done in the small fireplace in front of the stove or in the summer kitchen located in the shack outside.

Spinning and weaving was done on long winter nights. Mother's younger sister or nieces came to stay with us for weeks to do their spinning. They would spin all day long stopping only for meals. After the spinning was complete the weaving process would start. Again, one of my aunts or cousins came for a long stay to help Mother. They amused me by singing funny songs or telling fairy tales. Those were the happy days when I felt the extra love and care bestowed upon me.

During that same time, Father was often away working in the forest or on a trip to distant markets. He used to come home with icicles hanging from his moustache and teased me by pretending he wanted a kiss. In winter it was dangerous to travel at night. During blizzards the wind howled in the chimney creating scary pictures in my imagination. People got lost and wound up in the most unusual places like at the bottom of a ravine or on someone's roof. High snow drifts buried barn roofs making it possible to drive up and over them with a horse sled.

Common winter footwear was felt boots. They were made by a traveling bootmaker right at the kitchen table. First, wool was spread on the floor and beaten with a stick to remove any dirt. Then it was combed and spread on the table in the rough shape of a boot four or five times larger than what the finished boot would be. A folded towel was placed over the wool followed by another layer of wool like the first. Hot water was sprinkled liberally on the wool and it was kneaded until the wool fibers bound together. At that stage the wool was placed on a wooden form shaped like a foot and the wool would continue to be kneaded and rubbed (with many additional sprinklings of hot water) until it bound tight to the wooden form. The wool-shaped boot was then removed from the form and baked in a very hot oven until it was dry. I remember my first pair of felt boots, hot from the oven and smelling of burnt wool. The heel and sole were as curved as a half moon and I couldn't stay straight on my feet but with time and use they flattened out.

Every summer, right after spring sowing, a tanner would come to the village. He used our neighbor's summer kitchen as his workshop. It was a very messy and smelly process. First, he would collect skins from the whole village and soak them in a special mixture for several days. After the curing process was complete, the skins were dyed red or black. The red dye was made from red brick dust mixed in linseed oil. Oak tree bark was boiled in a large cauldron to make the black dye. Black was the preferred color for a skin coat, especially for future grooms. I daydreamed about being dressed in a black sheepskin coat but never even had a red one. All my winter coats were made from my parents' old coats.

My early childhood village had two fair-sized ponds. One was deep enough to be able to bathe the horses and to swim. I spent several summers sitting on the shore watching the older boys swim. When I was about six years old Ivan's two older brothers built a dam at the bottom of the ravine. Ivan took me there to learn how to swim. The pond was spring-fed and the water was so clear I could see the bottom but it was over my head in places. I was scared stiff but couldn't show that I was a cry-baby so following Ivan's instruction I undressed and walked into the water. The bank was steep on all sides, but I walked in with my eyes open, and before I knew it, I was walking out on the opposite side. After that my fear of getting into the water disappeared and soon I started to swim.

The second artificial lake was next to Ivan's garden, where his mother grew lots of cucumbers. It was our job to carry water from the lake to water the plants. Ivan's mother, whose name I don't remember, used to share her abundant crop of cucumbers with my parents. Cucumbers were pickled in a large wooden tub for the winter. People also grew lots of winter cabbage for sauerkraut and made it in similar tubs.

Ivan's mother was the head of the household and everyone in the village knew it. I saw her picking a fight with Uncle Ivan. They had a mean stallion that couldn't be castrated and she would not agree to sell or trade it. Every time Uncle Ivan got bitten by the stallion it created turmoil in their house because she said it was his fault that the horse bit him. My father said that Ivan had two curses in his life; one was the horse, the other was his wife.

In 1935, Cousin Ivan got posted as a teacher fifty kilometers away from our village. He wrote to his sister, Sophia, and on one occasion sent her a picture of a girl asking what she thought of her. When he didn't come home for summer vacation his mother got suspicious and decided to pay him a surprise visit. She travelled the distance on her mean stallion without incident. When she appeared unexpectedly at her son's residence Ivan was in a panic. He had married a village girl without telling his parents. The prevailing Communist culture deemed church weddings a thing of the past. Marriages were registered in the district administrator's office often times without any witnesses.

The following summer Ivan came home for summer vacation with his wife. I missed him and was anxious to meet his wife. After a couple of visits, I noticed that my presence was not wanted, especially when nobody else was in the house. I was old enough to know why. Opportunities for privacy or intimacy were rare and he wanted to be alone with her. To smooth over an awkward situation, he loaned me a book titled *The Complete Collection of Alexander Pushkin*. I liked Pushkin's verses from our school books, but here I had all his poems and prose. That summer I immersed myself in the self-study of Russian literature. It was a productive summer for learning. By summer's end, I could recite several poems by heart and could recall many pieces and which larger work they were a part of. Before my cousin and his wife left, I returned the book with my deepest gratitude and we parted like grown-up people, with a cool handshake not to see each other ever again.

In 1969, after my father died, I received a letter from Ivan. He described what transpired in his life over the past thirty-plus years. At the beginning of WWII, he was called to serve the Fatherland and spent four years in the military. He was not fit for the front line but was wounded several times and returned home with a concussion. Subsequently, he suffered from sudden headaches the rest of his life. He was still teaching and was interested in acquiring a Bible that was forbidden in the Soviet Union at that time. He asked me to mail pages of the New Testament in an ordinary envelope. I took apart my well-used Bible, printed on fine paper, and mailed it to him ten pages at a time. I remember sending him the last chapter of the Gospel of John when a teacher from a local college in Sudbury decided to visit the Soviet Union and asked me if I had anything to send to relatives. I gave him a Bible for my cousin, which he mailed from Moscow. I got a letter from Ivan thanking me for the book. He said his only disappointment was that the book of Proverbs was missing. Someone had cut it out. I told him that it may have been God's will to deliver the book to someone who needed it more than he did. Ivan thought the same way. We corresponded for several years. His letters became a long list of questions concerning the Scriptures and I would respond with long letters. He wrote that before getting the pages of the Bible they used my letters as preaching material and for discussion.

Around 1980, Ivan asked me to sponsor his son and grandson for temporary visas. He said they were good mechanics and if they worked in Canada for a year, they could return home with enough money to start their own business. I wrote back explaining that I would not be able to do it because of the complexity of acquiring work visas. He didn't believe me and wrote, "Well, if you don't want to do me this favor so be it," and that was the end of our correspondence. Thirteen years later my wife, eldest daughter, and I visited my village but Ivan didn't come to see me. After we returned home, I received a short letter from him saying, "What is going on? I was waiting for you and heard that you were here and have gone back." This time I didn't believe him.

Chapter 5

First year in School

Prior to starting school, I liked to look at books that belonged to Cousin Ivan. I don't really remember when I started to read simple phrases, like, "Here is Spot," and "Jump Spot, jump," but by the time I was six I was able to identify words. My first memorable event concerning school is the day Cousin Ivan took me there to meet the teacher, when I reached my seventh birthday. I was scared that the older boys would make fun of me, but they were excited too and I felt accepted. The teacher's name was Maria Michaylovna. She asked me how old I was and if I would like to come to school. I responded in the affirmative and she gave me a clean notebook and pencil. It was like receiving a treasure but the notebook and pencil were appropriated by my father. Reflecting back, I think he started bookkeeping because of that notebook. After returning from a long trip, he would take out the abacus, make some calculations, and write down numbers in the notebook.

Father had a trunk in which he kept two books, among other things. They had hard covers and glossy paper. The pictures in one book were about a faraway place, where people didn't wear any clothing. There were pictures of unfamiliar trees and animals and black people carrying babies on their backs like a backpack. I daydreamed about travelling to those places and seeing the people. The second book was called *God's Law* and had a shining cross on the black cover. All the pictures in the book were of Icons, which resembled the pictures on the walls of the church building. There was one separate picture of Saint Alexei. I was told that he was Father's patron saint. The Saint's clothing was torn in shreds. I wondered why saints were poor but couldn't gather the courage to ask my father.

I was eight years old and ready to go to school. That summer just before school started, I had a traumatizing experience. People talked about the trained, hunting horse that came from the Kalmyk steppes. Kalmyk is the name of western Mongolian people, whose ancestors created the Kalmyk Khanate in 1630–1724 in Russia's North Caucasus territory. Today they form a majority in the autonomous republic of Kalmykia on the western shore of the Caspian Sea. Kalmyks would hunt wolves and foxes on horseback and clobber them with a club. Their horses were trained to keep their head down to the left to avoid being hit by the club.

I was envisioning an occasion when I might ride this horse (who was reputed to be the fastest in the village), when the owner called me from a crowd of children and asked if I would like to ride it to a pasture that was three kilometers from the village. I was so excited for the opportunity that without thinking I ran to him and got on the horse. He released the bridle and slapped horse's rump. It took off like a bullet raising a cloud of dust. Turning the corner, I saw two little girls in front of the horse. One of them was my three-year-old sister, Vera. The horse jumped over them but looking back I saw only a thick cloud of dust. There was no way to stop or turn back. I just hung on by holding tightly to the horse's mane. I passed another boy with three horses going the same way. He was waving his arms in the air and yelling something to me.

Thinking that the girls had been trampled, I earnestly prayed to God to keep them alive. Reaching the pasture, I jumped off the horse and ran back as fast as I could. I ran past the boy with the three horses. He was coughing and spitting mud out of his mouth, but I was in a rush to find out what happened to my sister, so I just ran past him. Only later it became clear what had happened to him. Flying earth from the horse's hoof hit him in the mouth and he nearly choked to death.

I pictured a street full of crying women gathered around the maimed bodies of the two girls, so to avoid being seen, I made a wide circle to the back of our orchard and crawled under a cherry tree nearest the front fence. It was very quiet on the street. The only sound I could hear was the beating of my heart. Suddenly I heard giggles and saw my sister and her friend running down the street. The feeling of relief was beyond description. Later it became clear that the man had something against my father and used me to get back at him. Apparently, it didn't bother him to see me crippled or even dead. The other children told me that man wished to see me with a broken neck. After that I spent several sleepless nights wondering why some people were so mean. After all, what had I done for them to hate me so much? Mostly, I was bitterly disappointed with myself for being so naïve and trusting of people.

Finally, it was time to go to school. My mother sewed me a school bag from homespun, white material and Godfather made me a pencil case. In school we got a beginner's book and a blackboard the size of a book page. It was a sheet of slate mounted in a wooden frame. To write on it pencil-shaped graphite was used. A pincushion-like little pillow was attached to the board with a piece of string to wipe the board clean. In Grade One we didn't waste much writing paper that was scarce everywhere.

Maria Michaylovna was highly respected by pupils and their parents alike. She was a strict disciplinarian who didn't tolerate bad behavior in or out of school. After two years she was transferred to another school and we got a new teacher, Claudia Vasilievna. Claudia was not much older than some of the girls in our class. People were concerned that her young age would be a detriment but she proved them wrong. She organized different games and often played ball with us after school. During the winter we had snowball fights and sled rides. Once she asked me if my father would drive her to the store in next village. It was a very cold day, and while we rode on the sled, she cuddled me in her fur coat. I felt embarrassed and happy for the notebook and pencils she bought me at the store.

During the first three years of school all subjects were taught in the Chuvash language. Very few people in the village, including my mother, could speak Russian. My father was an exception. He was fluent in both the Russian and Tatar languages. Claudia Vasilievna started to spend her days off with us and tutor me in Russian from the beginners' book. Additionally, in the evenings I read short stories aloud and Father corrected my pronunciation. It was difficult to distinguish similar sounding words and translate them correctly. In the process I encountered some embarrassing moments. For example, once I was reading a story about a poor peasant who saw a rabbit sleeping in its burrow. The peasant sat down on the ground and envisioned how he would kill the rabbit with a horse whip, which was the only weapon he had. I translated it as the peasant saying, "I will kill the whore." I knew it was a profane word, but it sounded similar to whip. Father gave me a strange look and tactfully corrected my mistake.

The year before I started school our horse was kicked by another horse that resulted in a cracked shin. While our horse was healing, Father bought a Siberian mare for a very cheap price. She wasn't used to being harnessed and spooked easily. First, she would resist passing the gate, and then would run until she was out of breath. The following summer she had a foal (as small as a toy horse) and after that it was useless to try to ride her because the foal was always behind the mother, trying to suck and the mother was constantly turning back, trying to lick the foal. I would sit straddled on her back going nowhere, getting frustrated and crying my heart out.

In the early spring, Father took both horses to a fair and returned with a tall horse. It was the best-looking horse in the district. I was very proud and anxiously waited for an occasion to ride on its back. My godfather and his brother were ploughing the fields before spring sowing. In the evening they returned to their home and from there brought our horse home. Once I gathered the courage, they let me ride it home. They put me on the horse's back and I got home without trouble, raising my friends' envy.

In Grade One we were told that there was no God; that only uneducated grannies believed in God. School plays ridiculed priests and grannies for being religious. To hinder people from attending church services, the government changed the day of rest from Sunday to Saturday and later introduced a five-day week. Every fifth day people had the day off.

In spite of the antireligious propaganda churches were open and functioning. Religious holy days were observed diligently. The day of Pentecost, in particular, was a very important Holy Day. The day before Pentecost houses and fences were decorated with birch and oak tree branches. The courtyard of each home was swept and a table with an embroidered tablecloth placed in the center. A full loaf of caraway bread and bowl of salt were placed on the table to be blessed. On the Day of Pentecost, a procession with icons and banners marched through the village, stopping at every household to bless the family and buildings. After every house was blessed, the procession would continue to the cemetery where the priest would pray for the souls of the departed. At its entrance would be a large container of fresh water that the people would carry home in bottles, bowls, and clay pots to keep as a miracle cure from sickness until the next Pentecost. And finally, the village shepherd would lead the herd past the priest who would sprinkle the herd with holy water.

The village shepherd would also lead the herd past the priest when badly needed rain didn't come. In that instance a calf was slaughtered on behalf of the villagers and cooked in a large cauldron. When the meat was ready it was cut into small portions and divided amongst the people. Porridge was also cooked in same cauldron and for some reason was burned every time. Regardless of the smoky smell it was tasty. After the meal younger people doused each other with water. One time during this celebration a black cloud appeared on the horizon, which developed into pouring rain. The people were jubilant that God showed his mercy. Ironically, most of them didn't know the custom originated during pagan times. I was confused why people attended church and at same time, left offerings at designated spots for the pagan god, Kiremet.

Once, while carrying the blessed water I met my teacher. She asked me what was in the container but seeing my embarrassment she changed the subject and let me go my way. The following year I decided to avoid the whole ceremony and hid behind the barn while watching the procession through a hole in the wall. The procession came in, and Father looked around for me. Everything went smoothly without my presence but I had some explaining to do. I couldn't invent a plausible excuse so the only thing I could do was tell the truth, that I didn't want to participate. I was ready to accept punishment for my disobedience, but Father didn't say a word. He didn't have to. I saw such hurt in his eyes I would have preferred to get a good licking.

Before that I had only one physical punishment for a thing I didn't do. Father was growing apple trees from seeds and grafting them. Once he found a broken branch that was grafted the year before, lying on the ground. Nobody was around the trees except me and that made me a prime suspect but I wasn't guilty and refused to take the blame. That made him angry. He took me by the ear and struck me on the head with the branch a few times. As I remember that was the last physical punishment I received from my parents.

Regardless of our occasional pranks we learned responsibility at an early age. Several boys my age had to babysit their baby sister or brother. During harvest time we were left at home alone with younger siblings. Our food for the day was bread, boiled potatoes, and milk. The days were very long and boring. My sister was too young to be left unattended so I had to drag her in her carriage with me all the time but I couldn't go too far from the house because there were always beggars nearby begging for a piece of bread. Additional responsibilities where my sister was concerned included bathing her in a huge trough near the well, feeding her and putting her to bed. Occasionally Mother would come home early and save me the task of washing and feeding.

During the day my friends and I amused ourselves with whatever we could think of. We raced down the street pushing baby carriages. The carriages were home-built contraptions without any springs. When we ran with them on the bumpy road the babies were probably so scared that they didn't cry. In the evening we had to wait for the animals return from the pasture. Sheep often couldn't find their way home so I had to search for them.

During the best of times, my father kept one beehive in the garden. The second household down the street from us had over twenty hives and Andre, who was one year older than me, had to watch them during swarming season. Since we played together, we shared the task of watching for signs that the hive was about to swarm. When bees started to leave the hive, the queen would come out. Andre's job was to enclose the queen in a wire mesh box and put it in a bushel basket. The whole swarm would then gather in the bushel basket around the queen.

Occasionally a swarm would escape and fly away. They would be chased on horseback with a shot gun in hand. The trick was to catch up with the swarm and fire the gun close enough to make the swarm land. That often happened with my second cousin Gary's family. They had bee hives but they were so busy doing other things and didn't have a permanent watcher. They would bring escaped swarms from as far as ten kilometers away but rarely lost them.

Our reward would come during the honey harvest. Andre's playmates were treated with fresh honey and freshly baked, caraway rye bread. It was an awesome procedure to sit at the table and watch Andre's father slice the bread and put a bowl full of fresh honey on the table. Each boy was provided with a new wooden spoon painted in bright colors. We were told that fresh honey tasted best when served from a new spoon. We would hold our spoon full of honey over the slice of bread so it wouldn't drip on the table, and euphorically chew our treat with eyes closed.

Chapter 6
Changing Times

The summer of 1929 passed as many other summers. The harvest was plentiful that year, which indicated there would be elaborate celebrations during the winter but the older people were sad. The real reason for their feelings wasn't discussed in front of the children.

I remember hearing the first rumors about upcoming changes. It was unbelievable and scary. The rumor was that an order would be issued from Moscow to separate all the men, women, and children. Each group would live together in one building and husbands would only be able to see their wife by permission from a government official. All the children would be in boarding schools, being taken care of by teachers. It was a very scary time. I was worried, most of all, about how my mother would handle the situation. Who would cook for Father and how homesick would I be without my parents? I was too young to distinguish between what was real and what was a foolish rumor. All I wanted was to grow up and fight against foolishness.

The real trouble started in mid-winter. Government representatives came every week and called general meetings to teach the people about future changes. People were told that private households would be a thing of the past, that the village would be converted to a "collectivnoye hozaistvo" or "kolkhoz"—in short, collective farming. They were told they needed to submit an application to join the collective. Those who refused to join would be declared a "malicious defaulter" and would be exiled to Siberia. For the first time women started to attend the meetings with their husbands and voice their opinions. That had never happened before and some older people predicted worse calamities would result because women were interfering in what had traditionally been a "man's business."

Meanwhile new directives were streaming in from Moscow telling the local activists what had to be done but how to fulfill the directives was left to the local administration. To start with, the organizing committee was comprised of poor peasants who had nothing to lose. It was a generally accepted fact was that they were poor because they were lazy. They didn't have much to contribute to the kolkhoz but they would share everything on an equal basis with the people who made significant contributions. The people of our village acted instinctively in contradicting the Moscow directives. For example, the directive that forbade slaughtering animals resulted in a mass slaughter. People did it at night but the members of the committee were on hand to snoop around and report their suspicions to the police. Convicted offenders were sentenced to two years at a "correctional labor camp," where they worked without pay.

One year before the turbulent times began, a parochial priest, Vishnevsky, left his post. He locked the church building and disappeared without notice or explanation. Everyone was astonished when he returned as the government's representative to organize the kolkhoz in his former parish. He spoke about how wrong and how bad everything was until now. He told the people how they had been told a pack of lies by the clergy and government officials of the previous regime. As an example, he said that while he was a priest, he believed that the bone fragment of a certain saint sown into the Shroud of Christ was real. He tore the shroud with his own hands and found piece of wax instead of the remains of the saint.

My father was known as a man who didn't hesitate to speak what he thought. During question time he asked Vishnevsky, "Since you admitted you were a liar as a priest, how can you expect us to believe you now? Isn't it logical to assume that once a liar always a liar?" The former priest announced that my father was always a troublemaker and should be expelled from the meeting. After Father left Vishnevsky characterized him as an arrogant and disagreeable person, not suited to live in the new society. He said the only place suitable for dissenters like him would be Kamchatka. The question regarding exiling my father to Kamchatka was put to a vote.

Everyone at the meeting was afraid they would meet the same fate if they disagreed so they voted that he should be exiled.

Late that night Uncle Pavel came and told Father what transpired after he left the meeting. The following day I didn't go to school and was told to stay away from the window. The front gate remained locked and the dog was let off the chain. During the day committee members, led by a policeman, came to the gate but finding it locked and with the dog barking like she had gone mad they left. Father sat at the table writing all day. I woke up several times during the night and saw him still writing. The next day he slept through the afternoon and I had to be very quiet. Once again, I felt that I was a burden to my parents. I saw my godfather's baby die in his mother's arms. I was afraid to die. I thought, "It would have been better not to have been born but it was too late now."

When I woke up the following morning, Father was gone. Mother told me that he would be away for a while and I wouldn't be able to go to school or play outside until he returned. Days were long and boring. When the windows were not frozen, I could see children sliding on their sleds but when they were covered with thick ice, I couldn't see what was going on in the street. Uncle Pavel came over a few times to tell Mother what was going on in the village. Some families had been evicted from their homes and their relatives were not allowed to let them into their house.

The committee members probably didn't know where my father was or what he was up to. They didn't bother us but Mother said we had to be ready for the unexpected so we slept fully dressed. It was extremely uncomfortable lying in bed fully dressed. Lying awake I tried to picture the places where we might end up, in whose house we would live and where the previous owners had been exiled. Should I take my school books with me or I would I get new ones when we got there? Would I miss this place and my friends badly or would I quickly forget about them? I was thinking that undesirable people everywhere would be forced to leave their home and relocate somewhere else. At that time, I couldn't know that the majority of exiled people were unloaded in the Siberian forests, in the middle of nowhere, and perished from hunger and cold.

The winter of 1929–30 was joyless. People were absorbed by waiting for the unknown. The kolkhoz was organized; cattle and horses were gathered in one place. Women resisted having their cows taken away and some of them were arrested.

My father had been gone for a long time. It started to get warm outside. The sun was shining brighter and windows were clear of ice. I sat at the window all day watching my friends sliding down the street on their sleds and wishing I could join them.

The winter festival, called Maslennica, was approaching. It was the last celebration before Lent. Normally it was a great festivity with enormous parties. It was staged as a "show off" event where everybody and everything was judged according to their looks and performance. Everyone knew the showing off was a pretense but acted like it was the most natural thing in the world. The young people did their best to gain the approval of the village elders, who were sharp observers and conveyed their approval or disapproval of the goings on. Young bachelors rode with young ladies on brightly decorated sleds pulled by two or three horses. The most desirable brides were noticed, which led to new match making arrangements and weddings were performed on a grand scale. There was also the occasional brawling by drunks that was considered a disgrace but was gleefully accepted by the people.

On the memorable day of my father's return, I was sitting at the window watching my friends as they played outside. It was a bright, sunny day. I was watching the drops of water slowly running down the icicle outside the window. Every drop froze to the tip of the icicle making it grow longer before my eyes. Being preoccupied with the icicle I didn't see our horse walking slowly up the street. Father was kneeling on the sled. The horse stopped at the gate and Father got off the sled slowly as he looked up and down the street. It seemed he was moving in slow motion. Mother ran out to open the gate that had been bolted since Father's departure.

The horse walked in through the open gate and stopped near the stable. Father, with a wide grin on his face, was talking to Mother. She started to walk toward the gate to bolt it but Father shook his head from side to side, indicating that it wasn't necessary. Mother came in excited and told me that I could go outside to play with my friends.

I looked out and saw a band of people coming to our gate with a policeman in the lead. The policeman wore a black sheepskin coat and a belt with a shoulder strap. On the belt was a gun holster attached to his right hip. All government officials wore skin or leather coats in those days, while the so-called poor people's "committee members" were usually dressed in rags. The gate flew open and the policeman stepped in first. In the blink of an eye our dog jumped on his chest and he fell flat on his back. The dog jumped back in surprise and ran into her kennel barking all the way. The policeman jumped to his feet and drew his gun. In an effort to cover his embarrassment he pointed the gun toward the stable, yelling, "Where is she? I will shoot the bitch!"

Father came out of the stable and walked toward the group. He poked his chest with his finger as if to ask, "Are you looking for me?" He stopped when he reached the policeman and said, "Here I am." The police man removed a warrant from his pocket and started to read it, but Father stopped him and produced his own document. The policeman stretched out his hand to grab it, but Father pulled it back far enough to be out of reach but close enough for the policeman to read. The policeman stretched his neck to scan the document from a distance, turned on his heel and directed the rest of the group to follow him. So, they left and our family was left in peace, at least for a while.

The story behind the letter was as follows: After he was expelled from the meeting where he confronted Vishnevsky, Father came home and wrote a letter/report that described his status and assets, and the actions of the organizing committee. He traveled 700 kilometers by sled to Moscow to petition a government official who would be able to resolve his predicament. It took almost two weeks to reach Uncle Piotor's place in Himky, on the outskirts of Moscow. Eventually he got an audience in the ministry and received a certificate stating that the bearer of such a document couldn't be forced to join a collective farm or be evicted from his residence. It was signed by the chairman of the Supreme Soviet and was stamped with an official seal.

Officially, collectivization was completed by springtime. Those who didn't join the kolkhoz were called "yedinolichniky," meaning "individuals." The following summer surveyors came to divide the land, planning to give the most fertile areas to the kolkhoz and leaving the less productive land for those who refused to join. The "individuals" were outraged and their women went after the surveyors in the field with sticks. The surveyors ran to the village and barricaded themselves in a house. The women blockaded the house until police came and arrested few of them. Among those arrested was my mother. She was sentenced to a year of forced labor or a fine of 150 rubles. Father borrowed the money from relatives to pay the fine and Mother was released.

The land was finally surveyed and divided but there were no processes in place and the members of the kolkhoz encountered all kinds of problems. For example, they were supposed to gather their cows and horses in one place to be used communally but because there were insufficient buildings to house them, the animals had to be taken back to their original owners.

Those who didn't join the kolkhoz farmed as usual, helping each other during the heavy work seasons. Our relatives, with four horses between them, managed to plough and seed each other's share of land including that owned by the widow of Uncle Gerasim. My godfather, Nicolas was already an established homesteader with a horse and a cow. His brother, Inokenty married a girl whose parents were evicted from their home and lived in their steam bath. Her father was known as a gendarme because before the revolution that was his occupation. He was the only law enforcement of a jurisdiction that covered the whole district of about twenty villages.

Former government officials and people who were evicted from their homes by the Communist regime were called "Kulaks" and considered political enemies. Kulak is Russian for "fist," which could be used against the government. The government in power believed that as the opposing force it was necessary to eliminate the Kulaks, which was carried out in a campaign called "raskulachvat."

The next campaign to be carried was the expropriation of people's jewelry and silver coins, which were extensively used for adorning a woman's headpiece. These headpieces were family heirlooms collected over several generations and no one wanted to part with them willingly. Organized gangs of activists searched every household and confiscated whatever they found of value, including the icons that were adorned with silver or gold. That was followed by a campaign to close churches. Church bells and crosses from church domes were removed and sent to foundries. Icons were stripped of their precious metal parts and burned on bonfires, along with all birth and death records, mine included.

The last time I attended our parish church in Lutsk was for the Epiphany service. Father took me there, saying that it would be last time I would ever see anything like it. The church building was surrounded by throngs of people holding huge, lit candles. Women were wailing and everyone was praying with a loud voice. My hair stood on end as I experienced what was for me, really scary. Within a day or two after the service, the priest was arrested and the church vandalized beyond recognition.

I finished my second year of school. The following year was relatively peaceful and another school year flew by. Because of the law regarding elimination of illiteracy, which was instituted with the Communist regime, more children were added to the classroom and it was not unusual to find older girls joining younger children in the first grade. Cousin Sophia sat with us for three years until she was seventeen years old. Older girls often quit school after the third grade and older boys without fathers left after the fourth grade so they could help their mothers earn a living in the kolkhoz. The classroom became so crowded there wasn't enough room to accommodate all four grades.

In the fourth year we were transferred to a school in Polevye Shep-thovo, a village three kilometers from us. It was a more established school with two large class rooms and two teachers, Vasily Ivanovich Slesarev and his wife, Maria Stepanovna. She was Vishnevsky's daughter. They had been teaching school for a long time and continued to discipline children using methods that would be considered child abuse today, such as pulling students by their ear or slapping the palm of their hand with a ruler.

The most severe and embarrassing punishment for students was to kneel on the floor facing the corner and listen to everyone's snickering. Stories were told about this punishment in previous years when buckwheat was spread on the floor where the offender would kneel. One had to do with a village clown in his early twenties whom I will call Joe. Several years earlier Joe was in Maria Stepanovna's class. Being a smart aleck, he was often punished by the teacher. One day he made a bet with classmates that he could kneel on buckwheat all day long. He had a chance to prove it the next day. He was put on the buckwheat and fell asleep while kneeling, which made the teacher furious. She announced that he would be kneeling there the next morning as well. The next morning the teacher checked Joe's pants and found pieces of sheepskin sown inside on the knees of his trousers. She got so mad that she expelled Joe on the spot, which is what he wanted to happen. The government order for older boys to attend school was perceived as punishment and getting expelled was his reprieve.

Maria Stepanovna's daughter, Nina, was in third grade and her son, Nicky, in first grade. On one occasion our class couldn't solve a math problem. To shame us she called her daughter from the other room and told her to solve the problem. Nina couldn't solve it either so her mother slapped her across the face and chased her out. We thought it was funny but obviously didn't think then how Nina must have felt.

We were encouraged to join the Pioneers League and take an oath of allegiance to be vigilant members ready to do whatever the League asked. We were encouraged to follow the example of Pavlik Morose, the poster child for the youth of the Soviet Union. He was an eight-year-old boy from Siberia, who betrayed his father by reporting to government officials where the grain was hidden. The hidden grain was confiscated and Pavlik's father arrested and sentenced to many years of hard labor. Pavlik was supposedly strangled by his uncle for what he did but government officials declared Pavlik a martyr, who gave his life for the wellbeing of Soviet Society. I was not eligible to join the Pioneers because of my father's stance against collectivization and I wasn't sorry for it. I hated Pavlik's guts but felt really sorry for his uncle who was sentenced to be executed.

That winter I stayed with distant relatives during the week, coming home only on weekends and holidays. Their daughter, Ludmila, was my classmate and eventually became a teacher. Every evening we ate dumpling soup with finely chopped pork and garlic added to it. Garlic was a common staple in every household but here it was used in larger portions than I was used to. If for no other reason, I was glad to be home Saturday and Sunday without the garlic in my diet.

I graduated from public school with high marks and was awarded a pair of factory-produced socks but I didn't have suitable shoes to be able to wear them. Other awards were bars of soap. That evening, as part of the graduation celebration, we staged a play and sang patriotic songs.

The following year our school was reorganized to include a seven-year curriculum and three additional teachers. All three graduated from St. Petersburg Teachers College. A dismantled two-room house was added to the existing building. One room became our classroom and the other became the kitchen, which housed a large cauldron for boiling potatoes.

For three years our lunch consisted of boiled potatoes with salt. It wasn't much, but in those days, it was almost a luxury. In return, our class gathered potatoes for the collective farm during harvest time. During wintertime the boiling cauldron created lots of steam and when the kitchen door was opened the hall and our classroom were filled with steam. Occasionally, at mealtime, we misbehaved by throwing hot potatoes at each other. On one occasion, the principal came to check up on us. He stuck his head through the door at the same time someone launched a hot potato in that direction and was struck right in the forehead. He wasn't injured but the class received a stern lecture so we stopped our lunchtime antics.

The local cabinet maker built our desks as well as a bookcase with glass doors for our library. I was appointed librarian and was entrusted with the key. The school also acquired its first microscope and .22 mm rifle.

Two new subjects were added to the existing curriculum. One of them was a woodworking class and the other was a paramilitary program designed to teach endurance and target shooting. Pupils in the fifth grade came from four different villages and most boys stayed after class to work on projects in the carpentry shop or improve their rifle shooting skills.

The instructor of the paramilitary program taught at several schools and visited us once a week. We behaved well in his class and he trusted us but boys being boys, eventually we learned how to smuggle a few extra shells. Once I fashioned a miniature pistol-like contraption from an empty shell. I loaded the shell with less gunpowder than one pellet and shot it against the window pane at close range, making a perfect hole in the glass. Over a period of time, I successfully created several holes, which were discovered but nobody knew how they were created or by whom.

I spent the next two winters with Aunt Matrena, who lived with several children in a small hut. Her husband had been exiled and the family was evicted from the main house. Personal space was at a premium but we didn't feel crowded. I remember chopping fire wood occasionally with her oldest daughters. Once while cutting wood the axe slipped and cut through my felt boot into my foot. The boots were almost new and I was more concerned with how to fix the boot than with the injury I sustained so I didn't tell anyone about the accident.

We always had beggars but in 1933 they multiplied immensely. They came from the Ukraine and the lower Volga districts. Some beggars sang church songs, asking for compassion or mercy for Christ's sake. They went from door to door but not every household could afford to give even a small piece of bread to every beggar. According to the government the beggars were illegal drifters who couldn't be employed locally. The older people knew what was going on and kept quiet but I spent many sleepless nights trying to understand why so many people would be hungry at one time. People worked hard and lived frugally, following the government's slogan of the day, "Catch Up and Overtake Capitalist Countries," but why the government would starve so many working people was beyond my understanding.

In 1934, construction began on the first "paved" highway in our area. It ran between the Kanash Railroad Station and Ulyanovsk, and passed about three kilometers from our village. It was built literally with picks and shovels. Every village got a quota requiring it to supply a workforce and horse-drawn buggies to haul whatever material was needed. After the road was graded, men were hired to lay cobblestone as the finishing surface. My father was among them.

One day he told me to come to the worksite and read a newspaper article aloud during the noon break. The article was Stalin's "Constitution," which was to be read and discussed at every workplace. So, every day for several days I walked three kilometers each way to read to the workers. It was all just a formality since honest discussion could lead to imprisonment. The workers praised the article believing everything they heard. The Constitution contained many good points theoretically but they were hardly ever fulfilled by the authorities. In Father's opinion it was too good to be true and he was right. For my effort all I got was a pat on the shoulder.

After completion of the highway a tower was erected near our village. It was about ten meters high with a platform on top. Nobody knew its intended purpose but it gave us youngsters a place to climb and wait for something to appear. After climbing the tower several times, we became disappointed: the new highway was void of traffic. In art class I decided to draw the new highway with an automobile on it. Up to now I had never seen one so I drew my fantasy automobile with a smoke stack on its roof similar to that of a steam engine.

A few weeks later a real automobile appeared in our village. The district administrator obtained a car from the government and was touring the villages. Children surrounded the car like a swarm of bees. The driver asked me for directions to the chairman's residence. While I was explaining how to get there, he told me to hop in and show him where to go. I rode one hundred meters to the chairman's house and stepped out feeling like the luckiest boy in the village, who got to ride in a real automobile.

After the collective farms were organized, tractor depots appeared in district centers. The tractors came from Ford factories in the United States and were called "Fordzons." Trade schools were established to train eligible young people as operators and mechanics. Working on tractors was considered a prestigious profession and most of the operators were showoffs and braggarts. On one occasion I was in a clinic for a medical check-up when a tractor driver came in with an ear problem. The nurse took him in immediately and came out a little later carrying a basin containing the liquid that she had used to wash out his ear. In it swam a live louse that was extracted from his ear.

At sowing time tractors were dispatched to collective farms to plough their fields. After the harvest the farms had to repay the tractor depots with grain. Prices for everything were determined by the district autocrats.

The government also demanded "the first grain" of the harvest from every household; a quota based on acreage and not the quality of the harvest. In those years that produced a poor harvest people were left with very little for themselves. There was an additional quota for milk, eggs, meat, and skins. The government gave a token amount of money for delivered goods. Before collectivization the men would often travel to Moscow to earn extra money but after collectivization people were forbidden to travel without permission. They had to stay and work on the Kolkhoz.

Individual households were obligated to pay an income tax several times a year. Those who couldn't pay were declared malicious offenders and sentenced to two years in a labor camp. The strategy was designed to get as much as possible from people to force them to join the Kolkhoz.

Individual households and collective farm members worked hard on their garden plots just to survive but the government felt people were spending too much time in their gardens so they issued a decree to reduce the size of garden plots and forbade individual households from keeping a cow or horse. Without a large garden plot most households couldn't grow enough potatoes to feed a pig, the only source of meat for most families; and without a cow for milk, there was nothing to feed the babies. There was no way to survive except by joining the Kolkhoz and continuing a meager existence. There were many other restrictions that didn't make any sense but an order was an order and anyone who expressed an objection disappeared forever in the labor camps.

Between 1930 and 1932 our house was often searched by the police. They suspected my father of owning a rifle and hand grenades and they looked everywhere by poking the ground and straw roof with a pitch fork. I knew the rifle was often kept at a friend's place in a neighboring village but I didn't believe he had grenades. Eventually, Father took the rusted remains of four grenades from their hiding place and left them where the police would find them. The police found them on their next visit and arrested Father. He was released after one week's incarceration and was left in peace for a while.

One day his Tatar friend, a former merchant who had been forced to close his business, brought a heavy sack to our home. Before his goods were confiscated by the government, he took rolls of good quality fabric and brought it to us hoping it would be safe there. Initially the sack was hidden under the straw in the barn but toward springtime all the straw was gone so it was brought in and placed on the top of the brick oven. When my parents were out working, I would often open the sack and admire the quality of the smooth woolen cloth daydreaming about how it would be to have a coat made from it. I knew that it would be absolutely impossible for several reasons. Firstly, the fabric didn't belong to us and secondly, it would be impossible to wear such a coat without raising suspicion. In no time the police would be on our doorstep with a search warrant.

Eventually the police did come to search the house as was their habit. They found and confiscated the sack of merchandise and arrested my father. After nightfall that night someone came with the message from my father. He was being detained in our school building overnight and wanted to see me. I ran the three kilometers in the dark was let in by the policeman in charge, who didn't object to my visit. In a whispered voice, my father said that I had to deliver a warning to the merchant's family before daybreak. It would take four hours to reach the merchant's village if I went by the traveled road so I took a shortcut and by running through the snow-packed fields, cut the trip by an hour. I left home around three a.m. and reached my destination at six.

I woke the merchant's wife and daughters with a light knock on the window and delivered the message. Though we didn't speak the same language they knew enough Chuvash to understand what I told them and they praised me to high heaven for being fearless enough to walk that distance alone at night. During the course of our conversation, the daughters said they remembered carrying me around through their father's store when I was about two years old. They had a good laugh when I told them that mothers in our village threatened their children by saying that they would be sold to traveling Tatar peddlers if they were disobedient. My mother effectively used that threat against me until these two daughters spoiled me with candies and cookies in their store. The next time Mother threatened me I started to cry and said, "I want to go to the Tatars!"

Mother was relieved to see me return safely later that morning. I felt a deep sense of accomplishment even though I didn't know what the end result would be. After all, Father had been arrested many times before and was usually released within a few days. I expected the same thing would happen this time, but Father was kept under arrest until he went to court and was found not guilty. Father's merchant friend was sentenced to two years of forced labor.

Chapter 6

First radio

We first heard about radios in the fall of 1934, when one was installed in our school in Batyrevo, a district center. First, two tall posts were erected next to our school building and a copper wire was strung between them as an antenna. Then the radio receiver was installed in our classroom. We were told it was a talking box that transmitted a voice from faraway places. People were skeptical and old, superstitious grannies were sure that the voice was from devil.

School children were told to spread the news amongst the townsfolk encouraging them to come to the first demonstration of a news broadcast. On the appointed evening our classroom was packed with people anxious to hear the "talking box." The man in charge sat by the radio wearing huge earphones on his ears. Everyone watched closely as he turned the knob and dial indicator back and forth trying to get a signal and listened intently to the hissing and crackling sound that followed. Suddenly a voice came from the box and said, "Attention, attention, Cheboksary speaking here." The room fell silent and grannies crossed themselves. Someone looked behind the box to see who might be hiding there. Some even rushed to see what was under the table, suspecting some kind of trick. The broadcast lasted for over half an hour and afterward, everyone started to express their opinion. The same procedure was repeated the next evening.

The following day the man came to talk to our class about the radio. What he told us was very exciting. At recess time the principal asked me to remain in the classroom. The man showed me how operate the radio including how to connect and disconnect the aggregate (battery) and where to keep the dial needle to hear "the voice." As the librarian, with the key to the bookcase, I was also entrusted to keep the radio safely locked away when not in use. People gathered every evening for two weeks to listen to the news and I felt very proud to be able to wear the ear phones on my head and operate the radio, until the radio stopped working.

The battery died and my pride died with it. Nobody provided a new battery and the radio stood idle for two years, until I left the school. During that summer vacation someone broke the lock and stole the shiny tubes from the radio. I felt badly that all the cost and effort that went into installing and operating the radio came to such a futile end.

But back to some good memories. Extracurricular activities kept us busy during these school years and included building model airplanes, collecting bugs and butterflies, and participating in a drama guild; my favorite. We were encouraged to organize concerts, stage plays, sketches, and poetry recitals. While we were in Grade Five, everything was planned and conducted by the teacher, but the following year, I was given all that responsibility. I chose the play for each event and assigned the roles. I remember on one occasion when a classmate was not happy with his given role. I had an explosive temperament back then and slapped his face when he expressed his dissatisfaction. Later in life I recalled the occasion many times and felt remorseful for my mean spiritedness. I had an occasion to meet up with my old classmate sixty years later and I apologized for my imprudent action but he said didn't remember the occasion.

In addition to performing, we were responsible for building and tearing down the stage sets. We didn't have curtains and had to persuade the future brides of the village to lend us their bedspreads to use as curtains. It was risky for the brides-to-be because there was a chance their treasured bedspread would get soiled. At the same time, it was appealing because it was a nonchalant way of showing off their dowry. After the first girl took a chance and trusted us the others were easier to persuade.

That same year, the Kolkhoz Theater was organized in Batyrevo. The troupe of actors who were hired had some training and received a salary comparable to that of the teachers. They toured the villages and put on performances similar to what we did in school. The theater came to our school for the first time when I was in seventh grade. We set up the stage for their performance and rehearsed a play we would be performing at a future date. They watched us and gave some tips on how to act in some segments of the performance. After watching our rehearsal several of them suggested that I should apply to the school of performing arts in Cheboksary.

The last year of school was full of humorous and poignant memories. We developed a very close relationship with the three young teachers who had taught us for three years. They were born and raised in the same village and all three graduated from the teachers college in Leningrad. For me, the two male teachers were role models. I wondered if I would ever be like them, educated and well-dressed. I was always self-conscious of my poor clothing and it became painful when we suddenly realized how fast we grew up.

Three months before graduation our school received a more powerful microscope and our Zoology class became very interesting. The year was an awkward time of our lives. We felt all grown up and didn't know how to behave. The girls started to flirt with us and we, boys, felt embarrassed. The Zoology and Chemistry teacher was the sister of one of the male teachers. During one of her classes, she was explaining that frogs multiplied like fish, by spawning eggs. One boy asked, "Why then are frogs mounted on each other?" She probably didn't expect such a direct question and hesitated in responding. "Maybe he's squeezing the eggs out of her," came a response from the quietest boy in the class. Everyone roared with laughter, which was too much to handle for the young, female teacher. She announced a recess and left the classroom.

During that last year our drama guild was functioning really well. We traveled to the surrounding villages with performances and people were talking about how good we were. At the end of June, as part of the graduation ceremony, we gave our last performance. I was awarded with pair of socks and a bar of soap for successfully completing school. That was the second pair of factory-made socks I owned but I still didn't have the shoes to wear with those socks.

We were the first graduating class in our school. Of the eight graduates from our village, three were thinking of further education. There were special schools with three-year programs for training primary school teachers, book keepers, and nurses. Such schools would place advertisements in the local newspapers explaining what documents would be needed and what subjects the entrance exams would cover. At the bottom of the advertisement was an insert in smaller print stating, "Only the children of collective farmers need apply." That was my stumbling block or dead end. Father resolved not to join the kolkhoz so I was stuck in the village.

In October, after graduation, a government directive came out requiring each village to organize evening classes for their illiterate adults. On the recommendation of the local teacher, I got the job to teach the adults. I created a list of twenty people who fit the criteria and it brought to the chairman of the village soviet. He made it clear I wasn't the man that he would have selected for the position but he stamped his approval on the list.

The program was very basic, starting with learning the A, B, Cs. My pupils were, to say the least, not very bright or enthusiastic people. I was just a teenager and was completely lost as to how to handle the situation but after some sleepless nights I decided to try to be more like them by being less timid and it improved the situation slightly.

After getting my first pay of fifty rubles, I ran home thinking about where I could finally buy a new pair of leather shoes but a big disappointment was waiting for me at home. A distant relative had come for the money Father had borrowed to bail Mother out of jail sometime back and hadn't been able to repay up to this point. I handed the money to Father and went outside to cry. I was hurt and angry at the government officials for creating such a miserable condition for the common people. The second pay went to the same place as the first. The third pay was postponed with the promise that I would be paid after the class graduated.

The chairman kept postponing graduation and finally told me to bring the list to the office. He stamped and signed it with a smile, telling me that was the way to avoid unnecessary hassle. I didn't see the rest of the money, even though I kept going to his office every, so called, payday. A few months previously, I overheard him bragging that he could send an additional tax bill to anybody and make them pay. Understanding his dishonesty gave me the courage to be bolder and I kept coming back for what was rightfully mine.

The last time I went to his office, he refused to talk to me, saying that he didn't have time. A representative from the district office was visiting and seeing that I wasn't leaving, the chairman whispered something to the representative, who walked directly to me and asked, "Why does your father refuse to join the Kolkhoz?" I told him the reason I was there and that he was off topic. My voice was quivering from hurt and anger as I said, "Since you take me for a stupid kid, I have no right to lecture my father regarding what to do." Closing the door behind me, I heard the chairman say, "See, what can you expect from the offspring?" Finally, I wrote to the district attorney explaining the situation and then went to see him. I believed that somewhere there had to be fairness and honesty but got only empty assurances. I became convinced that an ordinary man was powerless against government representatives.

Eventually I forgot the chairman and the money he essentially stole from me. Four years later though, I ran into him and his family at the railroad station. He recognized me and acted as though he were happy to see me. He said he was going to virgin lands in Kazakhstan on the government's resettlement plan. I felt like saying something very nasty but seeing his snotty-nosed kids sitting there on duffel bags caused me to swallow my anger. He lost his post as chairman of the village soviet and figured that he would find a similar position if he relocated. Evidently, he didn't find it and wasn't used to hard work. The only thing he could do was to return to his native village with his meager belongings, poorer than when he left.

During the summer months after graduation, I scoured every available newspaper for the educational institution ads. Finally, Chuvash State Theater School posted their ad, which said it was looking for talented youth with acting abilities. The requirements included submitting a written application, a birth certificate and one passport-size photo. My birth record was burned during the church closing campaign and I couldn't find any records in the pre- revolution archives of the district. I explained my problem to the secretary of village soviet and he issued a birth certificate.

The next problem was the photo. There wasn't a photographer anywhere. Cousin Ivan knew one person who had a camera but he lived eighteen kilometers from us. I walked there once to be photographed and went back three times to get my picture. It cost me three rubles and seventy-two kilometers of walking to get a sad looking, barely recognizable print of me.

One week after mailing the papers I received notice that my application had been accepted and I should report to take the entrance exams on such and such a date. I decided to keep the news quiet until something definitely happened.

An overwhelming concern at that time was my clothing. I didn't have clothing for the city. Even shoes were homemade. An interesting story concerning footwear remains in my memory forever. Our neighbor saw a pair of women's shoes for sale at the market but the asking price was too high and they were not sold. The only thing he remembered was the village where the seller of the shoes lived. Father immediately decided to go and pay the asking price for the shoes. I knew he would spend all the money he had for me but the idea of wearing women's shoes wasn't appealing. I prayed that the shoes wouldn't be available and I guess my prayers were answered. Father returned without shoes, disappointed that he came a few minutes too late, but I was relieved.

Mother worried that I wouldn't be able to find my way around in the city. In those days most village people didn't travel farther than the local fair. I was short for my age and had never been far from home but ultimately everything turned out well.

Chapter 7

The School of Performing Arts

Over one hundred candidates came for the entrance exams. Looking at the crowd I realized that my worries about being poorly dressed were for nothing. We were all alike except for a few girls who wore city dresses. The instruction posted on the board was simple. First came a preliminary test of acting ability followed by a test on academic subjects and lastly, a final test of acting ability.

As names were generally listed in alphabetical order my name was usually at the top of the list so I was the one who would almost always be called first. I was used to being first on the list and found it easier on the nerves not having to wait too long for the unknown. Such was the case in this instance.

I recognized the examiner, with heavy rimmed glasses, from a picture in our school book. Maximov Koshkinsky was a playwright, founder of the Chuvash Theater and producer of the first film in the Chuvash language. My first encounter with him was shockingly short. The interview went roughly, as follows:

Koshkinsky: "What did you said your name was?"

Me: "I didn't say. This is the first time you've asked." My response was met with roaring laughter.

Koshkinsky: "Oh yes, I didn't ask, did I? What song can you sing for me?" I mentioned a well-known poem by Alexander Pushkin.

Koshkinsky: "Just recite the poem, please."

"Enough," he said after the first stanza. "See you later."

Everyone was anxious to see me come out of the examination room and hear what I had to say about my experience. In a couple of hours every person had gone through the first test and was waiting for the results. After an excruciating two hours a list was posted on the board and everyone rushed to it hoping to find his or her name on the list. From a distance I could see my name at the top of the list. Feeling relieved and ecstatic, I had the feeling that I would be admitted and my name would remain there for the years to come.

The next two days were filled with writing exams on general subjects and then came the grilling on acting. This time a formidable crowd of senior students occupied a row of chairs behind the table. A tall and exceptionally well-dressed lady acted as the chairperson and asked more questions than the others. She happened to be our future teacher of drama and acting, Valentina Savik-Saks. We were tested on our singing and dancing abilities, rhythm, and mime that was easy to understand. The interview and performance part of the exams took an additional two days and it was hard on everyone's nerves. Out of a hundred applicants, thirty were accepted on the condition that those whose performance fell below the accepted standard might be eliminated during the first year.

Because some of the classrooms in need of repair had not been completed in a timely manner the beginning of school was postponed for several weeks. I returned home to wait for the call to return and had to listen to the village gossips whisper that I had not been accepted. In the meantime, the local cabinetmaker built me a plywood suitcase that Mother filled with non-perishable, "biscuits" (dry home-baked, rye bread) that I could take with me. She also prepared a three-liter jar of hard-boiled eggs in clarified butter. The call came in mid-October and Father drove me to Kanash by horse buggy.

He didn't have any money to give me, not even for bus fare back to school, so he took a sixteen-kilo bag of flour from his meagre supplies and sold it on the open market. He handed me the proceeds and said, "Sorry son, and don't feel guilty about anything. This hardship isn't your fault and it won't last forever." Unwanted tears rolled down our cheeks and we gave each other a big hug. My heart split in half as I thought, "What if I failed and all his sacrifice would be for nothing?"

The bus discharged its passengers at 11:00 p.m. in the dark, city square. Carrying the heavy suitcase on my shoulder, I reached the gates of the school building only to find it locked for the night. Knocking didn't produce any results so I climbed over the gate, opened it to retrieve my suitcase and locked it back up the way it was. I walked through the dimly-lit hallway hoping to find the watchman but nobody was there. I found a few early comers asleep in the room where we stayed during the entrance exams so I quietly took the first bed in the corner and that is where I slept for the following two years.

The sleeping quarters contained twenty beds, each with a side table, arranged in two rows alongside opposite walls. We lived an army style life. Each student was issued one pillow, one bedsheet and two army blankets. The pillow case and bedsheet were changed every week. Every morning our beds were inspected by third-year student, Gregory Ovchinikov. He woke us up by blowing a shrill whistle and once we were out of bed, led us in a half hour of physical exercise. After washing our faces, we ran to the mess hall for breakfast; 500 grams of fresh bread and a cup of sweet tea. At 1:00 p.m., after four hours of classes, we broke for lunch. The afternoon schedule consisted of another four hours of classes and then we were free until the next morning. For supper I ate the supplies from home while they lasted. By January I ran out of biscuits so for the next four months I lived on two meals a day, except for occasional evenings. When it was my turn to peel potatoes in the kitchen for the next day, I made sure we got lots of leftovers.

For the first three months I was terribly homesick but for obvious reasons I couldn't go home for winter break. Even if I could afford the trip, it would put an additional burden on my parents. They would feel obligated to supply me with sustenance, which was beyond their ability. I was glad at having been successful in the first term of school. With that big hurdle behind me, I didn't have to worry about being expelled but it was hard to sleep on an empty stomach. Many times I cried myself to sleep.

But in April, along with the sunshine, my life brightened up unexpectedly. One of my classmates came up with a brilliant idea that changed our economic plight. The 1st of May and 7th of November were the biggest celebrations in the Soviet Union. Every establishment was required to decorate their buildings with red banners that had slogans written on them. My job would be to go to every establishment and take orders to write slogans on their material and my friend would do the work. I didn't have any idea how it was done but my friend said he had the experience and could do it quickly. I was a shy person and making cold calls for sales orders made me feel apprehensive but after careful consideration I decided to try and see what would happen. The first store I went into gave me an order immediately.

It happened that painting slogans on banners was a very lucrative business and I brought rolls of material along with all kinds of brushes and pens (per my friend's guidance) to do the job. The paint medium was toothpowder mixed with paper glue and both were available for a reasonable price. We got permission from the building manager to work in one room and turned out many meters of slogans per evening. We charged two rubles per meter and by month's end we had three hundred rubles each. For me it was a miracle because I now had enough money to buy food. A full stomach changed my outlook and demeanor. The Drama teacher noticed the change and asked if I had fallen in love with someone.

Up to this time, I was still wearing rubber galoshes over white socks and was terribly ashamed of my footwear. There was a working tannery on the outskirts of town but no shoes were available in the stores. Every week I walked through the open market looking for a pair of shoes. In the market one could stumble on all kinds of unexpected things sold under-the-counter. My lucky day came just days before summer vacation, when I purchased a pair of soccer shoes at a sports equipment store. I removed all the cleats thinking that they would then be like regular shoes but without heels the shoes were uncomfortable. Regardless I decided to wear them and after a while they didn't feel too bad.

We finished the first year. The exam results were posted on the bulletin board showing our overall standing. My name was second on the list, after Ludmila Chernovsakaya. I didn't feel any resentment that she was first. She deserved it by all means. She was an outspoken city girl revered by the whole school and a leader among her peers. She had studied German previously and knew more than what was presented in our study book. She could translate the whole book without difficulty and was always willing to help those who asked for it.

She knew that my father was under GPU (later KGB) surveillance. Later on circumstances brought us closer and we trusted each other. Her father occupied a responsible government position and during the purge, in 1937, was arrested and never seen again. Ludmila disappeared suddenly and came back after a few weeks. Probably the instinct of self-preservation was at work amongst the people. Nobody asked questions but everyone knew what was going on. She told me that the KGB had interrogated her.

After the graduation speeches and usual dances everyone was eager to go home. I travelled to Kanash by bus, found a horse cart ride with people who passed through our village and by afternoon I was home. Near the village gate I met my babysitter, Sophia, with her friend so I hopped off the cart to greet them and realized how much I had grown in the past ten months. I was now taller than her. We passed by a group of women sitting by the gate doing handiwork and gossiping, which was the custom during the slack period of the summer. I lifted my straw hat to greet them, received a polite response and kept walking behind the horse cart. As the horse stopped at our house to unload my cumbersome suitcase, I heard the women laughing. I turned my head and saw my mother running like a teenager towards me. She had been sitting in the crowd and didn't recognize her son walking by.

In spite of the home sickness, I had mixed feelings about being home. It felt good to be treated like a celebrity by most of the villagers, which made the young communist party members jealous. They were stuck in the village forever and I felt smug about it. The sad part was the change around our house. The barn and stable were gone. They were confiscated and sold by the village administration for unpaid taxes. Except for a few chickens no animals were left in the homestead.

There was no bread in the house and no flour to bake it. Father and I had to walk to the district administrative center eighteen kilometers away to buy bread. Each person was allowed two kilograms and often late comers didn't get any. While we were there, he surprised me by walking into the KGB office. I didn't want to ask him what business he might have there but suspected that he was coerced into becoming an informant and spying on the village officials. Listening to him talking I got the picture that he hated what he was forced to do and felt guilty. Eventually, he was issued a passport and left the village to work in Kanash.

Being home, I got bored quickly and started to count the days before I could leave. Father read my thoughts and sat me down for our first heart-to-heart talk. What I heard from his lips was confusing and scary. He repeated how sorry he was for missing the chance to go to America. Maybe he was trying to tell me not to pass up the opportunity if it came my way, but then I didn't dwell on it. He was sure about an imminent war between the Soviet Union and Germany that would bring more hardship and suffering.

Mother wanted to visit her sisters with me while I was home. I remembered happy times from childhood when people were glad to see relatives anytime but times had changed and I was hesitant to visit anybody. People didn't have the resources to receive guests anymore and an unexpected visit could turn into an embarrassing experience for the host and visitors alike. But I relented to her wishes as she reasoned that this could be the last chance to see some of my aunts.

We came there to find an almost empty village. It wasn't like in the olden days when one could quit working for the day because of visitors. People were expected in the fields. It was a collective farm on an army-like regimen, where every worker had a day's quota to fill. The second oldest in Mother's family, Aunt Mary, was a widow. Her job was to milk the cows on the farm and deliver the milk for processing. There was a time when she could treat guests with milk products. My mother was sure that her sister would treat us with cottage cheese but Aunt Mary could share only her grief with my mother and have a good cry together. She didn't have even a slice of bread in the house. We departed feeling bitterly sorry for putting her in an embarrassing position.

A similar meeting occurred with my godmother. She had been married to a well-to-do widower but during collectivization their homestead was confiscated and her husband exiled. Now she and her three small children lived in a small shack. Every time I returned from the market I had to pass by her place. The last time we saw each other I was still a young boy. Now, being all grown up, I decided on the spur of the moment to surprise her by stopping in to say hello.

She was excited to see me. In no time she boiled three eggs, put them on a plate with a slice of bread and asked me to the table. Reluctantly I sat down face-to-face with three hungry children. I didn't know how to act in the situation I was in. By the look in the children's eyes, I could read that they never had an egg in their entire lives. Their mother pulled stretching little hands away from the plate but their eyes were glued to the eggs. I was lost in my thoughts and didn't know what to do. Excusing myself as best I could I left the table and soon the house.

During my visit in 1993, I was told that one of those children grew up crippled and lived alone in a strange village but I didn't have a chance to see her and she died in 2000 before our second visit.

It made no sense to me to remain in our village any longer. Reluctantly I took sixty rubles from Father, knowing that was all he had. He knew a truck driver who drove to the city every day with a load of lime. We walked to the highway to catch the truck. I climbed on the pile of lime and after a two-hour ride reached my destination, covered with lime dust from head to toe, itchy all over my body and yearning for a steam bath.

The Second Year

Studies were going well. Drama and special disciplines required lots of practice but the rest was easy. Political Economy and History of the Communist Party were boring subjects but gradually I discovered that the teacher's mind was preoccupied with something else and he wasn't paying attention to our answers. Fast and continuous talking did the trick and I always got good marks.

Financially, I was better off than the year before. The city's preparation for celebrating the anniversary of the October Revolution on November 7th gave me the opportunity to earn extra money. This time, because I had some experience collecting orders, we made even more money. Occasionally we participated in a play's crowd scenes and were paid four rubles per performance. Even four rubles made difference in our budget. It was enough to buy four kg of bread or almost one kg of sugar.

That year, my sister, Vera, was in eighth grade and attended a school located in Komsomolsk. Mother was home alone. For the New Year break I decided to visit Father in Kanash and then visit Mother in the village if I could find the transportation. I met people from our village, who delivered loads of grain for the state and were returning home in empty sleds. I asked for ride with them to the village and they agreed, hinting as a joke, if I bought them home brew on the way. We left the city late that afternoon and after driving for two hours, reached the village where I bought a large container of home brew for five rubles. I had tried it before and didn't like it because it guaranteed a heavy hangover but this time, following the custom of the people that the first drink was for the buyer, I downed a full glass, which nearly cost me my life.

We resumed our journey. One glass of brew was enough to put me to sleep on the sled. After some time, sensing unusual quietness I woke up. All three horses stopped at a haystack to munch. I recognized the place as being three kilometers from our destination. I led one horse back out on the road and the rest followed. My head was spinning and I felt rotten. I thought about how the others must feel because they drank three times more than me.

The next thing I recalled was my mother's voice telling me to wake up. She was violently shaking me by the shoulder and calling my name. I got off the sled and leaned on her as I walked. My feet felt like they were making a creaking sound inside my boots. As soon as we reached the house Mother pulled my shoes off. My socks were covered with frost as though I walked in them through the snow. Mother brought in a pail of snow and rubbed my feet with snow until I felt the pain. And then I slept.

I awoke the next morning to the crackling sound of burning wood and Mother making breakfast for me. Apparently, upon arrival at the stables the night before, everyone got off the sled and walked home. There was a stableman to look after the horses but he was sleeping too. One of my travelling companions went to my mother's house and knocked on her window to tell her where I was. She had to run out on a cold winter night to save her son from freezing to death. I didn't experience any ill aftereffects and considered myself very lucky. I thought about my stupidity and about the power higher than we are who directs our steps.

While I was home, I went to see Uncle Pavel's widow. My uncle died suddenly a few months earlier. He was only in his mid-fifties then. I recalled how just the previous summer he complimented me on my soccer shoes without heels. He talked about his oldest son, Petya, and how he missed him. Petya left home without telling his parents and didn't write home for five years. Uncle Pavel died without seeing his son, and to me, that was very sad.

Across the street from our house was the village school where I had spent time teaching illiterate young people to read or substituting for the teacher when he had to go away for a day. The current teacher, Nicolai Skvortsow, suggested staging a play while I was there. Young people, including the Comsomol activists, were excited and anxious to participate. We staged the same play that I was working on at that time in theater school. It was one of the few pieces in the Chuvash language written by one of the founders of the theater. He was the chief surgeon at the city clinic but often came to rehearsals and knew most students by names.

Word spread fast and people from neighboring villages came to see "real artists" perform. To accommodate everyone who wanted to see the performance we played two nights. The performance was below my expectations but it was an educational experience for me and a memorable night for the villagers. That fall, when I was back at school, I told the author about it and he praised my daring act given the circumstance, comparing it to handling a hot iron with bare hands.

Before I went back to school, Mother presented me with a length of blue satin and other length of black satin for shirts as a gift. Both pieces were too short for a full-size shirt, but a seamstress figured out how to sew good-looking shirts with short sleeves.

Getting back to school was another adventure. On my own I could have found a way of getting to Kanash but Mother wanted to deliver fresh bedding to Father. There was only one person in the village who could lend us a horse. The roads were slippery and our sled had only wooden runners. It kept swaying from side to side and hitting the snow banks. In one place it swung wide and overturned. Mother and I flew out of the sled and landed in deep snow. I jumped to my feet to help Mother but she was worried about me and was on her feet sooner than me. She was a tough woman for her age.

Political unrest was manifesting itself in our world at this time. For example, the Soviet Union and Japan were engaged in border skirmishes in Mongolia, which started in 1932 and ended in 1939 at place called Khalkhin Gol. One of the major conflicts occurred in 1938 when Japan attacked Soviet forces in the Battle of Lake Khasan. According to legend, Officer Vinocorow was wounded by a shell that penetrated his tank. Japanese soldiers surrounded the tank and attempted to pull it with a team of oxen. Vinocorow bandaged his wound and sat quietly till nightfall. After dark he got out of his tank and ran to join his own forces. He was decorated for heroism with a medal and was awarded the title, Hero of the Soviet Union.

Vinocorow returned to his native city, Cheboksary, and was received with high honors. He told his story in every school and factory around. He was a role model for the youth as to how to serve their great country. For the working people he was an example of how selflessly they should work for the safety and wellbeing of the working class.

Another example was the civil war in Spain. Fascists, led by General Franco, fought against Republicans. Franco forces were supported by Germany and the Republicans by the Soviet Union, along with international brigades. The general public didn't know that they were directly involved in this war until pictures of Heroes of the Soviet Union started to appear in the newspapers.

In the theater a play was produced, which showed the heroic battle for a fortress called "Alcatraz." Villagers and factory workers were brought by buses to see the play that ran for weeks without interruption. We participated in the crowd scenes again and earned four rubles per night. When the May 1st celebrations came my friend and I created banners again and made additional money. Gradually I was able to save up enough money to buy clothing at an acceptable level, like a city dweller.

In late fall, Father surprised me by bringing me a brand-new suit. He got it "under the table" at one store. Because most stores were generally so devoid of merchandise, the word "buy "almost disappeared from the Russian vocabulary. People "got" things by standing in line at a store all night or by bartering, favor for favor. The suit was outstanding and even my teachers asked where I got it. The quality of the material, however, was good for nothing. By springtime the trousers developed two round holes in the seat. But fortune smiled on me again and I got myself a brand-new, dark blue suit.

Schoolwork continued without a hitch. I finished with the highest marks in the class and was awarded with two weeks at a health spa in Ilyinka. The place was a pristine spot on the right bank of the Volga about fifty kilometers from Cheboksary. Three or four persons were assigned per room. My roommates included a tractor driver and combine operator from a Kolkhoz. We were fed three sumptuous meals every day. The only strict requirements were to be punctual for meals and to go to bed at the required time. Otherwise, we were free to do as we pleased. I spent my time reading, taking nature walks, and occasionally playing volleyball. Every second day I sat in the steam bath for hours just sweating.

At bedtime the rooms were checked by a doctor. The tractor driver was absent every night and was reprimanded every time. According to policy a person who broke the rules three times was supposed to be sent home but it was never enforced. Men and women came without their mates and were using their freedom to have "fun." The beach provided an isolated spot cluttered with piles of logs. It was accessed by a wooden stairway with a platform between the flights. Railings and benches on the platform were covered with graffiti, and cave writings expressed who loved whom. One limerick described the quality of service one received there. It said, "At the rest house of Ilyinka we were fed very well. Every day we enjoyed fresh air, sunshine, water and porridge from pearl barley."

On the shore was a dock for local boat traffic but regular passenger steamers didn't stop there. There were no life guard stations like in Cheboksary so swimmers were on their own regardless of what might happen to them. Once we witnessed a man drown in the river. He was intoxicated and was arguing with a woman, most likely his wife. He took off his shirt and walked into the river. The woman was pleading with him not to do it but he kept walking. He swam to the middle of the river, turned around and waved with one hand as though saying good bye and disappeared under the water about 500 meters from shore. The woman was hysterical and we couldn't do anything to help.

After two weeks' rest, I returned to Cheboksary. With all the students gone, and the theater on vacation the city was desolate and boring. I walked to the bus station across the street and bought a ticket to Kanash for the next morning. To kill time, I walked through the street market and met a teacher from home. It was a pleasant surprise but the news I heard from him wasn't. He asked me, "Did you know that your father was arrested yesterday?" I didn't know but I wasn't worried because I felt sure that they would release him soon, as usual.

The next day, at 8:00 a.m., I was at the market place in Kanash looking for people I could hitch a ride with. I didn't find anybody traveling in that direction so I decided to walk the thirty-five kilometers. The only inconvenience was carrying my suitcase and lack of knowhow prevented me from devising a way to carry it like a knapsack. Fortunately for me I didn't have to make that journey alone. I soon overtook two fellow travelers, who were returning to their home eighteen kilometers past my village. As we neared my destination, we parted company. I wished them a safe journey and took a shortcut to Kaynlyk, the Tatar village a stone's throw away from my village. I bought a bottle of vodka in their store for Father as a present. Somehow, I didn't believe that he was under arrest like my former teacher said.

I didn't want to be seen on the main road carrying a cumbersome suitcase on my shoulder so I took a back road. I walked by the place where Cousin Ivan and I, along with our friends, Grisha and Vasily, nearly drowned in a washed-out hole so many years ago. It was a dangerous bog then but now was a peaceful meadow. I sat down for a short while on what used to be a steep hill that I was afraid to climb as a child; but now I could reach the top with an outstretched arm.

I walked in through the back and caught Mother by surprise. She was expecting to see me walking down the street with Father. My former teacher had told me the truth about Father's arrest but made a mistake with regard to timing. My father was arrested a week before and released after three days. The morning of my arrival Father had a strong feeling that I would be coming and walked to the highway to meet me. He met up with my two fellow travelers as they were passing by and they told him what road I took. He returned home to find me sitting on a chair with my feet on a bundle of nettles.

After that long walk, my feet were sore and my big toes throbbed in unison with my heartbeat. I took off my boots and looked at my toes, which seemed a lot bigger and sported huge blisters. Mother told me to sit still and not put any pressure on them. She ran behind the steam bath and returned carrying a big bundle of ripe nettles, which she spread on the floor at my feet. I stepped on the nettles and felt a soothing sensation. It felt ticklish and after a while my toes stopped throbbing. My blisters were gone in a short time and the skin didn't even peel afterwards. That was another wonder cure of folk medicine I learned about.

That summer, after many years of absence Uncle Piotor came from Moscow for a visit. After tea we stepped outside to look around at what was left of the former homestead. As we stood outside the gate looking at his former house, he took a long look at me and said, "How fast time flies. It seems not long ago you were a little boy: now you are grown man. I want to warn you that life won't be easy. Do not despair during the hard times and don't be overly exuberant during the good times. Nothing in this world is permanent. Good things will be replaced by bad ones and vice-versa. Remember that not everything in life depends on you, because your destiny is written in the book above."

I thought long and hard about what I heard. The immediate result was that any intolerance and explosiveness I felt left me. The awareness of being guided by a force greater than myself gave me the assurance that nothing so terrible would happen to me that I could not handle.

A sad event that summer was the death of a young girl, who drowned in the pond that was built two years before. She was in the water only a short time before she was pulled out but there was no one who knew how to perform artificial resuscitation. Her body was kept overnight in her family's courtyard and my father was appointed to guard it. The next day the doctor came to certify her death by drowning and she was buried. It was a tragedy that affected the entire village and was remembered for a long time.

I found the village to be a dreary place. My former classmates were gone and those who were still in the village were not my friends. One of them proved to be a real enemy. Alexei was my father's godchild and the "witch's" grandson. Our families were always at odds. Alexei came to our house for a visit. We had a tea with him and parted as friends.

In mid-August a rash appeared below my left elbow. Home remedies didn't help and, in fact, made things worse. Soon my whole body started to itch and tiny pimples appeared between my fingers. Instead seeing the local doctor, I decided to return to Cheboksary immediately.

Upon my return, I took a private shower in the public steam bath then went to the clinic. My hair stood on end when I saw the sign over the door, Skin & Venereal Diseases. I looked up and down the street to make sure no one would see me and dove in the door. I was met by a heavy-set female doctor, who looked at my hands and called for her assistant to come in. A good-looking young lady came in and was told to diagnose my illness. She looked at my hands and bare belly and told me to drop my pants. In order not to fall apart from shame I switched my mind to acting, pretending that she was a boy.

After looking at my legs she whispered something to the doctor. Somewhere I had contracted a highly contagious skin disease called "itch." I was prescribed a brown, ill-smelling salve to apply all over my body three times a day for three days and then take the bath. I followed the instructions and was cured of the disease in three days, just in time to watch the entrance exams of the new class.

When I returned to school, the Administrator handed me an open envelope. I read the letter that was written to the school principal about me by Alexei, Father's godchild. He wrote that I should be expelled from school for negative things, supposedly said by me, about the collective farm in my village. It was naïve, dumb, and illiterate. I was flabbergasted.

"I saw the return address was your village and suspected that it was some sort of smear letter," the Administrator said. He broke the law by opening an envelope addressed to the principal but I was grateful that he did. It was the way of survival. At first, I thought about keeping the letter until my graduation and then giving it back to him but I changed my mind, tore up and threw it away.

The Third Year

Watching the entrance exams was an enlightening experience for me and made me reflect on where we started and how far we had come. Suddenly we were grown-up people with bigger responsibilities.

Pravdin was replaced by Shesterkin as our school's principal. Four of us occupied one of Pravdin's former rooms. Ivan Botcharov and Piotor Ivanov performed in the National Dance ensemble. Ivan grew up without a father in a village about twenty kilometers from Cheboksary. For the first two years his mother carried a packsack on her shoulders to bring him food. I often got a piece of bread from him until I was in a position to reciprocate. We became close friends and shared all our secrets. Simon Karpov taught school for several years before coming here. He was married to a good-looking girl who worked at the pharmacy in his town. The first year she used to visit him every week but eventually they divorced and we never heard why from Simon. Later we understood that a young couple cannot be separated for long periods of time and stay married.

The room had an old-fashioned brick oven where we could cook or bake. A large glass door led to the back of the building, where we could sneak in or out without being seen and, it was closer to the outhouse.

We shared the courtyard with Shesterkin and his family; his wife and six children. We rarely saw them outside and often wondered what kind of a life they had. We didn't know much about Shesterkin's past except that he was a member of the Communist Party and his whole life revolved around fulfilling the Party's requirements. He was appointed to his post as principal of our school by the Party. He also conducted lectures on the history of the Communist Party, as written by Stalin, and Political Economics. Both subjects were boring and made no sense to me at the time. Every night at 11:00, Shesterkin would walk through the corridors of the school building to make sure everyone was in their quarters. He would cough at the entrance of the building before making his rounds to give "lovebirds" time to disperse.

Once I saw him on a dark street with his vice principal, Muratov. Both were very drunk. I found it funny to watch them alternately falling and getting up, encouraging each other to hang on as they helped each other walk. I took a shortcut to the courtyard and watched them approach. They parted at Shesterkin's door. After Muratov left, my curiosity led me closer to Shesterkin's window so I could eavesdrop on a potential argument from within. While I was standing there in complete darkness the door suddenly flew open and a beam of light caught me.

I took off to my room like a rabbit, cursing myself for my stupidity. My roommates were out and the whole building seemed empty. I didn't know what to do so I lay down on my bed and waited for what would come next. I was hoping that he didn't see me or didn't recognize me but his mind was clearer than I thought. I heard Shesterkin's familiar, shuffling footsteps approach as he came into my room. He suspected me of being a KGB informant and said, "If you have been engaged to spy on me you can go to them right now and kiss their asses. I don't care!" He choked and couldn't continue. He walked out sobbing and I felt rotten beyond description.

I had illegally kept a half-liter bottle of vodka in the night table. I uncorked the bottle and poured it down my throat. I felt that if I didn't wake up next morning it would be okay. Much to my surprise, I awoke the next morning without the usual aftereffects of drinking. I had slept soundly and woke up refreshed with my mind made up as to what I would do.

As soon as Shesterkin walked into the office I knocked on his door. He was surprised to see me. Looking straight into his eyes, I said, "Comrade Principal, I came to apologize for what transpired last night and to tell you that I'm ashamed of my stupidity. I am not a KGB informant and I sincerely hope that I never will be." He took a deep breath and looked at me for a long time, then stretched his arm across his desk to shake my hand, saying, "Forget it ever happened." I don' remember speaking with him eye-to-eye again except in class.

The following spring, Shesterkin went to a camp for retraining political instructors in reserve. He came home often to see his family, wearing a uniform that didn't sit well on his shoulders, but kept his distance from school. As students, we didn't dwell on political events seriously, even when we were bombarded with propaganda about imperialist warmongers, who were ready to attack our country. And we enjoyed making fun of the platoons of reservists, when they marched to the theater to watch performances.

School kept us busy with theater productions, in supporting roles, and attending rehearsals. According to the school curriculum we were to work on two plays in varying capacities, one of which would be staged in the theater at the end of the school year. One Sunday afternoon as I stretched out on my bed to rest, I was startled to hear the voice of Boris Alekseev, a leading actor in the theater. He said, "Boy, am I lucky to find you here! Listen, in two hours I'm supposed to read this poem on the radio but I can't be there. Go to the radio station and introduce yourself to Valentina Andreyeva and tell her that I sent you."

I was excited about the opportunity and ran to the studio. Entrance to the studio was prohibited without a pass so the security lady had to phone someone to let me in. I walked into the office and was met by the gaze of two ladies with forlorn eyes looking at me. One was Valentina, editor of the children's programs and the other was Serafime Mironova, the news broadcaster. I explained why I was there and several phone calls later I was admitted to the studio to read the poem. It was about the tragic end of twenty-six revolutionaries, who were executed by the White Guards. According to legend they were thrown alive into a steam engine furnace. Fortunately, I was working on this poem in my diction class and knew it by heart.

The reading took exactly the allotted time, twenty-four minutes, and was conducted without any problems. I was asked to wait for a call from the chairperson of Chuvash Radio, Comrade Alexsandrov, for feedback. He congratulated me and asked that I meet him the next day after school. During our meeting he asked a few questions about my school grades and how I felt, in general. Then he handed me a newspaper and told me to look over the editorial article and read it aloud when another gentleman came in. The gentleman came and I read the article aloud for couple minutes. They looked at each other and told me they were looking for a male voice to read the news alternately with a woman. I was told to get verbal permission from the principal and come to work the next day at 5:00 p.m. For the next two weeks I read the news with Serafime Mironova, twice a day. The early broadcast was at 7:00 a.m. and the evening news at 6:00 p.m. Serafime was a very calm and kind person. After every broadcast she praised my performance and pointed out where I needed to make changes.

It was the custom in every establishment to start the day with a short meeting of the collective. I wasn't required to attend those meetings and soon found out why. The youngest stenographer in the office provided me with minutes of the meeting, where my future was discussed every morning. The most critical person was one of the stenographers, an old maid with some kind of heart problem. I saw her passed out at her desk several times. She kept a small bottle of ammonia in her desk which was stuck under her nose every time she became unconscious. My feeling toward her was mutual and I was unsympathetic to her condition. Later her condition improved and I was told that she got married to a prominent person in the city.

Stenography was a skilled profession for women. They were required to know shorthand and type fast. The typing machines were noisy cast iron contraptions. I would sometimes spend my free time between programs at the typewriter and eventually was able to type somewhat proficiently with two fingers. Later on, I had to receive radio telegrams from Moscow. The current news for the day was dictated via short wave every morning at 6:00. It was read syllable by syllable at a slow speed and my typing came in very handy.

After the two-week probationary period, I was officially hired as a "dictor," with a monthly salary of 225 rubles. That was one of my happiest days in my life. One sure thing was that my financial worries were over. The radio station would also pay extra for reading articles on the air other than the news. Children's programs fell into that category and Valentina let me read many of those broadcasts as a favor so I could earn extra money. I was paid one ruble per minute.

I was always on the lookout for a bargain, so as often as I could, I went to the secondhand store to check out their merchandise, then walked through the variety store to chat with the salesgirls. They knew when a shipment of merchandise was scheduled for delivery and what was expected in the shipment; and they didn't mind doing me small favors by keeping items I requested under the desk for me. In fact, they got me the nicest pair of shoes I ever owned.

Once, while in the secondhand store I met a student from the teacher's college who left a suit there on consignment. The suit didn't sell and he took it back. I came out after him to ask how much he wanted for it. "If I can't get 300 rubles, then I'll keep it for myself," he said. I took down his address and promised to contact him the next day. I didn't have enough money and hoped to borrow the balance from Serafime. First thing the next morning I told her my dilemma and she lent me the money so I was able to get the suit.

I was also on the lookout for an overcoat as my winter jacket was badly worn. I had saved enough money but couldn't find one anywhere. On one of my visits to Father, he introduced me to the ladies working in his company's office. Later he told me how disappointed they were to see me so poorly dressed but by that time I was pretty sure of myself and wasn't bothered by people's opinions. Any spare money left I gave to Father because he needed it more than me.

Then, as now, military service was mandatory for all young men who were deemed physically fit to serve. I used to daydream about being in the army when I was eight years' old but now that we were facing that reality, it was not attractive at all. In May I passed the draft board medical but continued on at school. Two older boys from my class were drafted for service immediately. Another classmate, Grisha Gorshkov, send an application to the Military College and was accepted. He was a unique character who grew up in an orphanage and wasn't afraid to pull any pranks. One time, a group of us came out of the movie theater and were walking past a policeman on the square. Grisha walked by him and urinated on the ground just to see his reaction. The policeman gave Grisha a dressing down on the spot for his hooligan behavior and then took him to the police station. The rest of us walked home discussing the situation and that he would probably be released in the morning but smiling Grisha met us on the steps of our quarter. Another time, he made red pants "a la Taras Bulba," from stolen flags. He was summoned to the police station and ordered to dye them black.

Grisha was working full time in the children's theater, which was located next door to the home of the Republic's Communist Party boss. His sixteen-year-old daughter used to suntan on the balcony and Grisha flirted with her every chance he got. The girl's father found out about it and Grisha was summoned to his office. What was said by the girl's father remained a secret but Grisha's whole attitude changed. He joined the Young Communist League and left school for military college. We didn't hear from him for three months and then he started to bombard us with letters, saying that finally he found his calling and we shouldn't waste our time in a rat hole.

We finished the year with satisfactory achievement and high marks. Our final performance was validated by the spectators' reception. By public demand we gave three plays instead of one. After that, Ivan Bocharov, Piotor Ivanov and Maria Yegrashkina left on a tour with a dance ensemble and the rest of the class went home. I was left alone in the whole building, except for the administrator and one cleaning woman, who lived in a separate building across the courtyard.

Workdays were busy with long breaks between programs. I woke up at 6:00 a.m. and took dictation of the current news from Moscow. Part of the news was intended to increase productivity during harvest time by broadcasting how much was harvested by which collective and encouraging competition between neighboring collectives. I read the news for an hour and then was free until noon, when I hosted a one-hour broadcast of recorded music and local news for villagers called Kolkhoz Noontime. It was the rule that every song title, lyrics author and composer's name had to be announced for every recording. Once I made mistake, calling a song about Stalin something else and the next morning my name was on the front page of an editorial cartoon. In the cartoon a little girl was telling her mother how stupid I was for not knowing the proper title of the song. Happily, that incident didn't cause any problems but a slip of the tongue on another occasion did.

We were not allowed to say a single word on air that wasn't printed. During a Party Congress, Stalin delivered a long speech that occupied the entire newspaper, Pravda. We had to broadcast the speech in its entirety in the Chuvash language. I took turns reading it in half hour increments with the former announcer, who was a full-time student at the Teachers College. By the end of the program my jaw muscles were tired and convulsing. I mispronounced the last word of the sentence, which reversed the meaning of the whole sentence. Realizing the possible outcome, I was instantly in a cold sweat. I switched off the microphone and took a gulp of cold water. In this given situation I had to utter my own words. I switched on the microphone and said, "I apologize and would like to repeat the last paragraph." I finished it without mistake and, after announcing the end of the program, walked to the office across the hall.

Immediately the phone rang and a man's voice on the other end told me to stop by a certain address the next day. It was the address of NKVD, probably known by every school kid in the city. Since I knew why I received the call, leaving the visit for the next day was a good sign. It gave me time to calm down and consider how I should behave and what to say. Walking into the office I got a pleasant surprise. Behind the desk sat the former political editor, who signed off on the pages of broadcast material. "Do you know why I called you?" was his greeting. "Yes, I do," I said.

"Don't tell me why it happened, but I don't want similar things to happen again," he said. After exchanging a few less-official comments, I was free to go. I left the place like a cork exploding from a champagne bottle.

There were two parks facing each other across the street from where I worked. The one that faced my workplace had a dance platform and a brass band that played every night. From my third-floor window, I could recognize the dancers, and if there was anybody I knew, I would stop by and spend the rest of the evening there. The other had a large stage where a variety of performances were given free of charge. It had been recently renovated and a new monument of Lenin was erected.

One sunny day I was walking through the park with a journalist from the newspaper office, who edited articles from the Moscow newspapers for the radio news program. Rumors were that he was good at his job but he was an alcoholic. I didn't know then what alcoholism could do to a human being and regarded him as being a plain drunkard even though I never saw him drunk. Occasionally I met him in the morning at the post office entrance. I knew that he wanted to borrow one ruble and forty-one kopeks for the hundred grams of vodka his body needed to start the day. Eventually, he started to have hallucinations.

On this occasion, while we were strolling along, he grabbed me by the sleeve and pulled back, then vaulted over the fence and disappeared. While I stood on the sidewalk confused as to what to do next two policemen walked out from behind the bushes, holding him by the arm. During the night, someone put an empty container of asphalt on Lenin's head and the police were hiding there hoping to catch any suspicious individuals who might want to deface the monument. We walked to the police station and after some questioning, were let go. As we left, the journalist told me the reason for his bizarre behavior: he imagined that a troika of horses driven by a nobleman was trying to run him down.

I met him a year after that incident, pale faced and a lot skinnier. He told me he spent the year in a hospital to cure his addiction. The treatment he underwent was very difficult but now even an empty bottle was revolting to look at. He continued working as a journalist and didn't use alcohol anymore.

It was in around this time life for my parents became so difficult they had to leave the village. Father started working as a night watchman in Kanash and eventually became a foreman in the grocery warehouse. Mother and my sister, Vera (who was thirteen), worked packing gravel under railroad ties manually. In the spring they returned home to plant vegetables in their tiny garden plot as they didn't have any other land to plant or sow.

I earned ten days' vacation and decided to visit the village, and on the way back, spend a few days with Father. Mass transit had improved significantly and finally, a bus was running past our village every day. I got off the bus at the spot where, a few years previously, I had read the constitution to the road builders. Walking on familiar foot paths brought back memories of a past that seemed a lifetime ago. I often spoke with Father on the phone and knew all the details of their life. Because of his refusal to join the collective, our home was taken apart literally log by log by the village administration. Only the house was left standing, and that without a roof. Even though the old, straw roof was worthless it had been taken down out of spite. In my mind I pictured what our homestead looked like but what I saw was beyond my imagination.

Wiping her tears secretly, Mother tried her best to treat me but there was nothing. Even her homemade bread wasn't edible. All she had was apples on a few trees and vegetables. I wasn't sure about Father's wisdom in losing all his belongings on principle but couldn't judge him. I kept thinking about an old saying that stubbornness is good when it's reasonable but one can only reason with reasonable people. At the same time, I thought about pictures I had seen in local magazines that depicted American jobless workers, dressed in white shirts with neck ties and bowler hats on their heads, digging through garbage for something to eat. To say the least it was confusing to know what to believe because then, I didn't know how the propaganda machine worked.

Newspapers printed the caricatures of Japanese and British Imperialists, and Spanish and German Fascists. They were all enemies of the Soviet Union and the world's working class. "The Family Kogan," a movie produced in the Soviet Union about the fate of a Jewish family in Germany, was shown in every movie theater and Adolph Hitler was depicted as a joker or carnivorous beast ready to devour the USSR. Suddenly all propaganda against Germany subsided. The USSR's foreign affairs minister, V. Molotov, went to Berlin on a diplomatic visit and all propaganda against fascism stopped. On August 23rd, Germany's foreign minister, J. Ribbentrop, came to Moscow to sign a pact of non-aggression between the two countries.

Fourth year, 1939–1940

The school year started with a shock. On the evening news, I announced that Germany attacked the Polish borders and was conducting a successful military operation in Polish territory. Poland was our enemy, whereas our blood brothers, the Ukrainians and Byelorussians, were "exploited" by Polish landowners. Speransky, an actor from the theater was summoned to military service. Although we didn't know it at the time, he was a reserve lieutenant and spoke Polish fluently. A week later, a book came out describing the hard life of Ukrainians under Polish oppression. It was called *Winds Blowing from the East* and was written by an unknown author, Vanda Vasilevskaya. On September 17th, I started the news program with the following announcement, "In accordance with the demands of western Ukraine and the Belarus population the Soviet Government resolved to stretch a brotherly hand to those people and liberate them from the oppression of Polish nobility."

Sixteen days after Germany invaded Poland from the west, the Soviet Union did so from the east. On the seventieth day of war between Poland and Germany, Soviet forces crossed the border of Poland to occupy western Ukraine and Byelorussia. Soon after, Polish citizens appeared in our city. A group of young people, apparently the sons of Polish nobility, were put to work in the leather factory. They stood out amongst the local population by their exceptional clothing and defiant behavior. The following summer we witnessed Rumanian citizens being loaded on ships to be transported further north. Deep down in my heart I felt sorry for those people knowing that in a matter of months they were turned from self-reliant, well-to-do people to paupers.

It wasn't long before Speransky returned to the theater. Suddenly he was the best dressed man in the city. He had a full-length leather coat, leather jacket and several suits made from very expensive material. His wife was working at a kiosk that served cold salads and vodka. In a private conversation he told me about his wife's lucrative position; that by diluting the vodka with water she was able to make a tidy profit. He was probably trying to cover up how he really came by his leather coats by wanting me to believe it was due to his wife's illicit business practice. It was clear he trusted me enough to know I would keep this conversation confidential but why he would tell me a family secret that could jeopardize his wife's job and safety remained a mystery.

A couple months after the invasion of Poland, Finland was in the news every day. We were told that the Soviet Union asked Finland to exchange the Karelian Isthmus for a larger territory in the north because the border of the isthmus was too close to Leningrad (now St. Petersburg), the cradle of the October revolution. The Finnish government refused to negotiate so the Soviet army attacked Finland on November 30, 1939. That same day, our drama teacher's assistant and distinguished actor, B. Alekseev along with L. Agakov, a Chuvash writer, were summoned to military service. Officially they were described as volunteers, who asked to serve in the armed forces.

The bitterly cold weather, treacherous terrain and Finnish use of snipers inflicted heavy losses on the Red Army. The marshy terrain was treacherous with puddles of water under the snow. Factory-made felt boots absorbed water like a sponge and wet feet became frostbitten very quickly. The Finnish War was over on March 12 and soon after two "volunteers" returned home, one with frozen fingers and the other with a deep crease on his buttocks from a Finnish sniper's bullet. We made fun of him, saying that it taught us the importance of knowing how to belly crawl without sticking up our behinds.

Soviet losses during the war were kept secret. We heard about piles of frozen bodies from returning soldiers. In propaganda papers we read about individual traitors but nothing about prisoners. It became known fifty years later that returning prisoners were shot in masses in the forests of Finland by KGB units.

Meanwhile our school activities continued normally. We worked on one play up until the New Year and started to work on a graduation piece after that. Based on the political climate at the time we chose a highly patriotic topic. It was about the role model family of a Communist party official who was in a car accident and a selfless doctor who saved his life. Throughout the season we also took part in city theater plays. It was obligatory for us to be present for rehearsals and discussions of all the plays. In a play about Ivan the Terrible, I was cast as Boyar Morozov and had only one line to say before being executed by Tsar's hangman, Maluta Skuratov.

In another play Ivan Botcharov and I played border guards on the eastern border where Japanese saboteurs tried to cross. According to Soviet propaganda our borders were not penetrable. We captured a few Japanese and each time got a standing ovation. That was the time when Muratov was our school's principal. The second-year class chose to work on Nikolai Ostrovsky's play, "Thunder," but didn't have the translated version. Muratov asked me if I could translate the play into the Chuvash language in a week's time. I asked Simon Karpov to help me and we finished the translation on time, and got 250 rubles for our work.

At the first sign of war, vodka disappeared from store shelves as it was needed for the front. There was also an acute shortage of essential products in the stores. Now and then our news program advertised when and where butter would be available. Within an hour a queue would form at the store across the street. I was ashamed to face those people, who would spend all night on the sidewalk hoping to buy some butter in the morning, so I would use the back exit of the building to avoid the people in the lines. At the same time special distribution stores that served selected administrative personnel and party officials carried everything in abundance. I befriended a girl whose father was a high-standing official in another city. She had a pass to the store and occasionally would do me small favors and get me otherwise unattainable items.

One ridiculous ad I had to broadcast often was, "Smoke tobacco #6. It's available in such and such stores." It was evident nobody wanted the tobacco. One joker tried to nickname me "Tobacco # 6" but unfortunately for him it backfired because it was against the law to ridicule a product manufactured in the Soviet Union.

From Grade 5 on, it was compulsory for us to accumulate military skills. Additionally, before being drafted to military service we refreshed our skills in a special establishment. We had to know how to take off and put on a gas mask in a gas-filled chamber. Those who performed the task successfully were awarded the pin, Ready for Air Defense. The next course, Be Ready for Work and Defense, included performing exercises on cross and parallel bars, swimming a certain distance, and a ten-kilometer run on skis. We also practiced target shooting with a .22 caliber rifle until we were able to hit the bullseye several times in a row. Then we were led to a shooting range. Those who hit the bullseye three times in row earned a sharpshooter's pin.

Physically fit young people were encouraged to train as pilots. There were flight schools in every city. In three months' time, aviation students were flying biplanes solo, performing a few tricks in the air, and skydiving. I took the pilot physical just to see if I could qualify, but found out that I wasn't fit to fly planes. My classmate Alexander Karpov graduated as a pilot and was issued a pilot's uniform. He was so proud that he almost wore it to bed.

At that time Valery Chkalov, a Soviet and Russian aircraft test pilot, became a popular figure in the Soviet press. He flew a Soviet airplane nonstop over the North Pole to the USA and was made a Hero of the Soviet Union. He was described as a fearless legendary figure that flew his fighter plane under Moscow bridges. He broke a few rules but he became a hero. Inspired by his hero, Karpov flew over our school while performing a somersault and spend the next 24 hours in the guardhouse. Our teasing and making fun didn't have any effect on him. He was so serious about becoming a certified pilot that he neglected school completely. He achieved his goal by being sent to fighter pilots school. I'm sure that he met WWII as a pilot but did he become a hero? Who knows?

On the other hand, political indiscretion was absolutely not tolerated, even if committed by naivety or plain foolishness. An example that comes to mind is that of a former graduate, who was accused of sabotage and anti-government propaganda. A portrait of Lenin had been hanging on the wall for a long time and flies soiled it considerably. The young man wrote four lines on Lenin's forehead praising the flies as the smartest creatures in the world for knowing what to do on his forehead. Officials made an example of him in open court and made us watch the proceedings. He was sentenced to ten years at a hard labor camp for a silly prank and we never heard from him again.

Our graduation marked the last year of free higher education. From then on free education remained up to grade seven only. We graduated in an atmosphere of uncertainty regarding our future. Our individual and class pictures were printed in the local newspapers. The government assigned us to various theaters. We could not reject the appointment or change a workplace on our own. Being twenty minutes late for work meant losing a certain percent of our salary for three months and the sentence for missing one day was two years at a labor camp. We felt as though doomsday was approaching and often acted foolishly, thinking to experience life to the fullest.

I, along with three other classmates, was appointed to remain at the city theater. It was a prestigious appointment but I didn't want to quit my job at the radio station. I knew I would be drafted in the fall so switching jobs seemed senseless but my reasoning wasn't good enough for the administration. I found myself in very precarious situation. I could be penalized either way, for not starting to work in the theater or for quitting the radio station. The Minister for Cultural Affairs was the uncle of my friend and roommate, Ivan Botcharov. I explained my situation to him and the problem was resolved. I would remain at my present job until I left for the army.

Ivan was appointed to the same theater as me and received a salary from the theater. To save money we could stay in our room at the university until September free of charge but the building wasn't guarded and our room was easily accessible.

One evening while walking home from work I saw Ivan running toward me. He was pale and speechless. After some stuttering, he blurted out, "We've been robbed! Except for our empty trunks nothing was left. I've run to meet you so we can go to police station," he said. For some unexplainable reason I found myself being very calm. This wasn't the first time I felt calm in a precarious situation. Our dilemma was quickly solved, and to make a long story short, we were happy to get all our belongings back.

Finally, we left the school building for good. Ivan rented a room in a private home and I moved to an empty basement room in the building where I worked. There was an iron bed without a mattress, a small desk, and a chair. A few days after I moved in a radio receiver was put on the desk and I was told to receive the daily news dictated from Moscow. I accepted that as an unspoken understanding to compensate for my free stay in the building.

Olga Gavrilova

The whole story started as a joke during my last year of school. Olga was a second-year student. The boys in her class found her to be an enigma because she wasn't approachable like other girls. When a boy stopped her to talk, she would turn and run as fast as she could. They thought I would be the one who could "tame" her so in the spirit of friendship I agreed to go along. My first attempt to talk to her ended exactly the way they predicted. She took off like a deer. One thing I noticed was that she was a good runner. After several encounters I told her not to worry, that I wouldn't tease her anymore and would wait until she was ready to stop running. That would be soon enough, I told her.

Not long after, as I returned from work in the late evenings, I saw a shadow on the second-floor window that disappeared as I came closer. One time I sneaked in by the back entrance and caught her sitting on the windowsill. Quietly I backed away so as not to embarrass her. A short time later I asked her to the movies with her friend and they came. In the dark I took her hand in mine. She made a startled move but left her hand in mine. "Was it scary," I asked her at her dorm room door and she said, "No." She became friendly enough but I decided not to complicate the relationship by pursuing anything more serious.

Every second weekend her two older sisters brought her provisions from home. The oldest sister was married: the middle one lived at home with her parents. I met them several times, on the run, just to say, "Hi, how are you?" The younger sister once asked how her baby sister was behaving. I said; "She is looked after and she is safe." In the early springtime her father died suddenly and was buried with Church rituals in one of the churches in the city. I didn't know that any church was still functioning at that time. She was absent from class only one day for the funeral and endured the loss without showing her emotions.

Again, this was the year the Government stopped free education beyond public school. The tuition wasn't a lot of money but most village people couldn't afford it and Olga found it difficult to continue her education. Just in time she was given an opportunity to work in a Kolkhoz theater in the city of Uffa, capital of the Bashkir Republic. The theater's administrator, who graduated the same year I started my first year, asked me to persuade her. She just needed a little boost. I told her that this was the best opportunity for her given her situation and she agreed to go.

A few weeks after she left her first letter came, saying that she was grateful for me and for her job, and that she liked the collective and the city. Two months later she sent a second letter telling me how much in love she was with me. Her letters started to come every week and I found myself waiting for each successive letter.

Meanwhile, I passed the second medical for the draft board and got my backpack ready to go. Olga and I had a long talk on the phone and in parting she said, "I'm coming home for two weeks. I want to marry you and stay at Mother's home for two weeks before we say good bye." Deep in my heart I felt that would be the last time we saw each other. In fact, many of us felt doomed but couldn't talk about it. Three days before we were to meet, I got the summons to report for duty the next day. I phoned Olga to say a final goodbye.

The next day we spent the whole day in the commissariat. We were disinfected with stinky white powder and told that our departure had been postponed until further notice. As we walked back to town, people we met in passing stepped off the sidewalk holding their nose. We were the despised population for that time.

Waiting to be called up again was boring so in the evenings we went to visit the remaining students in our school. I hoped to surprise Olga there but didn't see her so we left; but before we reached the gate one of the girls ran out calling for me to return. When I appeared at the door Olga threw herself at me with a loud scream and then wrapped her arms around my neck. We spent the next few hours walking back and forth in the same hallway where she ran away from me the first time we met. She had grown and blossomed in every way in the past four months. We discussed our plans for the following day and I left her for the night with the girls. I went back to my basement room and slept on the bare mattress in my street clothes.

The next day we registered our marriage at City Hall and then walked sixteen kilometers to her village to meet her mother and relatives. We stopped at her oldest sister's place. The table was set in no time, her mother came and we celebrated our wedding. We stayed in her mother's home for a week and every day I phoned my workplace to find out if another summons came. When it was time for us to leave, her brother-in-law drove us back to the city by horse buggy borrowed from the collective farm. The steamship was there already. I bought two tickets and we floated down the Volga to the next stop, where I would say goodbye to my wife and get off the ship. That stretch of travel produced only tears and more tears. She was sure we would never see each other again (and she was right). A long siren warned of the ship's approach to the next stop. We got off and took a short walk. We were too numb to say anything and stood looking at each other, wiping away our tears, reluctant to say our farewells. After the ship sounded a second siren indicating it was ready to depart, we kissed goodbye for the last time and Olga went back onboard. She appeared on the upper deck and stood there waving a white kerchief until the ship disappeared in the morning fog. As I started walking away, I realized my galoshes went with her in the cabin. I returned to the city on the next steamship with an extremely heavy heart.

Drafted to the Armed Forces

Once I passed the medical exam the September following graduation, I lived on standby, not knowing when I would be called up but I was able to continue working up to the last day. I also called my father every day. In those days telephone operators connected the calls from station to station. The telephone operators were young girls. During the late evening hours their supervisor was absent and the girls could connect me with Father free of charge, which allowed us to talk for a long time.

My summons to report for duty came on October 15th. I let the radio station know that I had been called and received my final pay. Chairman Alexsandrov called me to his office for a chat. "Nobody leaves here without a special treat," he said. "We will have a farewell party this evening at my place. You bring five bottles of champagne and we will reimburse the expenses in the morning."

Vodka had not been available in the stores since the Finnish War but champagne and expensive Caucasian wines were available. I came to the chairman's apartment at the appointed time with five bottles of champagne. The table was set for five: the chairman and his wife, the sound engineer and his wife and me. I was flattered to be treated as an equal. I owed both men a lot for being supportive in critical times.

It was a pleasant evening that included rare food items not readily available locally. I knew my host traveled to Moscow using fake permits just to bring back smoked meat products and butter. By the end of the evening my legs were wobbly from champagne so the engineer walked me home. The next morning Alexandrov handed me a receipt to submit to the bookkeeper requesting that she reimburse me 150 rubles for the "toiletries" bought for me by the staff. That was almost double the amount I spend on the champagne!

The recruitment office was located two kilometers out of town and the only means of transportation to get there was on foot. On the day I reported in, there were over one hundred men, all from the city, who joined me. We were put through the shower and our clothing through chemical treatment that smelled horrible. That afternoon our departure was postponed again until further notice so we walked back to town, forcing passersby off the sidewalk with our foul smell.

The next morning everyone was surprised to see me again. The Chairman called me to his office and suggested that I continue working until I was called up again. It was the best solution to what would otherwise have been a lonely and boring time. After two weeks I received the call again, got paid off again and said a final farewell, again. The next morning, we walked to the recruitment center again. After a pep talk by a political instructor from the garrison, we were told that our departure was postponed yet again, but this time only till the following day. We walked back to town cursing those who were responsible for the lack of transportation to and from the recruitment center, although, compared with those who came from a considerable distance we were the lucky ones. For every postponement they had to travel a long distance back home and we walked less than one hour.

I didn't feel like returning to my room for the night and getting together with people who I had already said goodbye to several times didn't hold any appeal. Some friends and I decided to have supper at a restaurant, enjoy a mug of beer and then see what to do. After supper we decided to pay a last visit to our former classmate, Maria Yegrashkina, who lived just one block away with her coworker. They were glad to see us again for the very last time. We talked until midnight, mostly about the state of world affairs and about the possibility that we might never see each other again. It was disconcerting and scary.

Ivan and I went back to my place and for the very last time I slept on my bare bed and Ivan on the floor. The following morning, I phoned my father to let him know the approximate time of our arrival in Kanash. Ivan and I took our time getting breakfast and walked back to the recruitment center, where we were informed when we would be departing that afternoon.

This time everything went smoothly. After roll call, we marched one kilometer to the train station and boarded the train. The train rolled into the Kanash station after dark. My heart was pounding as I jumped off the train to look for my parents. We had only a half-hour stop. I saw my sister first, anxiously looking up and down the platform. Her image was burned in my memory as a poorly dressed girl with a frightened expression on her face. Then I saw Mother and Father come running toward me. They brought me a half-liter bottle of vodka as a present. We hugged each other and then were speechless. Everything I said sounded meaningless.

I didn't have a piece of paper to write down the name of the person with whom I had left my belongings so wrote it on a fifty-ruble bill and gave it to Father. We stood on the platform dumbfounded, looking at each other. Mother kept wiping her tears and saying nothing. Thirty minutes went by quickly. The train blew the whistle to board. We hugged each other one final time and Father said, "Well son, this is the last time we will see each other. You are a grown man now. Follow your conscience in all situations." And that was the last time I saw them as the train left the station, standing on the platform and waving goodbye until they faded from sight.

It was unusually dark when train left the station. Soon it resumed its normal speed on a well-used stretch of the railroad. We passed the next railroad station without slowing down. The engineer blew the whistle, which reminded me of childhood days in the village when I used to hear that whistle on quiet summer evenings. As a child, I would daydream about the future and about travelling on a train but never dreamed it would be away from everything and everyone I held dear, to war.

For supper we ate what we brought with us. Mothers supplied their sons with the best they could afford but we already felt like a family and shared everything with everybody. Someone invited our military escort, who was dunking dry rye biscuits in his tea, to join us. He declined the offer and said jokingly, "Soon you will learn that your stomach is able to digest nuts and bolts."

After supper I stood at the window staring into the darkness, trying to picture my parents walking home in darkness, shuffling their feet on the narrow footpath. Mother was crying for sure and Father was doing his best to assure her that God's will be done. I felt like I was falling into a bottomless black hole. Nothing of value was left anymore, only a fatalistic feeling that what will be, will be. The lump in my throat appeared again.

I went to the sleeper car and climbed on an upper berth to sleep. As I lay there, I thought about what the future held for them and for me. Images of the village and surrounding fields floated through my mind. I also remembered how surprised I was to see the dugout village in Kanash. The entire length of a deep ravine was populated with settlers. Most of them were former Kulaks, evicted from their homes as undesirable elements. These hard-working peasants were forced to work in construction at the railroad car factory. Their underground living quarters had an entrance door and a small window next to it, with a small flower box on the windowsill. On the other side of the door a smokestack came through the wall. Every living quarter had a number on the door. Those people couldn't hide from the government even in their underground quarters.

The rhythmic knocking of the train's wheels put me to sleep. I woke up when the train slowed down and the rhythmic knocking stopped. What I saw through the window surprised me; a snow-covered field with the shimmering city lights of Arzamas in the distance. Cousin Arcady lived there. We hadn't see each other for seven years. I thought, "If he knew I was here, he probably would have come to see me."

We were ordered out of the train with our belongings and after roll call we boarded a freight train whose cars contained only a cast iron stove and straw on the floor. It was similar to the trains that hauled convicts and exiles, or "unwanted elements" in Soviet jargon. The only difference was that this train didn't have iron grates on its windows. We were supplied with only a handful of firewood for the stove but soon a coal train stopped next to ours and within a few minutes we had enough coal to keep us warm for the next leg of our journey. Under normal circumstances stealing one chunk of coal could earn a person two years of forced labor but we were a different category of people. We were in this together and we learned that in togetherness there is strength.

The stove burned full blast for the entire trip and we lay down on the straw-covered floor in relative comfort to sleep. The next morning met us on the outskirts of Moscow, at a place called Luberetsk. The name was familiar to us because harvesting machines were built in that city. The train station was large, with rails covering an area fifty meters wide. Our freight cars were pushed back and forth for hours as they were unhooked from one engine and hooked to another.

As we waited someone discovered that the booths on the far side of the rails were grocery stores selling goods that were available only in Moscow. Those who ran to see what was available came back with bottles of vodka, smoked fish, and other goodies. As we resumed travel later that day, the whole train had a feast and by the time we reached our destination half the passengers were drunk.

The train stopped at Krasnaya Presnia, a place known to us from storybooks. Loudspeakers blared orders to disembark but only half the passengers were able to leave the car. A detachment of military nurses appeared on the run. Unconscious people were given liquid ammonia to smell and sobered up immediately. We were taken to a large building where we were ordered to undress and watched as our clothing was rolled out to a disinfection chamber.

There we stood, a line of naked recruits waiting our turn at the barber's bench. About a dozen barbers worked feverishly with hand clippers. Each head was shorn bald in a few minutes. When it came to my turn, I ran and sat on the concrete bench with my bare bottom. The barber jokingly said, "Say goodbye to your curls," and in a minute my long curls lay on the floor. We were given five minutes to shower, five minutes to dry off and dress in a hot room followed by mess hall and then back to our box car to continue our journey.

In two hours, we were rolling at full speed toward the west. After midnight the train stopped in Staraya Russa. We were marched to the mess hall, fed sauerkraut soup, and then re-boarded the train. The next day the train rolled at a slower speed and eventually stopped at the former Latvian border. Latvian railroad tracks were narrower than ours so our train could go no further.

Chapter 9

The Army

We crossed the border on foot and boarded a Latvian train. It was pulled by two ancient steam engines with funnel-like smoke stacks. The train was so slow that some jokers jumped off and walked at the same speed as the train. We rolled into Daugavpils Station late at night where we were met by junior officers of the 158th heavy artillery regiment. After a short walk we came to a large courtyard surrounded by long, red brick buildings. We were led into one of the buildings and issued uniforms. We undressed and put all our belongings in a sack with our home address attached to it. In two years' time, we would return home wearing the same, by then, stale and crumpled clothing. As a child I remembered soldiers coming home in brand-new uniforms. I couldn't wait to grow up and be a soldier. Now, being in the army was just a compulsory obligation to the country, not the priority of my life.

After showering and dressing in our military uniforms, we were led to the mess hall for a meal, then back to our temporary sleeping quarters. This would be our quarantine for two weeks. The floor of the large hall was covered with a thick layer of straw. We got two blankets each, one to wrap around part of the straw to make it like a mattress and the other to cover up. I felt exhausted and fell asleep instantly.

My first, full day of army life was spent doing nothing except eating three rich meals. The following day the menu was completely different, and typical of what we would be fed on a regular basis. Then it occurred to me that in the hustle and the excitement of getting to our destination I completely forgot about the 7th of November, the anniversary of the October Revolution. That is why the menu was so rich.

On the fourth day I woke up with a temperature and headache and found myself a patient in the medical unit. The medic was a good-natured man who liked to chat. He had re-enlisted twice already and planned to make a career of it. According to him the military was the best place to be with no worries about how and where to get the simple necessities of life. After I got over the headache, being in quarantine was a pleasant experience. Meals were brought to us and dirty dishes taken away. I spent the time reading whatever was available and watching my comrades performing drills outside.

After breakfast, on the last day of quarantine, we carried all the straw out of our dormitory, swept the floor, and were released to join the rest of the troops. Next, we stood in formation in the courtyard awaiting the arrival of the regiment commander. A tall officer with a Major's insignia on his collar stood at our right flank and glanced at his wrist watch repeatedly as we waited. Suddenly he called out, "Regiment! Attention!"

Two sergeants opened the gate and immediately a retinue of commanding staff walked through, led by a grey-haired officer. The first thing I noticed about him was his unusual insignia, four stripes; a rank that didn't exist before. The Major-in-charge approached him on the double, reporting: "Comrade Lieutenant-Colonel, the regiment entrusted to you is in formation!" It was surprising to hear the title of Lieutenant-Colonel in the Soviet Union and I felt I was witnessing a historical event that directly affected our lives.

We were given our crew assignments, introduced to our crew sergeant, and dismissed. This is where I parted with my friend Ivan, who was assigned to Regimental school to be trained as a mechanic and operator of a heavy tractor that pulled cannons. I was in the first unit of the regiment that had a special program. In addition to being a regular fighting unit we had to study and after two years of service, return to civilian life as Reserve Junior Lieutenants. But for now, we were like preschoolers starting our A, B, Cs.

Our first task was to stuff sacks with straw for a mattress and learn how to make our beds. Reveille was at 6 o'clock. At the sound of the bell, we jumped out of our beds and pulled on pants and boots. In less than two minutes we were to be fully dressed and standing in formation. Everything was aimed at speed and perfection. For one soldier's tiny infraction everybody had to repeat the task, be it making the bed or dressing on time. Then we went for a run outside regardless of the weather. Before the war with Finland training soldiers outside was forbidden when the temperature was lower than minus 15C. After the war the clause was removed from the training manual and we were trained to endure any temperature. After our physical training we were given fifteen minutes to wash up and get ready for the rest of the day. Some of the troops washed their faces with snow right after the morning run to get a head start.

Between breakfast and lunch, we practiced putting the cannon from the marching to firing position, repeating each step several times, until we were able to do it according the manual, in four and a half minutes. Once a week we cleaned the barrel, wiping it dry and applying fresh grease using our bare hands. The weight of the cannon, in marching position, was eight tons. That weight was enough to make us sweat in minus 30C weather. At noon, we marched back to the barracks in formation and, after washing up, we marched to the mess hall. We were given fifteen minutes to eat and after that, would retire to our barracks for an hour's rest. By that time everybody was tired and fell asleep immediately. Initially it was difficult to get back up after only an hour's nap but eventually we got used to it too.

Afternoon activities were conducted in the class room. One hour every day was devoted to the discussion of international politics and the dangers of being surrounded by capitalist countries. All theoretical subjects were taught by battery commander, Lieutenant Anton Kvashko. This included the manual and regulations, which we had to learn by heart as well as pass the test. Lieutenant Kvashko was from Ukraine, fresh out of the Military College located in the Ukrainian city of Poltava, and spoke only Ukrainian. We thought his accent was funny and although most of the words were the same in Russian not everything was understandable. He would lecture for long periods of time after which he would ask, "Is everything clear?" We would all nod in agreement but thought to ourselves, "Yah, as clear as a cow pie." Supper was at six followed by two hours of personal time for writing letters or reading. The next two hours were for lectures or movies.

After three months we passed the test and were a battle-ready artillery regiment. During the winter we had a few ten-kilometer sky runs with full combat gear. On one occasion we had a garrison competition where I covered the distance in fifty-five minutes and got a commendation from the regiment's commander. That day I bought the first orange in my life for one ruble and it turned out to be half rotten. Inside it looked exactly as my father described it during my childhood but its taste was terrible. It was a considerable loss for my meagre budget of ten rubles a month.

For the first two months we were paid ten lat in Latvian currency. With it I could buy butter and white bread every Sunday for breakfast. In January the lat was replaced by the ruble, which had a much lesser value. One joker managed to cheat a store owner by paying for merchandise with a bond. We were told about several such transactions in political instruction class and reprimanded for insulting our glorious country by conducting such underhanded behavior.

One night we were roused out of bed by an alarm and a short time later our whole division marched out in full combat gear for a training exercise, with twelve cannons in tow. After half an hour we stopped in the forest, placed the cannons in firing position and built a temporary cover over them with pine tree branches. That being accomplished we retired for the night. The entire crew lay down on pine tree branches back to belly to keep warm. The soldier on duty woke us every 30 minutes to make us turn around to the other side. That switching sides and sharing body heat helped to keep us from freezing. In the morning we built a fire and melted the snow in mess tins to make tea and concentrated porridge. We spent all that day maintaining a usual routine and retired, once again, to sleep on the snow-covered tree branches. After midnight we were awakened by an alarm and marched back to our barracks. Thankfully, we were given the next day off to recuperate.

For entertainment during our down time, we organized a theater guild and prepared concerts and plays. Rehearsals were conducted every evening in the hall where we were first quarantined. The female roles were played by the officers' wives, including the wife of the regiment commander. Ivan and I were working together again. In the concert program we danced the same dance during which I fell on my backside in school and I recited the same poems. A Byelorussian poet wrote a humoristic poem titled "The Pipe," about a soldier's life in the army. It was well-received and remained popular.

Outside the regiment club there wasn't any amusement place for the officers' wives and they had a good time with us during rehearsals. One of them developed a romantic interest in Ivan and he discovered a shocking secret that his 'equipment' didn't work. Apparently, our tea was being laced with some chemical, which temporarily eliminated sexual desire. Someone told us to be mindful of the strange smell in the tea and one morning nobody wanted tea. Immediately after that silent protest a high-ranking political instructor gave a lecture about the necessity for artificial impotence in the current setting. Ivan's romantic interlude was short-lived. Soon the lieutenant's wife stopped coming to rehearsals. We couldn't find out if she had been sent home or if her husband was transferred to another unit.

Officers received high salaries so they could afford made-to-measure uniforms and to send parcels to relatives in Russia. After the devaluation of Latvian currency, all the goods disappeared from shop windows. The Latvian railroad tracks had been rebuilt and freight trains ran regularly to Russia and back. We didn't know what was going out to Russia but returning cars bore the slogan, **For Needy Latvia**, on the doors. I knew that this was pure propaganda aimed at duping the Soviet population into believing that they were helping poorer countries. The division's sergeant major and his friend lived in private quarters. Both befriended Latvian ladies and decided to marry them, so after the women underwent considerable brainwashing, they got permission to marry.

After the May Day celebration our regiment left for summer camp in Lithuania. We conducted live-fire exercises at the shooting range and earned high marks for our performance. We were a full-fledged artillery regiment ready for any eventuality. On one occasion, after our firing exercises were over, lightning struck the ground nearby and started a bush fire. Luckily it was in a marshy place and with the exception of a few spots of fire we extinguished, it burnt out by itself. It was an interesting experience to see peat moss holes burned out in the ground.

A major propaganda scheme of the Soviet Government was issuing bonds and an intensive campaign was conducted about the importance of the current bonds. Every organization and individual were encouraged to challenge others to subscribe. The government would issue bonds as in previous years but these bonds wouldn't accumulate interest at maturity. Instead, a drawing was to be held on the maturity date and the winning number printed in the central newspapers. This was more like a lottery. Nobody believed in the reality of the drawing and nobody subscribed willingly. People called it compulsory-voluntary subscription.

While I was on duty in our tent the senior political instructor came in. He told me to sit down and sat next to me. He handed me a folded piece of paper and said, "This is the outline of the speech you will make today in front of the regiment, challenging each one of them to subscribe to the new government bonds in the amount of six months allowance. In half an hour the regiment will be in formation and I will see you there."

The meeting started on schedule with every officer present. The assistant to the regiment Commander of Political Affairs gave the usual praise to the government and Comrade Stalin and expounded on the importance of Government Bonds. At the end of his speech, he introduced me and asked me to say a word on behalf of the rank-and-file. I repeated the political instructor's words from the note including a promise to sign for sixty rubles worth of bonds and challenged the regiment to follow my example. That was our allowance for six months. I knew that nobody would thank me for my challenge but everyone knew that I did not have a choice in the proceedings.

After the meeting the instructor came to congratulate me for a well-done speech. He handed me a fifty-ruble bill and shook my hand wishing me well. "I'm leaving tonight and we won't see each other again," he said. The instructor was a man I felt I could confide in, so before he left, I asked him a deeply troubling question. In his last letter, my father complained that he was still paying high taxes. He asked if there might be some exemption for parents whose only son was serving in the army. He wanted me to send a certificate from my superiors to show local authorities. I wanted to know what I could expect if I asked for a certificate.

"Most likely you won't get it," he said. "Even if you did get a certificate, it wouldn't help him," was his conclusion. I wrote back to my father and tried to express my sorrow for not being able to help him with his situation. I don't know if he received my last letter. My heart would have ached for a long time over this if worse situations didn't develop soon after.

The next evening our regiment was on alert. We slept in full dress but nothing extraordinary happened. A small unit of Lithuanian army was located not far from us but the only personnel we saw were older officers, with a lot of insignia, in uniform. The next day the place was empty as though they moved to another location.

Being stationed in the dense forest we didn't see anything of the outside world. In thinking back on those days, the only joy I had was receiving letters from home and from classmates. Olga wrote often and her letters were full of a naïve girl's fantasy. She was pregnant, expecting our child in July. She wrote that if our fate was not to see each other again at least she would have this child to remind her of me. By this time my boyish fantasies had evaporated completely. Impulsively getting married just before going off to war was a foolish act and she would be the one to suffer the consequences. I thought, "She will have a hard time raising our child if I don't survive."

We heard rumors about moving back to winter quarters and hoped the rumors were true. One evening all the equipment was loaded onto flatcars and we moved out. The train moved west at a slow speed and after a few hours it stopped in the middle of nowhere. But this place wasn't just a plain field. There was a platform two box cars in length. First, a verbal "no smoking" order was passed. This wasn't unusual as it was part of the training to be cautious at all times. Then the order came to prepare unloading, which meant removing safety bindings from the equipment. It took just minutes for a tractor with a cannon hitched on to get off the flat car. There were forty tractors, thirty-six cannons and several trailer platforms loaded with ammunition. Once on the ground each division separately parked the equipment under the trees.

Morning was quiet and serene as usual with chirping birds and bright sunshine. Field kitchens prepared breakfast. After breakfast we lay in the grass and waited for further orders. At noon the regiment commander appeared with his political assistant and called the division commander to a meeting. Meanwhile each division stood in formation.

The commander came out of the meeting and reported updated orders to us. He said, "Yesterday afternoon we received orders to load the equipment for the purpose of moving to the winter quarters. While on the road an order came to disembark at such and such place and wait for further orders. The latest order is to move to a designated position after nightfall, place the division in battle-ready position and mask the equipment before daylight."

Tractors with dimmed lights pulled the cannons on soft ground parallel to the highway. Their operators made sure they were spaced some distance apart to reduce the noise made by so many tractors. After an hour they turned right onto a farmer's road and came to a clearing. The firing position for each cannon was already indicated. The sandy soil there was easy to dig and soon each cannon was placed in a dugout and covered with a masking net. The rest of the equipment was parked under the pine trees and was not visible from the air. Before us lay a swampy clearing with a full-grown forest on the opposite side that didn't obstruct the firing range of the cannons.

Except for eating three meals a day and listening to political information every evening we idled away the time by writing letters to schoolmates back home. We knew that every letter was read by the political instructor before being mailed, which made it impossible both to write the truth or to brag by making up some story. We waited and hoped for the day we would leave this place and move to our winter quarters. Imminent war was hanging in the air but nobody wanted to think about it. We were already fed up with macaroni, porridge, and oat biscuits instead of bread but worse things loomed ahead.

We were located six kilometers from a border town called Taurage. We got a description of the town from the orderly, who ran between the divisions and the observation point. It was divided by a river, which served as the border between Germany and Lithuania. It had one church with a tall steeple that was observation post of the regiment. There were barracks for border squads stuffed with new draftees. Soldiers drafted in May, yet not fully equipped with uniforms, marched on the parade ground in full view of the Germans. There were a few interesting questions that we couldn't ask. For example, why were a group of untrained soldiers located at the border? Why was the observation post in the church steeple, contrary to regulations? Why were a few foot soldiers digging trenches in an open field? Probably it was to show the Germans that we were not expecting an attack.

June 21st passed like any other day. There were two announcements: the arrival of a senior political instructor and a movie would be shown in the evening. The political instructor would take outgoing mail so everybody wrote a letter to loved ones. We also hoped against hope he would announce some good news, like moving to winter quarters. The movie title was *Chapayev*, a saga about the Civil War hero who fought against the White Guards and was killed by an enemy bullet while swimming across the Ural River.

The instructor, Smaydel, was of Jewish nationality. He said that a provocateur, who was captured crossing the border, told the Soviet authorities that Germany would attack us the next morning. Smaydel continued, saying that as long as we trusted Germany to keep peace according to the non-aggression pact signed recently, we would not fall for this kind of disinformation. The Soviets had a saying, "Anybody who dares to trust their snout in a Soviet garden, will be destroyed in their own territory." That was an often-used slogan of the day.

The German side of the border was rowdy, with loud singing and shouting continuing late into the night. The only thing we knew about them previously was that the silhouette on the target board resembled a German soldier. If we learned nothing else about the German army, we recognized the term "Seig Heil!" At last we heard a loud hurray, then it was dead silence. Someone said that the bastards got their fill and shut up.

It was late when we finally retired for the night. Crews slept in a tent on the tractor platform. It was a warm night and everybody undressed to their underwear. I decided to sleep fully dressed in the cab. There wasn't enough room to stretch out but I could open the side flaps to create little draught. I kept drifting off and waking up every time a bird started chirping. In the early morning I woke up again and decided to step outside to attend to nature's call. The fog was so dense that I couldn't see my fingers if I stretched out my arms. My ears were ringing from the total quietness. I climbed back into the cab, snuggled up on the soft bench and fell into a deep sleep.

Chapter 10

Into Battle

I heard rolling thunder and listened intensely to determine where it came from. Rumbling was coming from the depths and the earth was trembling. Suddenly it came to me that thunder doesn't happen during a dense fog and I woke up! It took some time to realize that the thundering sound was coming from the German side of the border. It was their cannonade. "It's started after all," I said to myself and uttered a rarely-used profanity at Germany. Although I acknowledged that it was difficult to wake up at four o'clock in the morning, I couldn't believe with all this noise everybody continued to sleep.

I yelled, "Reveille!" as loudly as I could. Within seconds everybody was on the ground scrambling to get dressed. One troop was so groggy he put his arms in his pant legs and was searching for the hole to stick his head through. The division commander, Major Grechko, appeared as calm as one could be. "Keep calm, boys," he said. "This is not the worst yet so get used to it." Each man took his post and we awaited further orders from the observation post in absolute silence.

A barrage of shells continued falling on the Howitzer regiments' position. At that time, we didn't know about the position of other artillery regiments between us and the border. It appeared that the Germans didn't know about our location. Suddenly, some women with small children were running towards our position, most of them dressed only in night gowns. One mother carried her naked baby wrapped in a towel. According to them the town was wiped out. The first shells hit the church steeple and military barracks. That explained the missing communication with the observation post. The women were in shock and even the babies didn't cry. They were directed to a side road behind our position, where they would be safer.

Selecting a likely target on the map we fired a couple of shells and soon enemy shells started to explode closer to us. We kept firing at every farm on the map within our reach. According to the manual, the cannon's firing range was seventeen kilometers, but with a full charge, shells reached as far as twenty-five kilometers. At least we surprised a couple of German farmers. After forty minutes of constant bombardment, the firing suddenly stopped. At nine o'clock, observers on the highway reported that a light tank and tank load of German soldiers drove by. We packed unused shells in boxes and loaded them on the trailer "just in case." We still had no orders nor were decisions made about what to do next. According to the observers, the highway seemed to be open for German vehicles to be able to run unobstructed. We wondered if we had been left behind enemy lines or if there was any line at all. Where were our infantry and the tanks? There were dozens of questions and no answers.

At noon we got an order to get ready to move out. Cannons hitched to tractors stood on the farmer's road facing away from the highway. To prevent a surprise attack, every vulnerable spot was posted. Just as the Column was starting to roll, the head tractor got stuck in the mud. Several roadside trees fell across the road under Caterpillars and the tractor moved forward. Soon we were in an open field moving between rolling hills. While descending the slope a leading tractor towing a cannon, jackknifed. While a lieutenant was directing the driver from the front, he couldn't see what was occurring in the rear. The cannon's wheel started to sink and I yelled for the driver to stop!

The lieutenant was new to me, someone I had never seen before and he probably took my action as being insubordinate. He ran toward me with a drawn pistol. I was at loss: he could shoot me on the spot. While I kept pointing my finger toward the sunken wheel a shot rang out from a nearby bush and the lieutenant hit the ground. His instinctive reflex of self-preservation sobered him up. He returned the pistol to its holster but continued dressing me down. I didn't know if I should be scared or angry, but I showed no emotion. The confused expression on the lieutenant's face told me to that I had done the right thing in remaining impassive. I turned around and walked away.

After dark we got on the highway and drove non-stop for two hours. For the purpose of maneuverability, the divisions split up. We stopped under a small patch of trees just off the road and with one cannon in firing position, stayed there until daybreak. In the morning, as the tractors were starting up a commotion developed near one of the cannons. A sergeant had fallen asleep behind the cannon and was run over by one of the wheels, which pushed his body deep into the moist earth. He had to be transported to the medical unit but nobody knew where to find it and we had to take care of him until it was located. Because of this situation we couldn't pull the spare trailer loaded with remaining shells and leftover powder so we moved the shells to other trailers.

I was ordered to torch the trailer after the last cannon left and catch-up with the column on foot. After leaving the bush, the column made a forty-five-degree turn to the left. I had to cut through the field diagonally to catch up with the last cannon. I heard a shrill whistle and shouts and turning my head to the left, saw a line of Germans walking just fifty meters from me. They were shouting, "Ivan, come!" I ran like a deer, expecting a bullet to hit me at any moment but that didn't happen. As soon I got on the cannon and stretched out next to the barrel the Germans opened fire. We got away without damage. I climbed on the tractor's platform to check on the injured sergeant. He was quiet and pale, opening his eyes often and looking at his palm. Eventually we handed him over to the medics. The Column stopped to assess the situation. One crew and cannon were missing.

After getting away from the Germans we drove up a steep hill into the forest. The sound of a fierce battle was coming from there. Soon wounded soldiers were being taken out on trucks. That was the first time I saw so much blood on people. We heard the firing of our lost cannon. The battery commander decided to go there and ordered me to accompany him as I always did, with a surveying compass in hand. The ammunition truck drove us to the edge of the forest, where we got off. Suddenly a volley of rifle fire rang out mixed with loud Russian profanity. Six Germans were captured by our infantry soldiers. The battery commander said there was no point in searching for a cannon in a hand-to-hand skirmish situation. He ordered me to remain where I was and wait for the cannon. His parting words were: "Take care of yourself and don't try to be a hero." That was a very dangerous thing for anyone to say under normal circumstances but I was glad to hear that from him. I never forgot his words and believe they helped me to survive.

Soon after, the lost crew showed up on foot. They used up the last of their shells and abandoned the cannon after removing its firing mechanism. It was easy for them to be suspicious of our motive for being away from the battlefield. Only our artillery uniforms could justify our being there: No cannon, no shooting.

As soon we reached the others, the column moved out. Division commander, Major Grechany, and battery commander, Lieutenant Sheppel, took me (with the surveying compass) and sped ahead to survey a firing position. Just before darkness fell, we had our cannons positioned alongside the forest ridge. We faced a deep valley with a narrow road at the bottom. A German tank fired at our position from the opposite ridge. Its location was visible and we destroyed it in a single shot.

After an hour of complete silence, the Germans started machine gun fire aimed at our position and we silenced them with a couple of shots from our guns. Shortly after, two rockets shot up from the German side of the valley and slowly descended on our position, lighting up the whole territory. After the rockets extinguished the night turned pitch black. The Germans resumed machine gun fire followed by small caliber artillery. Our side answered with equal force. We weren't aware of the presence of our infantry but they were there. Our division was ordered to retreat. The escape road lay between two fighting forces. Tractors were lined up bumper to bumper on the road leading to the bottom of the valley. Tracer bullets and gun shells flew over us in both directions as our column moved through a tunnel of gunfire.

I hadn't eaten or slept for forty hours and was tired beyond description. I climbed on the reserve trailer loaded with sixty-four rounds of shells. Each round weight sixty-five kilos. I removed two boxes from the center of the platform and slid down to the floor. Tracers were still flying over us and I thought that they might be the last thing I saw. If one of those tracers hit the trailer nothing would be left of me.

I awoke the next morning and saw bright sunshine. Except for the murmur of voices near the trailer there was dead silence. The crew was surprised to see me alive. I didn't have any idea how far we had traveled and when we got to our current location. Compared with the scenery of the previous night this place appeared out of this world; a small lake surrounded by several cottages, a church with a tall steeple and not a living soul around. It seemed as though the whole of creation was on stand-by waiting for something to happen.

We moved out from the village in low gear and positioned our guns in an apple orchard. It was a large homestead that appeared to have been temporarily abandoned by the owner. At noontime an elderly man appeared from a hothouse. He appeared not to understand Russian so we left him alone, thinking he was a harmless, old man. But he had a mission to fulfill. One of our troops observed him spreading spare windows from the hothouse all over the pasture behind the barn as a marker for German airplanes to drop a bomb and he was shot on the spot. The field cook decided that this gave us justification to pillage the farm for food. One of the treats we found was cocoa, which we boiled in the field kitchen.

We spent two days there firing occasional shots with a low trajectory. One shell hit the tree top and exploded fifty meters from the cannon, injuring two soldiers. They were sprayed with gravel and sustained some minor injury to their foreheads. Both refused treatment, saying, "That's nothing," but delayed shock set in and overwhelmed them the next day, and both were handed over to the medics.

The first few days were so crowded with impressions, it is impossible to remember everything that transpired in its proper order. For example, on the second or third day one of the young men from Cheboksary, by the name of Yegorov, fell off a cannon and got run over. Forty years later, an old classmate sent me a clipping from the local newspaper with his obituary, as the first casualty of war from the Chuvash Republic.

Early the next morning we hit the road again. We didn't meet the enemy on the ground but their fighter planes were constantly flying overhead. Flying low they would ambush columns on the road and spray them with bullets. As soon as we heard the sound of a plane, we would jump off the tractors and scatter like ants. Up to now we hadn't seen any Russian planes and we were all wondering where they might be. That question was answered a short time later when we passed by an airfield with a dozen fighter planes burning on the ground. German planes dropped their bombs on the airfields minutes after they opened fire on our borders.

We were coming around a bend in the road when we were hailed by a civilian waving his arms at us to stop. "I am the manager of the dairy over there," he said, pointing toward the building. "There is a lot of milk, cream and cottage cheese that will be wasted. Go and help yourself." We ran into the building and, lo and behold, I couldn't believe my eyes. There was so much milk one could swim in it. We filled mess tins and field flasks with cream and cottage cheese. Our tasteless oat biscuits actually tasted good when washed down with cold cream. The only setback was that we had to do everything on the run. We climbed back on the tractor still munching the biscuits.

The Germans hadn't bombed the highway but the road was pockmarked with the spray of machinegun fire and the surrounding area had been set on fire. We came to a stretch of highway where our columns had been ambushed several times. A one kilometer stretch of road was crowded with the burnt skeletons of vehicles. Seeing burned, lifeless corpses hanging out from the cabins of burned-out trucks against a backdrop of cows peacefully grazing in a pasture close by, created an indescribable surreal feeling.

Suddenly a plane appeared over the tall pine trees and I was jerked back into survival mode. Every one vaulted overboard and ran between the cows in the pasture. I jumped out on the opposite side and hit the ground. The plane passed over spraying bullets so close to my head that it covered me with gravel. "Boy, this was close," I thought to myself. Then Uncle Piotor's words came to mind: "Many things in life will not depend on you, because your name was written in the book above at your birth." I thought, "If God set the length of my life why should I fear death?" The relief I felt in that moment was like cool water pouring over me, washing away my fear. The trembling in my stomach that persisted from the start of war subsided. I didn't have to worry anymore where and how I would be buried or whether my parents would know where my grave was. It was in God's hands.

Soon we were off the main highway on a farmer's road. The road led down a long hill to the bottom of the valley. Toward evening it started to drizzle and turned to torrential rain during the night. The ground became too mushy to support our heavy machinery. Tractors skidded and cannon wheels sunk in the mud up to the axles. Everybody got muddy and soaking wet. Every unit managed to get off the muddy road and park on the grassy slope under trees. Crews huddled close to their tractors. The body odors from our steaming bodies and wet clothing became unbearable so we opened the tarpaulin flaps for fresh air. Half a dozen infantry guys who joined us also stood close to the tractor's engine to stay warm. Compared with them we were the lucky ones. We could sleep on our tractors on the move while they had to carry so much weight on their shoulders.

It wasn't raining when we woke up, so without the benefit of breakfast or hot tea, the column started to roll again and soon we left the muddy road. The road sign on the highway indicated that Riga was ten kilometers away. We traveled at a slow speed and eventually deployed another firing position. We were very happy to see the field kitchen appear, full of concentrated porridge and hot tea. Someone stumbled on an abandoned storage depot close by, stockpiled with boots, uniforms, and underwear. We washed ourselves in a nearby creek and put on new underwear and new uniforms. I also replaced my well-worn, dirty boots for brand new ones. Out of nowhere, I had a random thought that if I were killed, I would at least be wearing clean underwear and for some reason it had a calming effect.

We didn't see any enemy airplanes that whole morning. A little later in the day the division commander briefed us about the plan for the coming evening. During the night we would drive through Riga. Each crew would sit on the tractor platform with rifles ready to fire since there was a strong possibility of being fired upon from the rooftops or upper floors of buildings. The column drove into Riga under total darkness. This was the first time since the war started that we saw our tanks. They were posted in critical spots to prevent snipers shooting at our passing troops, as there were incidents of our troops being fired upon by overzealous Latvian patriots or German paratroopers (who were dropped at night to create havoc on overcrowded roads). Some of them were captured and shot on the spot.

After we left Riga fighter planes stopped pursuing us. Our division was still fully equipped, with the exception of the cannon that was left behind on the third day of the war. In passing through small towns, it was hard to believe there was a war. Everything was quiet and peaceful. Friendly population was out on the streets greeting us as we passed by and wishing us well. Those who hated our guts were not there. They were in hiding, anxiously waited for the Germans to appear.

We kept moving toward the northwest, periodically assuming a firing position and then resuming our march. A few times bombers flew over without paying attention to us but we still ran and scattered in the fields. On one occasion we got caught up in heavy traffic and the column stopped on an open stretch of highway. Four bombers flew over us as we were standing there, and one of the troop started to shoot at the planes with his rifle. Someone was shouting to for him to stop firing while others urged him on. There had been a story going around about a soldier who brought down a German plane with a single shot. I don't know if one could actually believe such a story but it made for good propaganda and for this soldier, it seemed a good opportunity to fire a couple shots safely.

On one side of the road was a meadow with a dozen cows grazing and on the other side, a field of rye. On the meadow side was a drainage ditch that ran parallel to the road. I looked around, thinking about what I would do if one of the planes returned and dropped its load on us and decided the safest place was the muddy ditch next to me. As though reading my thoughts, one of the planes started to make a U-turn.

People started to run in every direction. I stood amongst the cows looking up and clearly saw three black dots separate from the plane, accompanied by a whistling sound. The cows took off with their tails straight up in the air. There was no time to run so I dove for the ditch. Bombs fell in even intervals alongside the ditch and I felt the force of every explosion pressing me deeper into the mud. The last bomb exploded less than ten meters from me. A sizeable chunk of earth hit my backpack and I blacked out for a short time. When I crawled out of the ditch the planes were still visible but moving away from us.

The Germans inflicted significant damage to our column. Several trucks containing the deceased bodies of their drivers were burning nearby and the unmistakable smell of burnt human flesh filled the air. A cacophony of human voices was heard calling for help, moaning, crying, and cursing heaven and earth. A young soldier from my unit called to me for help and I ran to him to see what I could do for him. "Something hit me in the back. It hurts," he said. His shirt was still smoldering from a large splinter lodged in his skin. I pulled the splinter out with a sharp yank. Curiously, the burned flesh around the splinter didn't bleed at all. We ran into the forest ahead of us and found the medic, who bandaged him up.

In a short time, our column was on the move again and we slept through the night on the tractors as they rolled along. As dawn began to break it seemed that we would be reliving the same events over and over.

It was pouring rain in the morning. We were on a muddy road again and cannons kept sinking in the mud. I tried to wedge the cannon's wheel with a log and fell in a creek full of water again. Bombers (probably the same ones that fired on us the day before) flew overhead and we fired our rifles at them. One plane made a U-turn again and started toward us.

We were near a fortress-like structure with brick walls about forty meters high on each side. Initially, I was in a corner hidden from the plane's view but when I realized that he was flying in circles around us I ran to the next corner. Just as I reached the corner, I heard a short burst of machine gun fire. With added speed I ran on to the third corner and heard another burst of gun fire. Seeing no chance of surviving, I was ready to give up when I stumbled and fell on my face. When I looked up the plane was directly over me and continued on without firing a shot. This was third time since we deployed that I was like a sitting duck and could have been killed by a single bullet, but wasn't. I thought, "Maybe the Germans are fighting the war by different rules."

In a town called Bauska, the truck towing the cannon jackknifed. A few old men came out to watch us as we tried to get the truck straightened out. A detachment of border guards happened to pass by and we exchanged a few phrases but their appearance seemed suspicious and out of place. Each was armed with a new rifle, wearing a clean uniform, and in possession of new bicycles. They were detained, interrogated, and shot on the spot as German paratroopers.

We exited Latvia and entered Estonia. As we drove through the city of Tartu it seemed abandoned for the most part. Windows were boarded up and window panes were crisscrossed with paper tape to prevent shattering from artillery concussion; and the quiet streets were deserted except for the appearance of a few old well-wishers. About twelve kilometers past Tartu our division took up a defensive position in a clearing near the edge of a dense forest. The fifty-meter-wide clearing wasn't indicated on any map and later we found out what a blessing it was for us.

In the next two days we built a bunker with two layers of logs overhead and covered them with a pile of dirt. We were expecting the Germans to show up at any time but they didn't. The Germans assumed that we were positioned at the edge of that forest and their shells kept falling there. Soon we fell into a routine of sorts. Every afternoon an urgent call came to us from the observation post directing us to fire on a certain object. Often the object was a German tank showing up on the road somewhere and disappearing around a corner. We would fire one shot and soon heard a sound like the uncorking of a champagne bottle. That sound came from a German Bertha 250mm cannon located somewhere on a railroad platform. On hearing the whine of the Bertha shell, we dove into the dugout to wait out the explosion. A loud bang that fell short of its target was followed by jubilant laughter in the dugout. It missed us again and again but I wondered how long would our luck hold out.

While we were there, we were informed that the lost tractor and cannon had been found and were being detained in Pskov. The senior political instructor, who lectured us the night before the war started, was there. We were told that he would be charged for exceeding his commission by ordering the crew to go the wrong way.

Most of our provisions came from surrounding farms. Farmers were given a certificate for anything that was taken. The certificate would be reimbursed by the government after the war. Farmers were not generally willing to give but didn't have a choice. They didn't believe that the Soviet Union would govern their country after the war. On one occasion I was running to the command post with a message and witnessed a steer being butchered by some of our men. The steer had been shot in the farmer's yard with his whole family watching. I found the whole scene revolting and after seeing it couldn't eat any of the beef.

One time a couple of the men picked a sack full of mushrooms and brought them to the cook, saying they were not sure whether or not they were edible. The cook knew they were not poisonous but he didn't let on. He fried the mushrooms and ate them all, saying that if he didn't die in an hour, it was safe for everyone else to eat them. It was a big joke.

We spent three weeks playing cat and mouse with the Germans. Every afternoon we received a shell from Bertha that fell short of its target although on one occasion one of its shells exploded very close to us and two soldiers got concussions. Both were in total shock. They didn't want to come out from the dugout at any price. They moved about like zombies and didn't' shave or dress according regulation. They didn't show any reaction to anything and were eventually dispatched to the field hospital. I was absolutely ignorant as to what was going on at the front but knew that we were doomed. We were stationed between two large bodies of water and closed in by German forces from the rear. Our only exit was between Lake Chutskoye and the Baltic Sea.

Eventually we started running out of ammunition. During the night we moved one cannon to the edge of the forest, next to the field where Bertha's shells fell. We were facing a clean field to the horizon about three kilometers away. The following afternoon we received an urgent order to be prepared to meet up with German tanks. They managed to cross the river unseen and were heading our way. The turret of one tank came into sight on the horizon moving to the left then turned and moved to the right. We knew the tank driver was trying to provoke us to fire but we remained quiet. Suddenly three tanks were heading toward us down the slope. We fired at one and hit it on the underside. The tank launched into the air and flipped over belly up. The other two turned around and disappeared below the horizon. We waited anxiously but nothing happened until morning.

In the morning orders came to retreat. One by one the tractors started to move toward the road when our tractor lost its caterpillar chain. We were ordered to stay behind to make repairs and catch up once repairs were made. The chain was on in an hour and we headed out. When it was not towing a cannon, the tractor could travel on any terrain so we got on a cart road and wound our way between the rolling hills at full speed. As we were coming down a hill, we observed a bus on the opposite slope. The passengers took us for Germans and panicked. Women and children were crying. Everyone started to jump out of the bus and run. Once we reached them, they were told to return to the bus and follow us.

My battery commander sent me and two other soldiers ahead for reconnaissance. We came to a paved road that ran perpendicular to the one we were travelling and upon hearing the sound of an approaching vehicle, we hid behind some bushes nearby. A German car was speeding our way and as it came closer, I threw a hand grenade on the road a few meters ahead the vehicle. The grenade ricocheted off the road and exploded in a ditch on the opposite side. The car sped by undamaged but a motorcycle that was following the car swerved toward where we were hiding and slid into the ditch a few meters from me. The motorcycle driver's hands were up over his head before I said a word. I was impressed by his nonchalant behavior, thinking he must have had some experience in warfare. He looked the rifle I had pointed at him, then looked at me and smiled. One of us knew enough German to ask him some questions. According to the prisoner his battalion was located three kilometers down the road.

We handed over the prisoner and continued our reconnaissance. Soon we came to a homestead on the slope of a hill. An old man came out from the house. He didn't appear to understand me and his demeanor indicated he not want to understand. I told my partner to keep an eye on the old man and searched an old barn on the property. There was nothing but dried cow manure on the floor and a moldy hay bale hanging from the roof. Outside the barn stood an empty water trough propped up by two rotten logs.

I heard the sound of an approaching motorcycle so I lowered myself next to one of the logs and propped my rife on it for support. I could feel my heart pounding, getting ready to jump out of my chest. About a hundred meters down the slope was a bridge over a narrow creek. I felt that was a good place to fire at them. As the motorcycle, carrying three passengers, came closer I kept the rifle aimed at the driver. In an almost dreamlike state, I squeezed the trigger. The motorcycle swerved to the left and dove into the ditch. Two Germans got up and ran. One disappeared into the field of rye to the left of the road but the other kept running alongside the road. I kept firing at him and missing. After the fourth shot he went down, then got to his knees and raised his hands over his head. He still couldn't see me or anyone else. I could hear the low murmur of a tractor engine behind me and waited for my comrades to show up. Finally, the tractor appeared followed by a crowd much larger than our unit. I thought, "That must mean the forests were full of our disorganized army."

We came to the motorcycle in the ditch. The driver was pinned and couldn't get out from under his vehicle. The knuckle of his left hand was bleeding. The German I shot sat holding his wounded arm. Below the elbow was a bullet hole but his arm wasn't broken. Drops of sweat rolled down his long nose. He kept mumbling what sounded like *comrade*. If I knew how to speak German, I would have probably congratulated him on this being his lucky day. I would have told him that, ironically, I was his benefactor in that, because of his wound, he might not be sent to the front line and might ultimately survive the war.

Our tractor kept moving ahead slowly as we came to a rise in the road. Ahead of us was a dense forest. Suddenly a small caliber canon fired two tracer shells from the forest followed by machine gun fire. One shell hit the farm house we just left and it was consumed in a ball of fire. The second shell hit our tractor head on. One of the men in my battery got hit by a bullet. We brought him down the slope to bandage his wound. He insisted that we leave him where he was and run. By the time I looked around everyone else was gone. I crossed the road behind our tractor, jumping over the puddle of leaking oil, and followed the path of others to the drainage ditch behind a farmstead's garden plot.

One curious family was out in their yard, probably watching us run. I was thirsty beyond endurance and contemplated stopping to ask for water but couldn't determine if they were friend or foe so I kept moving. I kept running and almost fell over two soldiers sitting in the ditch. They were looking at a puddle of muddy water and one of them attempted to filter it using his dirty hanky. At least we were out of immediate danger and could afford a short rest. We continued on after a bit and, after walking a whole hour, came upon a field hospital where there was plenty of drinking water. After quenching my thirst, I slept under a fern bush until dark. Someone woke me up after the last horse cart, carrying wounded soldiers, drove by. There were a lot more casualties than I originally thought. The medics didn't have enough room for the wounded on the carts and the overflow were carried on stretchers.

There were several lieutenants and one major who took charge over us. We traveled on a cleared path in the forest for a long time and came out on a paved road. After a while we came to a recently burnt building with embers still glowing here and there. This was the same homestead where I shot at the motorcycle and wounded the German soldier. Rather than moving forward we had walked in a large circle. The motorcycle in the ditch was gone but our tractor with a gaping hole in the radiator was still there. Oil and fuel from the tractor had run down the road creating a puddle and in it lay our ransacked back packs.

We reached the edge of the forest and turned right onto a narrow path off a farmer's road. We passed by the remains of a horse team that was hit by a shell. The stench was unbearable. Swollen carcasses lay with their legs extended looking like they could burst at any minute. Regardless of the night swarms of big flies buzzed over the carcasses.

Just before sunrise we heard a burst of machine gun ahead of us. Soon a homestead came into view with a German tank parked in the yard. There was a grenade explosion followed by a short skirmish. One of our men snuck up on two Germans sitting at a machine gun waiting to ambush us and threw a hand grenade at them. One German was killed instantly. The other raised his hands to surrender but he was bayoneted by an overly zealous soldier before anybody had a chance to question him. A third German stood on the open turret of the tank waving his raised hands. Someone yelled, "Look, he is surrendering! Let's go! Get him!" Several men rushed toward the tank, yelling Hurray, but when they were close enough the German jumped back in the tank and sprayed them with machine gun fire. A dozen people were killed instantly and the rest ran for cover in the trees nearby. The medics and injured were captured by the enemy and their fate remained unknown.

We found ourselves in a thick growth of aspen. We followed a barely visible foot path through a swamp accompanied by exploding mortar shells behind us. Fortunately, most of the shells fell without exploding. We had to stop at the edge of the swamp until nightfall. Those at the observation post reported light traffic on the roads and indicated that there were only a few Germans around but that didn't help us much. We were disorganized and confused.

In that melee I met the injured soldier whom I had helped to bandage the day before and to see him again was a big deal to me. He witnessed what transpired after I left him in the rye field and stayed in the same spot until we returned the following night. He said a German tank came out of the forest and stopped at our tractor for a short time. Three captive Germans ran to meet the tank and they had a happy reunion. Whoever had been guarding them just left them and took off.

One of the lieutenants from my division suggested that we break up into smaller groups when we were on the move. It seemed logical that a small group would be less noticeable, making it easier to advance at night. We tried to stay separate from larger crowds but each attempt proved unsuccessful. As soon we started to walk someone would join is and by morning the group would have grown upward to over a hundred people.

Our last attempt to walk in a small group brought us near disaster. We reached the edge of the forest when we heard the sound of motors behind us. We hid ourselves under some fern bushes and within minutes heard Germans voices close by. Three German soldiers were walking our way with submachine guns hanging around their necks. One of them walked by just three meters from me. We followed them at a safe distance to see where they were headed. They walked to the nearest farmhouse, where a man with a white armband met them at the gate. He was one of the local German sympathizers. They shook hands and went inside. If we went after them, we probably could have killed them but would have been killed by other Germans for sure. At that time our goal was survival so we ran back to where we had been hiding.

After darkness fell, we resumed movement, quietly walking past the same farmhouse and after several hours joined a large group led by a captain on horseback. Soon the column stopped to rest, and the captain left us to look at what was ahead. It was almost daylight when he returned and had a short talk with the lieutenants and an older man in a leather jacket. Later we were told that man had been a Red Guard in the Russian Revolution. I remembered learning about the Latvian Legion in History class; how they were a most ferocious unit used for coercion and punitive actions amongst dissatisfied peasants and I instantly disliked him.

As we continued on the move, we passed by huge blocks of peat used for heating by the local people. With the first rays of sunlight, we came to a hill thick with trees. The top of the hill had been cleared at some point in the past and was bare except for a few bushes growing here and there. As soon as we settled on the hill top we heard the sound of a trumpet, which was to be our signal for action. We were divided into three groups and ordered to dig foxholes. The sandy soil was easy to dig and in a short time we sat in waist-deep holes facing the direction of the trumpet sound. The left flank was under the captain's command. The center was under the lieutenant's command and our right flank was under the command of the Red Guard Latvian "civil war hero" who constantly walked back and forth behind us, trying to bolster our morale with his profanity-laced speech.

On my right sat a tractor driver from a collective farm, who was in civilian clothing. After his tractor ran out of fuel, he had abandoned the vehicle and was dispatched to our regiment. He was a belligerent person, who kept cursing the "bastards who would get their tails cut off." He was a direct contrast to the fellow on my left, a school teacher from the Chuvash Republic, who had been conscripted at the same time as me. He was in a near panic and spoke repeatedly about being killed. I tried to reassure him that we were all in the same situation but to no avail. As we waited somewhat quietly for a call to action, my growling stomach reminded me that I had not eaten in several days but with all that had gone on, I didn't feel hungry.

Around 6:00 p.m. the trumpet sounded at the foot of the hill and within a few minutes all hell broke loose. Several machine guns were firing up the slope, cutting down an avalanche of branches on our heads. Suddenly the fellow to the left of me jumped up and ran in the opposite direction. He stumbled and fell on his side dead as a log. Our Latvian leader was behind me yelling something about the panicking SOB so I knew that it wasn't a German bullet that killed him.

The left flank and center got ready to attack and ran down the slope yelling, "Hurrah!" Immediately the enemy stopped firing. Our flank rose and ran to the edge of the forest and stopped when we got to a ditch. Ahead of us was a clear field of about forty meters with thick brush growing in the swamp around its perimeter. Our commander screamed for us to advance, threatening to shoot every SOB who panicked, but with little effect. Four of our men ran out and were cut down almost instantly in a short burst of gunfire that came from an old barn to the right of us. The commander ordered me and another soldier to get those SOBs in the barn. We ran toward the barn not knowing what to expect but upon reaching it, found only empty shells lying on the floor. Whoever was there was long gone.

Our group was in the shrubs far ahead of us, shooting and yelling, "Hurrah!" We followed a foot path through the shrubs in ankle-deep, muddy water to rejoin them. Two Germans sitting behind a machine gun saw me and one of them pointed his finger in my direction and started to scream. I jumped behind a bush and ran to the left, skirting them. They gave two short bursts of fire when I flipped my last grenade over the bush and hit the ground. When the debris from the explosion settled, I jumped to my feet and ran as fast as I could. To the left and ahead of me the battle was in full force with yelling, clanking metal and exploding grenades.

Suddenly I realized that my partner was missing. I whistled a couple of times but got no response. I started to run and came upon the bodies of a Russian and German soldier, lying on each other in knee-deep water. Most likely they had engaged in hand-to-hand combat and they both lost. I came to a clearing and there were more Russian bodies. I came upon a lieutenant lying on his belly with half his scull missing. What remained was filled with blood and let off steam into the air. Daylight was fading so I ran ahead and came to a spot where Russian rifles stood with their bayonets stuck in the ground. That meant our soldiers had been taken prisoner by the enemy. I heard a moaning sound and saw the tractor driver sitting against a tree stump, soaked in the blood that still burbled from a hole in his chest. "Friend, finish me off please," he begged. I took his hand and told him that everything would be okay soon. I was ashamed to lie to him but he relaxed and I remained with him until I knew he was gone.

I was on the edge of the forest, with a clearly visible road going toward buildings on the horizon. A large group of people appeared on the road yelling, "Hurrah! Hurrah!" I knew the logical thing to do was to join them until I came running close enough to see German soldiers leading the column of Russians. The Germans saw me and called, "Come, Ivan, come!" But I turned and disappeared into the forest. I knew I couldn't remain that close to the enemy so I kept walking but it seemed that with every step another person would emerge from the trees and soon there was a crowd. None of us had a map or compass and there were no officers to lead us. I knew that we were walking back to where we had been in the past few days but there didn't seem to be any other choice.

Suddenly a lieutenant appeared on the trail and took charge. According to him we would cross a creek and join our troops. We came to the creek after dark. A large strip of reeds grew along the shoreline. I removed my boots, took off my shirt and waded into the water. It wasn't a creek by any means. The current was strong enough to push my feet off the ground. Putting the rifle across my shoulders I started to dog paddle to the other side. Soon I felt a branch strike my head and I got ready to grab the next one that came along. I pulled myself out of the water and listened but there wasn't a sound. Heavy fog covered the place like a grey blanket.

Then someone whispered and I whispered back. Two men appeared and we started to walk. We passed a barren field that had once grown vegetables. Soon the stench in the air became heavy with the smell of putrefying flesh. We came upon a machine gun with a dead body behind it and parts of another body were hanging on a hedge. The sight and smell were so odious we began running to leave it behind us as fast as we could.

The fog eventually cleared and visibility got better. We came to an overturned horse buggy loaded with loaves of bread and another cart with a barrel of lard and a bag of sugar chunks (like rock candy). I took a loaf and put a little piece of bread in my mouth. It was tasteless, and my mouth was sore because for a whole week the only nutrition I had, came from chewing clover leaves. I tried eating some lard, which was tasteless, but it felt soothing in my sore mouth. I took some sugar in my hard hat and kept sucking on it as we continued to walk, listening to my stomach gurgle and produce all kinds of sounds the whole time.

By the time we stopped at the edge of the forest to rest the fog had cleared completely. A sergeant appeared from the trees and told us about the previous day's battle and how their unit was destroyed. He told us they were hiding out in a farmer's barn. After he left, I fell asleep and was awakened by a voice saying, "Don't shoot! We will surrender." Instantly I was on my feet as I listened to the man repeat that he and those with him would surrender. I thought to myself, "You surrender but I will not," and I ran deeper into the woods. As I ran, I was joined by three sheep, who decided to step all over my bare heels with their hooves.

I hadn't run more than a hundred meters when I saw a row of German soldiers walking toward me with submachine guns in readiness. I stopped and looked at them, then turned and started walking away. I thought, "If they don't shoot me now then what I feared most would happen." I didn't want to be captured and be a prisoner of war but I wasn't ready to shoot myself either. I was apprehended on the spot where I slept. A blonde German asked me where my comrades were, in Russian. He noticed my startled expression and smiled. "There are no more comrades," I told him.

He removed my helmet and threw it away saying, "You won't need this anymore. Your fighting days are over. Keep your hands on your head and walk that way." A lot of thoughts entered my mind as I followed his orders. I almost asked him where he learned to speak Russian so well. I thought about how well prepared the Germans were to fight the war against us. And I wondered if this man might have been the "lieutenant" who directed us where to cross the river the previous night.

Chapter 11

Prisoner of War

I was ignorant about the International Red Cross and the Geneva Convention agreement concerning POWs. The Soviet Government did not sign the Geneva Convention because its leader, Josef Stalin, did not believe its soldiers should surrender to the enemy. He also declared that there were no Russian prisoners, only traitors. By surrendering we automatically became traitors of our country. During military training we were told that Germans didn't take prisoners. Once captured we would be interrogated, tortured, and shot. Our oath of allegiance forbade us from surrendering. Our duty was to shoot at the enemy until were down to our last bullet and with that last bullet, shoot ourselves.

Several days before being captured I saw a German leaflet dropped from a plane showing Stalin's son Jacob with German officers. Prior to this we didn't know that Stalin had a family or children. All we knew was that he was the Father of the Soviet people, our leader who lived solely for the welfare of the people. I didn't care whether or not the story was true. In this current situation, I had a much bigger problem to worry about.

Walking out from the forest I passed a row of German soldiers with drawn pistols, everyone chanting, "Russ. Russ."

"I know that I'm Russ without you telling me," I thought to myself. We, prisoners, were led to a road crowded with civilians, the majority being women and children. Twelve of us, in uniform, were ordered to sit down in the culvert. A motorcycle with three riders stopped next to us and a private got off first and stood at attention while an officer dismounted. The private ordered us, in Russian, to stand at attention and said that from now on we must stand at attention before an officer. Then turning about, he faced the officer and snapped a Heil Hitler salute. The private reminded me of a wooden soldier, with all that turning back and forth and snapping a salute for every question and answer.

The first question from the officer was if anyone understood German. Then he directed his attention to me and asked me my age, my regiment number, where we abandoned our cannons, and how we felt about being prisoners. "When will the war end?" asked one of us. "Three weeks," snapped the officer climbing back on the motorcycle. We were left sitting in the culvert without a guard. It didn't look like Germans were anxious to shoot us yet.

A detachment of soldiers on bicycles stopped to look at us. Everyone had their sleeves rolled up to the elbow and an automatic weapon hanging on their neck. The army flasks on their belts reminded me of how thirsty I was. Since we engaged in battle, I was wet on the outside a good deal of the time but couldn't remember when the last time was that I had a good drink of water. I felt remorse for not studying German when I had the opportunity and I was sorry for the foolish actions in class that made our teacher cry. We looked for opportunities to make fun of her like for being late, for uncombed hair, for torn nylons that slid down her ankles.

Pointing at the soldier's flask I blurted out two German words, "Trink Bitte" (Drink please). Without hesitation the soldier poured steaming liquid into a cup and handed it to me. Carefully I took a small sip and swallowed slowly. The hot liquid ran down my throat like a fireball and then I realized that it was tea. I took another mouthful and the cup was empty. With much appreciation I handed the cup back and managed to say, "Danke." Grinning, he made some comments to his detachment and they continued their journey.

It didn't look like we would be shot here in the ditch. "They are following some rules that we are not familiar with," I thought. At this point I started to feel sleepy and didn't care what they would do to us. I suspect that there was schnapps in the tea I drank and that led to feeling good. Before much longer we were joined to a passing column of prisoners and marched for two hours.

We came to large courtyard with a two-story house and large barn, likely owned by a land owner. During Soviet rule it was occupied by an army command post. It had a storage building full of provisions left behind by our forces. According to our propaganda the Germans had limited supplies. Regardless they didn't use our supplies for themselves. Two field kitchens cooked macaroni and porridge around the clock. The courtyard was filling up as more prisoners continued to arrive. We were kept there for three days and I ate and slept as much as I could. Laying on the grass all day gave me enough time to think. I had lost count of the days and didn't know the date when I was taken prisoner. In counting back the days, I came to startling surprise. The day I became a prisoner of war was on my 21st birthday, 27 of July 1941.

Early in the morning we woke up to the sound of machine gun fire coming from some bushes nearby. It seemed that some of our men were trying to liberate us from our German captors. We were directed toward the road on the double and ran past a detachment of Germans taking a defensive position in a culvert as several small units rushed toward the homestead we just left.

We soon came to a similar homestead with a similar crowd of prisoners. A lieutenant and junior officer met our column. Standing in formation we listened to the lieutenant as he gave instructions through an interpreter. We would be grouped based on our nationality. Those with German ancestry or who spoke the language were called first. Then came the Ukrainians, then Russians, and the rest were counted as Asians. After being grouped by nationality came a startling question: Were there any Jews? Anyone with features that might be considered Jewish was checked for circumcision and separated from the rest.

I met a fellow from my regiment and we decided to stick together for as long as we could. He still had his field tent and that was a blessing at night or during the rain. It was better to sleep under a tent than under an open sky. We heard that the following morning we would be marching again and at sunrise the next day stood in formation on the road. We were counted several times and told that we would be marching eighty kilometers in two days. We had to avoid drinking water during the march and not step out of formation. Those that did would be shot. The only thing I could think about was how hard it was going to be to march eighty kilometers in bare feet. Some people who had sustained minor wounds walked in the column supported by comrades. We all knew we had to depend on each other and nobody wanted to be without a friend.

We walked all day under the baking sun without food or water. Village people turned up by the side of the road with large tubs of water but they were overturned or cordoned off by the soldiers so we would not have access to it. Women threw pieces of bread and potatoes at us in an attempt to give us food but they were chased away by soldiers. After walking for twelve hours, we stopped on a road lined with tubs full of water and were allowed to drink our fill. Some people lay down on the ground and put their feet up on the fence that lined the road, moaning because of muscle cramps. My soles were bleeding but compared with them I felt I was much better off.

Before dark we were marched out to a potato field and ordered to lie down and not get up during the night, unless we wanted to be shot. We slept on the ground that was still warm from the sun's heat. As we lay there someone started to feel around in the dirt and found a potato so word spread quickly for us to dig around where we were laying to see what we could find. In the morning the potato field looked like a freshly ploughed field. All the potatoes we could find were eaten raw during the night.

After being counted and recounted we started to march again. The going was much harder than the day before. We heard a few shots fired at the tail of the column and soon news traveled to the head of the column that two prisoners had been shot. Apparently, those who were weak and couldn't keep up with the rest were told to sit down by the roadside. The exhausted person would gladly sit down and close his eyes. After the column had walked by the last guard would shoot the prisoner and keep walking as though nothing happened. Unfortunately, that became a common practice and was seen many times during the war.

At noon a truck drove by us and stopped at the head of the column to distribute food. This was our first meal in two days. Four Germans were on the truck with rolled-up sleeves handing out a handful of sauerkraut right from the barrel. I received my share in my bare hands. Toward evening our column was ordered off the road for a rest. Three military vehicles stopped on the road and a high-ranking officer stepped out of one of the cars, followed by several lower ranking officers. He walked for a short stretch looking at us. He saw my bare feet and asked in Russian where my boots were but completely dismissed my answer and kept walking. I was surprised to hear him speaking Russian and wondered if he might have been a former Russian White Guard, who fought against the Bolsheviks during the civil war.

Soon we were walking across a field and before dark we came to a temporary detention compound. The compound, a piece of field surrounded by barbed wire, was packed with POWs. We were led inside and ordered to sit down near the entrance. We were not allowed to leave the column and wander around. The next morning, we were loaded onto a train that ran on a narrow-gauge rail. It was a temporary track for transporting potatoes and sugar beets from the farmers' fields. There were so many of us, we stood in the boxcar like wooden matches in a box.

After several hours the train stopped at the railroad station in Riga, where we disembarked. After a short march we came to a former military compound, now converted into a prisoners' camp. The commandant was a fairly amiable person who spoke Russian. We were fed real macaroni from our supplies. We were also able wash up and walk around within a limited area but whoever stepped outside the boundary set was punished. In one corner of the camp there appeared to be a dump and I was hoping I might find some sort of foot ware but was told that I would risking my life if I left our assigned area. As an alternative I wrapped my feet with rags I found. Even that felt better than being bare foot.

After four days we left the camp and walked through the narrow streets of Riga to the harbor. A German destroyer, painted to resemble a shark, was docked at the pier with sailors working on deck. Two soldiers walked by, saluting an officer. Not a single civilian was around except for an elderly man, who stood on the street corner with tears running down his cheeks, constantly repeating, "Boys, you don't realize how lucky you are. You will work on farms in Germany and survive this ordeal."

Our column stopped at a wide stairway leading to a barge docked at the foot of the pier. The walls and floor of the barge were covered in raw petroleum. We were crowded onto the barge and left the harbor towed by a tugboat. I wondered if we were really being transported to some destination or if we would be drowned in the Baltic Sea but the tugboat kept close to the shoreline and suspicion left me. Eventually it turned and we travelled up a river for several hours until we docked at a town called Jelgava. At the dock we were met by a detachment of Germans and marched to the prisoner camp. The camp, a former agricultural exhibition facility, was enclosed with barbed wire fencing. We were marched to a building with a glass front and slept on the bare floor that night.

In the morning we encountered startling news. We learned that the camp was run by prisoners of Ukrainian descent. They were fed in the German kitchen and housed in the barracks outside the camp gate. They wore brand new uniforms and lived by military discipline like in peace time. At that time, I believed in my mind they were the real traitors. Some of them were real villains, ready to do anything to please the Germans. All the camp's police, known as Capos, were Ukrainians. Among the camp police I met one sergeant from my regiment. Officially he ignored me but, occasionally, tried to be helpful. Later, we found out that some of them were actually agents of Soviet counterintelligence with the special task of creating a miserable existence for the prisoners. This served a two-fold purpose: it would cause Soviet soldiers to think twice about surrendering and it would paint a bad picture of Hitler's politics in the eyes of the international community.

We spent the first day in registration, which included giving our name, home address and regiment number. We surrendered all personal belongings including money and family pictures and were issued a dog tag with a number to wear around our neck. My number was 4664.

Several hundred people were packed in the hangar-like building. We were divided into groups of twenty, with an appointed leader, and slept in a designated spot. The leader was responsible for the headcount every morning. Our daily routine began each day, waking to the sound of several Capos running into the building and shouting, "Get up! Fast! Fast!" We would run outside and stand in formation. Those who weren't fast enough were beaten with trounces. After the headcount was taken, we stood in line to get a cup of "coffee" made from roasted barley. The hot drink was welcomed in an always empty stomach.

After that we hung around near the front gate in hopes of being assigned to a work gang that would get us out of the camp for the day. Every day hundreds of people would rush toward the gate sometimes trampling the weakest prisoners to death. I remember one morning being caught up in the crush of people and being pressed against the barb wire fence with so much pressure several barbs punctured the skin on my backside. After the work gangs were gone, those of us who were left behind wandered around aimlessly from one group of people to the next. Every group had a storyteller reliving his heroic deeds on the battlefields.

In late afternoon we got our second and last meal of the day. It was thin barley soup, most likely made from abandoned Soviet supplies. My empty stomach didn't bother me much but the thought of how long we could last on such poor nourishment was constantly on my mind. I knew I had to get out of there, even temporarily, and the safest way would be to get assigned to a work gang and try to slip away. I thought about my uncle's words and how much (or little) control I had over my life. I believed that I was not my own boss and prayed that God would not allow me to put myself in a regrettable situation.

Then one day something completely unexpected happened. A civilian truck backed up to the narrow entrance and instantly a crowd pressed against the gate. One by one forty prisoners were let out the gate, loaded onto the truck and driven away. It was rumored that we would be let out to work at the local farms. The truck showed up twice more, then stopped. Every day people were packed near the gate waiting for the truck but nothing came and gradually people stop gathering there. One rainy day I was close enough to be first at the gate when two guards started to count prisoners. About forty of us were escorted to the railroad station, where we loaded sugar beets on boxcars all day. I prayed the whole day for a chance to slip away, picturing the outcome if I got caught escaping. At worst I would be shot on the spot, which, for me, was better than slow starvation.

As an answer to my prayer, we finished late and by the time we were counted and ordered to march it was already dark. Walking four abreast we occupied the narrow street from wall to wall. I was in the last row on the outside, my heart pounding like a drum. It seemed the head of the column was not moving fast enough for the guard so he took a few fast steps forward ordering them to move more quickly. In doing so he left the rear unguarded. "Now or never!" I thought and dove into the pitch-black archway of the building next to me. My trembling legs barely held my breathless body as I squeezed myself into the dark corner. Slowly the clacking sound of wooden shoes disappeared into distance.

Holding my wooden shoes in my hand I hastened to the back of the building and ran over already harvested fields until I came to a farmer's road. What direction I went in really didn't matter but deep in my mind heading east seemed more desirable. It would be good to get to some hiding place before daylight and as far as possible from where I was. I passed several arrow-shaped road signs and later learned they indicated the direction of certain homesteads. In one place I heard roosters crowing and thought it might be midnight. I walked for a long time after that.

Though I felt tired beyond description, I was afraid to sit down and rest in case I fell asleep. A few times I dozed off while walking and stumbled on my own foot hurting my toes. When darkness started to turn to gray, I slowed down and started to pay more attention to my surroundings. It was time to look for hiding place for the day. I didn't know how the Latvian people felt about Russian soldiers and kept thinking about the Estonian with the white armband coming out of the farmhouse to meet the two German soldiers. Maybe there were Latvians wearing those armbands as well.

I saw the looming silhouette of a building ahead and stopped, thinking the road must be passing right in front of a homestead. There was no dog barking so there should be no danger of waking anyone. I walked along next to the fence thinking it would be safer to be in its shadow than on the open road so close to the house. Next to the gate I found a platform on two posts and on it was a wooden bowl covered with a board. I uncovered the bowl and what I saw was so incredible it seemed unreal. The bowl was full of buttermilk and next to it lay a thick slice of bread. I took a little sip of the buttermilk and found it to be thick with some strange but wonderful mixture in it. With every mouthful I had to chew a little before swallowing and I was full before the bowl was empty.

I took the bread and kept walking. It was not long before daylight and in less than a kilometer I came to a huge barn on the opposite side of the road, where the local farmers stored all their harvest. I climbed up onto the hay loft, lay down under a pile of hay and fell asleep. I woke up late that afternoon feeling as though I had slept through the night. Except for feeling thirsty nothing else was lacking. Through a hole in the wall, I saw a house and another long building across the yard. The stable and barn were constructed from boulders but the house was a wooden construction with a limestone floor. Next to the entrance door stood a large tub of cold water with a milk can in it. A large pitcher hung next to the tub.

In the field, turnips or sugar beets that had been pulled out of the ground lay in rows and a man worked late into the evening chopping off their leaves. I tried to get a good look at the man's face when he came close to the barn to decide whether or not to approach him. His face looked plain and without a sign of malice, so when he reached the end of the row I walked out. He was startled to see me and asked if I was an escaped prisoner. I told him I was from the prisoner camp. He asked me, "Do you know in what a dangerous position you are? There are local people hunting after the likes of you. One of your officers was shot just a week ago for refusing to take off his boots." I told him I had no choice and that I would starve to death in the camp anyway.

"Did you know that the Germans took Leningrad?" he asked. I didn't know that and didn't believe it either but said nothing. "What are you going to do now?" he wanted to know, but I couldn't answer that. "You know what?" he said, "You come with me back to the farmhouse and have a good meal and I'll ask the landlady to see you. "My name is Zep, short for Joseph, and I'm a farmhand here. The landlady is a very kind, old woman and she may allow you to stay here."

We came to the house and Zep suggested that I wash up in the trough of water outside. He went inside and returned with a towel. I dried myself off and followed Zep inside to a large kitchen, with a long fireplace on one side and a long table on the other. Zep showed me the bench by the table and told me to sit. He spoke in a low voice with the women there. They put a few boiled potatoes and a small bowl in front of me. The bowl contained the same milky substance that I had discovered and tasted earlier. I learned that the mixture was called *pootra,* buttermilk mixed with barley porridge, and everybody drank it to quench their thirst instead of water.

While I was eating everybody left the kitchen. After finishing, I dozed off and woke up when someone touched my arm. It was a very small, old woman. Looking up at me she said, "Hi soldier. You can sleep on the hay loft in the barn. Zep will wake you up in the morning and show you what to do." She wished me a good night and disappeared in the darkness. Zep showed me the hay loft and wished me a good night. I think I fell asleep before my head touched the hay.

Morning came and Zep had to call me several times before I was fully awake. Night seemed very short and I felt as though I could have slept another day. We started the day by feeding the livestock before breakfast.

Zep showed me where to get the hay for the horses and straw for the cows and how much I should give.

I met two old men at breakfast, one Latvian and one Jewish. Zep told me the one with the red moustache was a temporary worker named Ozol, which means oak tree in Latvian. The other man, whose name I don't remember, was placed there temporarily by the police. I had never seen anyone dressed like him before. He wore a black suit and a black hat with a wide brim. Ozol constantly mumbled derogatory things at him and made gestures with his hand like cutting his throat or hanging him from the gallows. Zep told me that Ozol hated Jews. He didn't approve of Ozol's behavior but did not say or do anything to indicate his displeasure.

At suppertime I was surprised to see so many fried pork chops on the table. Zep suggested that I shouldn't eat meat for a few days until my stomach got used to a steady diet of solid food. The Jewish man didn't eat pork and Ozol ridiculed him for that. Once the Jewish man was given three hard boiled eggs and Ozol protested, saying that he deserved eggs too. The Jewish man believed that he was going to be sent to Israel. Soon after he was taken away, most likely to a concentration camp.

After supper I was given clean underwear and told to take a bath in the horse stable. Latvians didn't have steam baths like we did in Russia but used bath tubs instead. Obviously, there would be no bathtub in the stable but I carried a pail full of hot water to the stable and had a good wash while standing on clean straw.

Meal time provided me with an opportunity to observe what was going on around me as I sat at the dining table. It appeared that every major activity was carried on in the kitchen. Cooking, baking, and laundry were done in the same room. Two women did all the household chores. They didn't speak to me initially but they were friendly in their attitude toward me. Biruta was a Russian from the Latgalia province in Latvia and had worked at the farm for over ten years. Zep's wife, Vera, helped her in the kitchen and milked the cows. They baked the most wonderful rye bread in a low oven with a cast iron plate for a stovetop. The bread had caraway seeds that were larger than those I remembered from home and didn't get moldy for a long time

Biruta was like a member of the family and would probably work there until old age. Before the Soviet occupation she earned forty lati per month clear money, which was the equivalent of one bicycle. This allowed her to support her elderly parents at her birth place.

Zep and his wife, Vera, had three small children. He earned sixty lati per month, while his wife's help in the kitchen and milking the cows paid for the family's food. I sensed from his words that he was happier during the Soviet occupation because the government gave him one of the landlady's cows. His reasoning was that he had nothing against Stalin because Stalin (via the Soviet government) gave him a cow. He said that there was always a shortage of milk for the family when he didn't own a cow. I tried to explain the false economy because now he had to pay for the cow's food but my logic wouldn't penetrate his skull because owning the cow made him proud.

Zep was an experienced, hard worker and could carry on his back twice the weight I could. He challenged me every chance he got and then would show off his ability and brag about it during meal time. Sunday was his day off so every Saturday evening he would leave the house to play cards with neighbors and return late Sunday evening.

On the first Saturday of my stay Zep told me that the Master was coming for a visit. Seeing my confused look, he explained who the Master was. The Master, a professor at the university in Riga, was the landlady's son-in-law. When she was younger, the landlady also taught at the university as a professor of foreign languages. She was fluent in Russian, German, and French. I realized I hadn't seen her in a while.

I was washing up at the trough just before supper and as I was drying my face, I saw the landlady's son-in-law watching me. He introduced himself and asked what I thought about the way of life in Latvia as I experienced it thus far. Was it better than the collective farms in the Soviet Union? I told him that what I saw definitely looked better. Our conversation progressed to him asking what I did before joining the army, whether or not I had siblings, what my parents did for a living, and so on.

The following week, Zep took the landlady to town and upon returning told me the good news. She went to town to bribe some German official on my behalf and used a sizeable chunk of salt pork as enticement. In those days a chunk of salt pork could buy many things so I cannot describe the gratitude I felt toward this dear lady who sacrificed so much on my behalf. My status was established as having been legally released from the prison camp to work on the farm. I was provided with well-used civilian clothing and another pair of patched underwear. The two women joked that I was better looking in civilian clothing than in uniform. They looked after me like sisters and I tried my best to help them whenever possible.

One day the landlady approached me and said, "You need to learn German. There must be some books in the attic. Go and see if you can find a book in German." I didn't find any German books, but there were some Russian classics like Tolstoy's *Resurrection*, and *War and Peace*, and a book I saw for the first time, called *What Could We Do Now*. There were also some of Dostoyevsky's books. I read them in the evenings and on Sundays but neglected to study German.

The Master visited the farm regularly with his wife, a heavy-set woman, his sister, and her gentleman friend. Although his sister and her friend were both well over forty years old, I was told that she was a student at the university. The man introduced himself as the future husband of the "young lady." Once he offered to help me chop tree branches for firewood, and as we were working, he asked me all kinds of questions and finally asked if I believed in God. Did I read the Bible? All I could think of in that moment was the antireligious propaganda we were taught about God at school. I felt very uncomfortable and didn't know what to say so I blurted out that I didn't believe in God. He took a long look at me and calmly said, "Even if you don't believe in God the Bible is a beautiful book to read." I felt extremely abashed but didn't have the guts to apologize.

In the beginning, my ignorance of farming was evident in everything I attempted. The women laughed every time I did something wrong. One time I tried to mow green vetch to mix with oats for the cows. Using a scythe looked easy enough but I didn't swing low enough and left most of the plant attached to ground. The women had a good laugh as they tried to get it out of the ground with pitchforks instead of raking it up the way they normally would.

I helped Zep and Ozol to butcher a pig once. The process was so different than the way we did it back home. The pig was blindfolded, hit on the forehead with a sledge hammer, and then had its throat slit. The carcass was then rubbed with powdered pine resin and scalded with hot water. After that the bristles were shaved off with a sharp knife. It left the skin clean and pale as a corpse. I told them how we did it in my country and Ozol suggested we try it the next time. When that time came, we tied the pig's legs and I plunged a long knife into its heart. After draining the blood, we turned the pig onto its belly, covered it with straw and lit the straw to burn the pig's bristles. The straw burned about half the pig's body when the pig gave a loud snort and galloped off. Both my companions fell on their rear ends and laughed until they turned blue. I'm sure they remembered that event all their lives. Luckily the pig didn't go far. We finished the burning where it fell and scrubbed it clean.

Farmers were obliged to provide the Germans with a certain amount of grain. As compensation they were given a bottle of vodka and a promissory note to be paid after the war. I spent one night at the flour mill grinding wheat for delivery. The mill produced bran and five grades of flour. The next day I mixed all five grades of flour together on the floor of an empty room. As I stood bare foot, shoveling the flour with a wooden shovel, I thought of my parents and how they were having a hard time surviving on their meagre supplies.

The stable initially housed three horses but the German soldiers decided they needed one of them so the farm was left with two. The smallest horse was the landlady's favorite and she used it when she took trips to town by herself. The remaining horse was not selected by the Germans horse because at times it was uncontrollable. It had a long stride and extremely nervous disposition. It was impossible to hitch the horse to a sled with short shafts because as soon as its hooves touched the sled it would take off like lightening. The only way to stop it was to run at a blind wall. For some unknown reason the landlady wanted me to use only that horse. I rigged longer shafts to the sled so its hooves wouldn't touch the sled but this solution was not foolproof.

Once a week I delivered milk to a dairy twelve kilometers away. Milk cans were separated from each other in a specially constructed frame. The road through the forest was bumpy and I was extra careful not to run the horse on that stretch. Once the horse got startled by a jackrabbit, hit the shaft with its hoof and took off at full speed. Every time the sled hit a bump a milk can flew off the sled and in no time the sled was empty. I let the horse go at full speed until it ran out of steam. It stopped at an apple orchard three kilometers away. I let it calm down and gently turned it and the sled around. We retrieved the cans and successfully delivered them to dairy.

The next episode happened with the landlady on the sled. The horse got startled and just took off. The sled hit a bump and she flew off and landed in soft snow. I ran the horse to the same orchard to stop it and came back a short while later hoping no harm had come to my patron. I found her to be in good spirits. I picked her up like a baby and gently placed her back on the sled. We finished the trip without further incident. The maid told me later how impressed the landlady was by my action. She praised me to high heaven for being such a good man.

As for my state of mind during that time, I existed literally day by day, not knowing what the next day would bring. The people in the household did their best to make my existence comfortable but there was no one there that could relate to what I was feeling, nobody in my position with whom to share thoughts. I didn't know what was transpiring on the front line. Most news was brought by Zep on the weekends after he returned from his card game. Once, just after the New Year, he brought a political cartoon from a German newspaper. It was a caricature of Stalin sitting on a three-legged chair holding his pipe and looking at an old broom with a sickle and hammer hanging on it as a decoration.

That particular winter was brutal and we heard that German soldiers were freezing on Russian soil. People talked about trains loaded with wounded and frostbitten soldiers going to Germany. "They deserved it for inflicting so much suffering on us," I thought. I also heard about prisoners starving in the camps. My mind was blank as far the what the future held for me but I refused to speculate on that and focused on getting through each day as it came.

It was in that state of mind that I met with the landlady in her apartment one evening, when she said she wanted to talk to me. "I have really bad news for you, soldier," she said. "Tomorrow morning you have to be at the district office to pass a medical examination and after that you are supposed to be sent to Germany. I will talk to the official and try to offer him something to exempt you but there is no guaranty as to the outcome." I thanked her for everything she had done for me since my arrival and promised that I would never forget her. The following morning, I ate breakfast alone. Zep harnessed the landlady's favorite horse to a cart and she and I, with Biruta at the reins, left the homestead.

The district office resembled a bee hive. Some farmers shook hands with their "soldier" and left while others hung around to hear the results of the medical examination. My landlady, assisted by Biruta, went inside to talk with the official while I waited on the sled. She came out sooner than I expected and knew that it was no deal. "I tried but it didn't work," she said. Biruta gave me a sack she had prepared for me the night before, just in case. We shook hands and parted forever.

Once inside we were ordered to undress to the waist and approach the table to face a German soldier at the desk, who asked everyone the same question. "Where did you work before the war, on a farm or in a factory?" Farmworkers got marked twice on the forehead with a wet stick and factory workers on the cheek. The process was over in two hours and at the end of it each one of us was marked by two blue streaks on either on the forehead or on the cheek.

We were all declared healthy and fit to go to Germany. For the first step in the journey, we were loaded on a truck and brought to jail in Jelgava. It was a tall building surrounded by a brick wall and several rows of barbed wire. We were led to the second floor, which was occupied by our junior officers. Discipline and order were maintained, just like in the army, by a few selected or appointed officers who were subordinate to the jail administration. We were not starved like the detainees in camps but existence was boring because there was nothing to do. Most of the inmates were extremely frustrated and bored. Some started talking to themselves. Some retold their heroic acts in the battlefield over and over and got beaten up by others for not shutting up. We were told that one lieutenant succeeded in killing himself by jumping from the fourth floor. After that all the windows were blocked and inmates were provided with a few Russian books to help pass the time.

After few days we were transferred to a prisoner camp. It was a much more eerie place than jail. We were led to one of three empty barracks. The barracks were brand new buildings and we were its first occupants. Two rows of bunk beds lined the walls. A quarter of the building was the washroom with rows of faucets over a wide trough. We were led one by one to the "warehouse," which contained big piles of uniforms left behind by prisoners who died of starvation. The interpreter, the guard's assistant, ordered me to approach the pile and empty my improvised back-sack. My treasured, clean underwear fell on the ground and the guard kicked it on the pile. Instinctively I made a step forward to retrieve them when I heard the clunking bolt of the guard's rifle as he aimed it at me.

The interpreter jumped between us and slapped my face, hissing at me, "Don't be stupid! He can shoot you on the spot!" Judging by the force with which he hit me he did it to save my life. I was allowed to pick out one pair of underwear and an overcoat. The overcoat was almost new but was stiff with dried human excrement from the waist down. After thoroughly soaking the coat in water I scrubbed it for a long time with a piece of wood and then rinsed it several times to get rid of anything that might still be clinging to the fibers. I hung it over a crossbeam near the stove and by the morning I had a clean, dry overcoat. I wore that same coat until the end of the war.

Twice a week we were led to the showers and our clothing was steamed to get rid of lice. The man in charge of cleaning the showers told me when the steaming first started, he swept up two full pails of dried lice every evening. We were not allowed to keep leather or items made from animal skin because after steaming they shrunk. One man's sheepskin hat shrunk to the size of a fist after steaming and everybody had a good laugh.

Our part of the camp was divided from the rest by a row of barbed wire. In warmer weather the prisoners from the other side would come to the fence for a chat. They were walking skeletons surviving on sheer grit. Not far from them lay the pile of frozen carcasses. Dead bodies were added to the pile every morning and hauled to a common grave every Saturday. The corpses were loaded on a specially built wide sled pulled by two well-fed horses. Twenty grave diggers worked every day digging the frozen ground.

Every morning we got about 200 grams of black, very moist bread and half a liter of boiled water that was supposed to pass for tea. For dinner every day we had turnip soup. The turnips were washed clean and chopped into cubes. It did not taste bad when there was enough salt but without the salt it was terrible. I learned that farmers were allowed to bring bread for their former workers. After two weeks at the camp, I was a very hungry man and decided to try my luck by writing a letter to my landlady and asking her if she would be able to send me some bread. I gave the letter to one of the prisoners whose name was called to the gate, hoping that he would give it to his visitor and the visitor, in turn, would get my stampless letter to its destination.

Three days later, I was surprised to hear my name called. I ran to the gate and saw Biruta waiting for me. She told me that the landlady received my letter yesterday and sent her to see me with a whole loaf of bread and a huge slab of salted pork. The guard looked in the sack, gave a short whistle and handed the sack to me. She told me that after I left, the Germans brought a new party of prisoners. I thanked her and the landlady from the bottom of my heart and we parted forever. The bread and pork lasted almost until we left the camp for Germany.

All three of the barracks in our section were filled with prisoners like me who had been returned from farms. Late one evening someone saw a steam engine pushing boxcars next to our camp, and said it may be an indication that we would be departing soon. The next morning the capo announced that we needed to take all our belongings with us. After breakfast we were loaded onto the boxcars. The doors were slammed shut and the train started to roll. It kept rolling at a slow speed without stopping until dark. Once it was dark the train stopped and the door swung open. We were ordered to get off to relieve ourselves and dump the slop pail in a hole. Once we were back in the car the train continued on at a much faster speed, eventually rocking us to sleep.

Chapter 12

Germany

I woke up to the sound of a German's barking voice shouting, "Rauss!" We were stopped a well-lit railroad station. A few steam engines stood puffing and emitting steam in all directions. A dozen young women in military uniforms and a couple of soldiers snapped a Heil Hitler salute to a passing officer. We walked in formation down the platform to a well-lit building. There we were ordered to take a metal cup and, walking by a large pot, we received a ladle of honest-to-goodness apple compote. Most likely it was leftovers from the soldiers' kitchen but it was sweet and tasted good. Then we were ordered back on the train. Walking back, I saw a sign over the large door identifying this location as Konigsberg. We were in the capital city of Prussia.

The train kept rolling through the night with short stops along the way and at noon the next day we reached our destination. The door opened and a barking voice again commanded us to disembark. "Rauss! Shnell! Shnell!" This was one of the first phrases we became familiar with as part of learning German.

After a careful headcount we were flanked by a dozen guards and ordered to march. We marched along the paved road, our wooden shoes clacking with every step, past homesteads with grain silos and long buildings that must have been barns. The smell of steaming earth and green grass on sunlit slopes heralded that life goes on regardless of our fate. In that moment I almost felt happy just for being alive. Close by was an open field where Serbian POWs played soccer. They were under the protection of the International Red Cross and were supplied with care packages every month whereas we were walking skeletons, who had been abandoned by our government as traitors.

From the crest of the hill, I could see the panorama of the POW camp surrounded by several strands of barbed wire and a dozen towers with projectors. The camp looked like a checkerboard with its hundreds of dark brown barracks arranged in an orderly fashion. A wide gate rolled open before the column reached it and we walked through without stopping. We were led to the farthest corner of the camp by three capos and a German soldier with an eye patch.

The German dictated the rules to us in Polish. "You are not allowed outside the barracks for any reason other than to go to the latrine. I'm the supreme law here and I'm not accountable to anybody. If I see any of you in any other barracks, I will whip him to death with my own hands." He continued, "I think that you are well-rested from sleeping on the train and could use some exercise. You will march as you marched in your army, with a song. Forward march and start singing!" We marched but weren't singing with the enthusiasm he expected so he made us march until we sang to his satisfaction.

Our column stopped once it reached the barracks entrance. A well-fed capo stood on each side of the entrance and another two stood at the head of the column. We were ordered to run into the barracks two-by-two as fast as we could. The capos at the door whipped each one of us with their long whips as we passed by. I got a hit hard across the shoulders and stumbled through the second set of doors into a table with two capos standing on either end and the German with the eye patch sitting in the middle. "What is in your pockets? Everything on the table!" My pockets were empty and after a quick search by the capo and I was free to occupy my spot on the sleeping platform.

During the first week we slept on a bare platform and spent all day marching and singing our patriotic songs. Twice a day we received a half liter of boiled turnip soup. After that week we didn't see the German with the eye patch any more. We didn't know if he had been disciplined and re-assigned or what. He was just gone. We were led to the office building at the gate. A young officer explained that we would be registered and needed to surrender all personal belongings, which would be returned to us after the war. Someone in our group said that our personal belongings had already been confiscated by such and such.

The next day sixty of us were marched back to the train station and loaded onto a boxcar. After a short ride we were ordered out and marched an additional eight kilometers. We came to an empty house by the side of the road, where we dug in posts and strung barbed wire around the house in literally one hour. We were then marched to a mess hall for supper served by Polish speaking girls dressed in blue uniforms where we ate an unlimited amount boiled potatoes with hot skimmed milk.

The house where we slept was warm and clean. Mattresses were large sacks stuffed with straw and we were fed three meals a day. During breakfast we received our ration of bread for the day along with boiled potatoes and black coffee. The coffee was made from deep-fried barley grounds. Dinner and supper consisted of the same boiled potatoes and hot milk.

We learned that the farm belonged to the government and was managed by a retired colonel. There were sixty Polish workers and a few elderly Germans. Our guard was a Polish-speaking joker. When no strangers were around, he completely ignored us, but when someone from management showed up, he started to yell and swing a stick pretending to hit the prisoners. He was quite helpful when I asked him how to say certain words in German.

Our job while we were there was to sort potatoes and remove the rotten ones. Potatoes were kept in long rows a meter high covered with straw and a layer of dirt, often right on the field from which they had been harvested. Two men turned the sorting machine and two men shoveled potatoes onto the machine. The rest of us were busy uncovering the piles and picking out rotten potatoes by hand.

One Saturday, our guard told me that the following morning he would select twenty men and send them to work on smaller farms. He asked if I would like to go. Seeing my hesitation, he continued by saying that life would be much better at a small farm so I thanked him and agreed to go. On Sunday, after breakfast, he separated me and nineteen others from the formation, told us to get our bags and get ready to go. He ordered us to take off our wooden shoes and put them in our bag and run. We thought he was joking until he started to swing his long stick. We jogged back to the train station slowing down for short intervals to catch our breath. In the meantime, he rode alongside us on a bicycle nudging those who fell behind with his stick. As he handed us over, our guard commented that we made the eight kilometers in record time. He wished us luck in Polish and pedaled away.

Two boxcars pulled by a small engine stopped and we got on. The train rolled on at a slow speed and stopped often. At every stop, our party dwindled by two or three men. I decided to stay until the last stop and at the end five of us were ordered off the train. We walked out onto the street to a waiting trailer, hitched to a very small tractor on rubber tires. The driver was a French POW, Michel, who greeted us like a long-lost brother. The guard was an older draftee in his fifties. They were waiting for someone and soon that person appeared in the distance.

The guard pulled himself to attention whispering, "Chef." Chef (German for boss) was a very good-looking man in his early forties. He wore a hat with a small feather on it, a military tunic with a swastika arm-band, riding britches and shiny boots. He approached us with a brisk stride and looking us straight in the eye, asked in broken Russian, "Are you familiar with peasants' work?" After getting an affirmative reply from everyone he said something to the guard and walked away.

We got on the trailer and rolled out doing about twenty kilometers per hour. We passed a station building with the sign Lubz on it, past some kind of factory with a typical barracks for POWs in the yard and finally, passed between green fields of farmland. We passed a village and some foreigners working the field waved as we passed by. We waved at them in return. As we approached the next village the tractor turned right and drove down the street. There were about a dozen houses on each side and a church building surrounded by a well-kept cemetery. I wondered if the church was being used for anything other than burying the dead.

We drove into a large courtyard. The driver made a wide circle behind countless woodpiles and stopped at a long building with several doors and two large windows with heavy iron grates. Seeing several smiling faces behind the grates I realized that we were an addition to the existing work force. The guard unlocked the door and we joined fifteen comrades, who had already been working there for three months.

The room was about four by six meters, and was furnished with a long table and benches. In one corner was a small brick stove with a built-in kettle. One door on the back wall led to the sleeping quarters, a two-tier wooden platform. Large burlap sacks filled with straw served as mattresses and smaller bags as pillows. The second door led to a smaller room, which led to a courtyard enclosed with a wire fence. A two-seated latrine stood in the corner of the courtyard. All doors were locked at night and our clothing was taken from us and locked in the smaller room to prevent a possible breakout.

At six o'clock every morning our barracks were opened by one of the guards. They would let out the stableman to feed the horses and the cook, to start the fire to cook potatoes for breakfast. The rest of us would get up at seven, eat breakfast and get ready for work at eight. We were divided into four groups with a guard overseeing each group. One of the guards would open the door and yell, "Raus!" and we would walk outside and wait for the Chef. If we weren't fast enough, we would see him running across the yard, often pulling on his jacket as he ran toward us. He would grab each of us by the sleeve and count, "Eins, zwei, drei," pulling each man out and kicking some in the rear end. This went on for a few months until we gained an understanding of the farm operation and learned to move out quickly and walk to our assignment before he had time to kick.

At noon we returned to our barracks for dinner. The menu was the same every day: barley soup and three pails of potatoes. The soup was prepared in Chef's kitchen by two sisters from Poland, who worked as housemaids and kitchen helpers. Our soup was brought in a pail to our door by the younger sister, Stephanie. The potatoes were boiled by one of us, whose main responsibility was to look after the pigs. Dinner was followed by a one-hour rest during which everyone slept like a log. We returned to work for the afternoon and at six we were returned to our barracks and locked in. We ate supper, which included our daily ration of bread, and then were ready for bed but were not allowed to sleep until we were counted and our clothing locked in a separate room.

Normally we were supposed get nine grams of margarine everyday but on one occasion we got a tiny square of pork fat in the soup. It came from a seven-year-old male pig that was kept for mating. It was castrated a few months before being slaughtered but that didn't make it digestible. The fat was transparent and as hard as a piece of leather.

During the first week, we excavated a large hole behind the barn twenty meters long by four meters wide by two meters deep. The guards kept nudging us to work faster and faster and we tried to comply, sweating accordingly. After we finished digging, we built a wooden form around its perimeter and poured cement. That took another week. The manually operated cement mixer was very heavy and difficult to turn for even for two men. By the time we were finished everyone's hands were full of bleeding blisters.

We soon learned about Chef's habit of spying on us. He would be hiding around a corner, then appear unexpectedly and kick someone's backside to encourage him to speed up his efforts. I didn't think he really wanted to hurt us. We were working for him at full capacity for a pail of barley soup and three pails of potatoes per day. He fully believed in the propaganda about the superiority of the Arian race that was destined to rule over the *untermenschen* (subhuman races) and acted accordingly, until Germany lost the battle of Stalingrad. After that his attitude toward prisoners changed drastically. He stopped hitting and kicking us and the tone of superiority in his voice disappeared. Instead of screaming orders at us he calmly told us where to go and what to do.

For the first six months that we were there, the guards followed their manual to the letter, avoiding personal contact with us. Every three months we signed a promise not to talk to German women and not to have personal contact in any circumstance. There were cases of public hangings for prisoners who became sexually involved with German women. The convicted women were shorn and incarcerated in a concentration camp. Our compliance to the rules eliminated the necessity of so many guards. Chef was closely connected to the local military authorities who allowed him to run the camp as he saw fit so he started reducing the number of guards. First, he eliminated four guards, then two more, and after a year only one guard was left. Chef didn't like guards who treated us like human beings and they didn't last long. Consequently, our guards were unreasonable, mean characters most of the time.

After the fields had been prepared for planting, four of us were assigned to mix fertilizers. Chef stood there telling us how many bags of each kind of fertilizer should be emptied into a pile. One kind was a black powder like chimney soot and had to be handled gently. Just a light breeze would cause it to fly into the air and would end up getting in our eyes and up our noses. We mixed the pile three times by turning it with a shovel and then shoveled the mixed fertilizer back into bags. We worked on that job for two weeks and were glad when it was finished. For me it turned out to be further torture for almost for whole summer.

Chef selected several men to spread the fertilizer to see who could do it the best. It was like sowing grain by hand. My rhythm was good partly because of the training I had at school and I couldn't hide my ability by faking it. I was selected to spread the fertilizer by hand, and walked over fifteen acres of sugar beets three times that summer. The fertilizer caused my fingernails to turn blue and cracked the skin on my knuckles. The dust residue left behind on my pants also caused them to fall apart.

One time, after unloading bags of fertilizer, Michel made a wide turn over the field squashing some plants under the tires. Seeing the damage, Chef went berserk and started screaming and cursing at him. Michel knew his rights under the Geneva agreement and didn't tolerate any abuse. He yelled back and told Chef that he had cultivated more beets than Chef and had purposely run a roller over the young plants to make them grow thicker. Three days after the argument Chef ordered Michel to run a roller over all plants. He was eager to experiment and continued rolling the young beet plants every summer.

Seeds for sowing came from a warehouse in the city. On one occasion, we received a sack of sunflower seeds by mistake but rather than get upset, Chef asked how sunflowers were used in Russia. He was told the seeds were used to make oil and the plant was good for silage so he ordered two more sacks. Three sacks sunflower seeds were sown and the plants harvested to fill the new silo. From then on, we sowed sunflowers after harvesting the barley and everything green went to silage. Chef learned everything he could about making silage and came up with a solution for us to use. We sprinkled the sunflower stalks with the solution and had horses walk over the plants to compress them. During the process, one in our group had some splash on his face and he was scarred for the rest of his life.

Carrot seeds were sown between rows of wheat. After sprouting the carrots remained in poor shape until the wheat was harvested. After that, they grew fast and were ready for harvest in October. Plants belonging to the cabbage family were cultivated the same way and harvested up to the snows of early winter. Harvest time usually came during the rainy autumn season. To keep from getting soaking wet, we were sometimes able to steal unused paper sacks. We wore them like shirts as protection against the wind and rain but they were hard to come by as they were under lock and key all the time.

Chef liked to hunt on weekends and would ride out on his thoroughbred horse to shoot a couple of jackrabbits or a deer. In late fall he would invite influential people to a hunting party. On such occasions he would come to our barracks, put a package of a hundred Polish cigarettes on the table and ask who wanted to join the hunting party. Everyone joined willingly because it was a break from the daily routine and it was fun to be able to walk through the bush free of guards.

The smokers were glad for Polish cigarettes. Occasionally they got tobacco that resembled sawdust. It was produced from the stems of the tobacco plant. The print on the package revealed that it was made in Grodno exclusively for Russian POWs. One year, one of the longtime farm workers, Paul Mayer, gave us tobacco seeds and we grew enough tobacco for a year. It grew in an obscure corner of the field and Chef didn't know about it.

Hunting for boars was a short affair. Chef would scout the territory ahead of time to find out where they were. The hunting party would arrive as quietly as possible and post themselves in advantageous spots. In the meantime, we POWs would circle the area and start walking toward the center making lots of noise as we moved. The boars would run away from the noise towards the hunters. We would hear dozens of shots and the hunt would be over. There would be a couple of dead or injured boars and the rest would run away. Usually the old, male boars would run directly toward the noise occasionally knocking down the noisemaker. One time we surrounded a boar with a broken hind leg. While a young officer approached the boar and took aim at its head the boar made a last dash at the officer and ripped his riding boots to the ankle. He killed the boar but was noticeably embarrassed.

Rabbit hunting was done in an open field but using the same strategy. We would surround a large field and walk toward the center with sticks in hand. All the rabbits would run to the center. When the circle got sufficiently narrow, we would stop and the hunters would shoot at the rabbits as they ran in circles. A typical hunt generally resulted in over one hundred rabbits being shot and another dozen clobbered to death with sticks. The dead rabbits were hung in pairs on a horse buggy and counted. They were then taken to a room in the mansion's basement to be stored.

Shortly after one of these hunts, we returned to our barracks for lunch and found our room totally dismantled. Out of one hundred twenty rabbits one was missing and Chef turned our mattresses upside down looking for the missing rabbit. Unbeknownst to him we had eaten rabbit stew the same evening of the hunt and had burned the remains in the boiler room stove. Several days after the search, Chef came to me promising a full pardon if I could tell him what I knew about the lost rabbit, but I couldn't divulge our secret. The remaining carcasses hung in a locked room in the basement for some days before being delivered to a restaurant in Lubz, where he spent his weekends.

In the knoll of birch trees nearby was a colony of crows that nested there every year. In May, when the young chicks started to spread their wings and sit on the edge of their nests, Chef organized another hunting party. Hunters, armed with .22 caliber rifles, shot the chicks in their nests. For that occasion, he needed only two POWs, which he selected, because nobody volunteered for this very dirty job. We had to rip open the birds' belly and remove the guts with bare hands. The birds were left on top of a retaining wall in the hot sun for two days. They were dry but their unpleasant odor wafted for a great distance and big flies buzzed all over them.

On Pentecost Sunday of 1943, Chef told me to harness the thoroughbred and bring the dead birds to the restaurant where he spent his weekends with friends. He told me to load the birds in the luggage compartment of the phaeton and leave the cover open. The flies caught up with me soon after I left the village. A few times I ran the horse at full speed hoping to leave the flies behind but they flew as fast as the horse could run. Two Ukrainian girls met me at the gate cursing everything under the sun because they had to pluck the feathers and wash the stinky carcasses.

While they unloaded the birds Chef came out with a mug of beer and handed it to me. He said, "Here, have a real beer." I took a long sip and stop to savor it. It was real beer, not the kind we had while I was in military training. That was when we started to receive coupons as a salary. A good-hearted guard offered to buy us beer with our coupons and we became the owners of an oak barrel full of "beer." Chef asked me if I want another one but I declined. I already felt tipsy from what I drank. I walked the horse all the way home singing Russian folk songs. I felt good being alone in quiet surroundings.

One day we were given a pail of very tasty soup with bluish pieces of meat floating in it. Chef asked us how we liked the soup and we said it was tasty. Then he asked if we knew what kind of meat it was and when we hesitated to answer, he flapped his arms like wings and said, "Caw! Caw!" We had eaten crow without suffering any ill effects but didn't show any appreciation that Chef might have done us a favor.

On another occasion, the girls brought a pail of soup to the barracks door and ran away holding their nose. The whole leg of a deer stuck out from the pail. It was rotten and stinking meat. We called the guard and he nearly threw up. He told us to stay in the barracks and called Chef to show him the meat. Chef sniffed the leg and declared that there was nothing wrong with the meat. The guard insisted that until we receive normal soup we wouldn't come out to work. The guard was a fifty-five-year-old and had been a former school teacher. He didn't agree with Hitler's theory of a superior race and treated us as equals. After the incident with the stinking soup, he was replaced by a young soldier.

Returning to the barracks for dinner we found a tall soldier, in excess of six feet, standing at the door. He stood there looking straight ahead and did not acknowledge us as we passed by. After the meal I went outside hoping to start a conversation. I really didn't know what to say and he sensed the uncomfortable silence, so he lightly kicked the pile of window frames lying on the ground and asked, "What is this stuff for?" He stuttered heavily so after answering his question I asked him where he was born and his family status. He was a single man and was content with his job because his speech impediment made him unfit for regular duty. He had something akin with the stable boy, Willy. Because of Hitler's law regarding pure race Willy was forcibly sterilized when he reached his 16th birthday. After the surgery he suffered constant muscle spasms at work. It wasn't a pretty picture to watch him rolling on the ground, crying, and moaning from the pain.

We treated the guard as a normal human being and he was very friendly toward us. During this time, fifteen young ladies from Kiev and the Poltava district of Ukraine came to work on the farm. The Germans forcibly evacuated young people from occupied territories, often ambushing them in the market places. Some of those young women didn't have a chance to say goodbye to their mothers and were hysterical for several days. They were placed in one large room in the basement with bunk beds. Their food was prepared in Chef's kitchen but their menu was exactly like ours. Each was given a coverall for work.

We were kept apart from them but soon every one paired off with one of the young ladies. The guys did for them what they could and in return the ladies did their laundry and ironed their shirts. When Chef was absent on weekends the young guard let the prisoners out until midnight. The guys were told to be on alert in case of an unexpected development. The guard would whistle and everyone will be in the barracks in a jiffy. Chef wasn't happy with this guard but his replacement didn't happen immediately. We were sorry to see him go and parted almost like brothers.

The replacement guard was the complete opposite, which pleased Chef. He was mean to us and friendly with the ladies. On the plus side, he spent more time watching them than us. Eventually they give him the nickname, Cybulya, which means onion in Ukrainian. He was told that Cybulya meant guard in the Ukrainian language so he called himself Cybulya, which gave them a great laugh. He didn't mind having the girls call him that but appeared uncomfortable to hear it from the rest of us.

The girl's supervisor, seventy-two-year-old Kraviec, didn't like the guard hanging around his gang. He also spent more time watching us. Kraviec spoke Polish and we could understand each other. He wasn't a talkative person unless he was in a really good mood, but gradually we were able to find out about his past one word at a time. He lived his entire life in the village working for the former owner of the homestead. In his younger years he traveled to Poland every year, with lots of cash in his pocket, to recruit seasonal workers. After recruiting was done, he would spend a few days having a good time with the Polish girls. He was a big man and always wore a jacket and loose corduroy pants held up by suspenders. Every morning we would ask him how the war was going, to which he would reply, "Ours are on the top; yours on the bottom." After the German forces lost the battle in Stalingrad his answer reversed to, "Yours on the top and ours on the bottom."

Another lifelong worker on the farm was Paul Mayer. He suffered from scrofula, (a condition where the bacteria that causes tuberculosis, causes symptoms outside the lungs, like inflamed lymph nodes) and was exempt from military service. He worked with a team of strong horses. He had a wife and ten-year-old son, Rudy, who wasn't in Hitler's Jugend (Youth). Paul bought me a toothbrush and supplied with me with tooth powder (Tooth paste was not invented yet).

The other stable boy was Stanislaus. He was a single, good-looking young man, who spoke fluent Polish and German. He didn't want to tell who he really was and we didn't bother him with questions.

In the spring of 1943, Chef received two teams of oxen from the Ukraine and asked if anyone knew how to work with them. Two men volunteered to work with the teams. One was Paul from the Tatar Republic and the other was Ivan Poltaranin, who lived his entire life in the Siberian jungles. As a voluntary prospector searching for gold along the Siberian rivers, he was exempt from military duty until the war started. Before the war, Ivan spent the whole winter in the forest felling lumber and floating it down the river in the spring. In the summer he traveled on horseback up the small rivers prospecting for gold. Ivan didn't go to school and was totally illiterate. I spent several weeks teaching him to sign his name. He saw a train for the first time in his life after mobilization. Compared with his primitive existence in Siberia he felt like he was living at a spa.

The oxen were slow animals like him, which suited him perfectly. They were kept in the stable with cows. Every evening Ivan returned from the fields during milking time and volunteered to help the Frenchman milk the cows. He chose to milk a young cow located in the far corner of the stable. He drank as much warm milk from the pail as he could and then rinsed the pail when he was done. He did the same thing every morning. Then he learned to skim the cream from the milk can. Chef noticed Ivan's growing belly and his red neck. It took him no time at all to figure out the cause. One morning Chef caught Ivan with his field flask in the milk can and slapped him a few times before Ivan ran away. Ivan ran back to the barracks moaning, "Oh! what is going to happen now?" Nothing happened right then but punishment came later.

In the summer of 1943, Chef appointed me to work in the pigsty. And because I understood German better than the others, he wanted me to be available as an interpreter whenever needed. The position required to me to clean the pigsty, feed the pigs twice a day, wash and steam a half ton of potatoes every day to feed the pigs, sweep the barracks floors and boil potatoes for twenty persons three times a day. I had to do everything on the run to keep up with what was expected of me.

The potato cellar was next to the pigsty. I had to carry potatoes in a bushel basket from the cellar to a water trough, and from there, to the steamer. After steaming the potatoes, I dumped the whole load into a huge box, added barley groats and mashed everything with a contraption I invented to make my work easier. Once, in the early days of this job, Chef ran into the barracks waving his arms and calling me a sparrow's head, meaning stupid, (that was how he cursed at me) for not knowing how to feed the pigs. He had looked into the pigsty and found all the pigs asleep. He imitated how pigs should scream with hunger every time I opened the door because, when I overfed them, they slept, and when they slept, they didn't grow. He chased me out of the barracks to the pigsty to show me what he meant. I was expecting that he might try to punch me from behind so upon crossing the threshold I ducked and turned around to face him. I caught him standing with an outstretched arm. "This time you missed, sir," I said, grabbing the shovel. He turned around and walked away.

I didn't feed the pigs that evening and in the morning I'm sure their screams were heard by the whole village. The pigsty was a mess. Some of the pigs managed to lift the tight-fitting screen from the drainage hole, plugging it with straw. Some broke out of their pens and ran back and forth in the corridor. First, I beat the free runners until each found their pen. After cleaning the whole area, feeding the pigs, and fixing the broken doors, I started to clean the plugged drainage hole when Chef walked in. He saw me pulling out a few straws at a time with a hook fashioned from a thick wire. He called me a sparrow head, took off his jacket, rolled up his shirt sleeve and stuck his arm into the drainage hole full of excrement. He pulled out a handful of soggy straw and said, "This is how it is done," and walked out. This was his lesson for me not to be squeamish about anything and there was no work in the world that was beyond my dignity.

When the piglets reached a certain age, they were considered weaned and would be separated from the mother. Chef said it was to prevent the piglets from injuring her with their tusks. After Chef showed me how to do it, separating them became part of my job. The piglets joined the rest of the pigs in the common compound. Occasionally, some of them got squashed during the night and then got sick and died. The first time I reported the death of a piglet to Chef he went berserk. Michel, the French POW, told me that he never told Chef when a sheep died. Instead, he would bury the carcass in the manure pile and in a few months it would have disintegrated completely.

The next time Chef saw an injured piglet he asked me if I thought my comrades would eat it. I said we would certainly eat the piglet and thanked him profusely. After that we got daring and slaughtered a couple of healthy piglets but stopped after that because the fear of getting caught made it too risky. In the summer of 1944, the farm had a more than usual amount of skimmed milk. Chef ordered me to feed the piglets with it but my comrades and I had another idea. I kept the milk in the cans until it curdled. We removed the solids and enjoyed eating cottage cheese. There was enough cheese to share with the girls but I decided against it. It was safer when less people knew our secret.

French POWs lived on the opposite end of the village in a new barracks, away from the manure piles and chicken coop. Every month they received a sizable care package from the Red Cross that contained items not even available to the Germans. Those who worked for a small farm such as ours were mostly treated as equals. They wrote letters home once a month, kept a hidden radio and listened to BBC. Important news was conveyed to us on the same day by two blacksmiths, who worked next to our sleeping quarters.

The French POWs had the opportunity to sign an allegiance to the Vichy government and be free as a civilian person but such POWs were rare. One such person was Henry. He fathered a baby with the kitchen maid, Ala, and to avoid punishment he signed the papers to become a civilian. Henry had a wife in France. When she came for a visit, we expected her to be outraged about Henry and Ala but nothing happened. All three looked happy. Henry's wife stayed with Ala in Chef's mansion, carried the baby in her arms during the day, and in the evening went for a walk with Ala and the baby. After she left, Henry got transferred to work in the dairy.

Two Frenchman looked after the sheep and a herd of sixty cows. One of them was a veterinarian. He limped heavily on his right foot but worked as though he had no impediment. Every day he led the cows to pasture in a column, reading a book as he walked with them, much like a priest leading a religious procession. He was accompanied by a pair of dogs, who were trained to look after the herd. In addition to milking the cows and cleaning manure from the stable he handled the thoroughbred bull and the horse during mating season. In season that job was a full-time affair by itself. Farmers from surrounding villages within a twenty-kilometer radius came with cows, mares, and sows for mating.

He was also the butcher for the farm and every time I was his assistant. Once he had to butcher a steer. After cutting the animal's throat we went in separate directions looking for a rope. Upon coming back, we found the animal standing on its feet, leaning against the wall, and looking at us with bulging eyes and bellowing. The Frenchman dropped the rope on the floor and ran. I toppled over, laughing at his reaction. After regaining his composure, the Frenchman returned muttering his usual profanities.

Chef had a pet dachshund that was trained to go down into foxholes to scare them out. It was let outside every evening for a stroll. A couple of times the dog got stuck because a fox wouldn't leave its den and blocked the dog's passage. The dog couldn't backup so we would have to come to its rescue and dig it out. On one occasion, after the veterinarian and I had finished butchering a steer, I dumped the entrails behind the barn. The dachshund came out to sniff around behind the barn and was attacked by the two shepherd dogs. We searched for him the following morning and found his carcass in the forest, 300 meters from the barn. We had to bury the remains in the park, behind our residence.

In the fall of 1943, I was assigned to the sugar refinery to unload the beet harvest. I arrived early in the morning with the first load of beets and returned late in the evening. I unloaded six to eight truckloads a day using special pitchforks. During wet weather a lot of the mud remained on the truck after the beets were unloaded. Chef told me to throw the mud in with the beets because he was being paid by weight and that could be the equivalent of two or three truckloads of beets.

After the unloading had been completed, Chef got a truckload of dried remnants soaked in molasses. Some guys figured out how to dissolve the molasses in boiled water and ferment it. We had an oak barrel to hold the brew and the yeast was provided by Paul Mayer. We hid the barrel in the attic under some sawdust. The brew turned out strong and did not taste bad. We enjoyed the results for two Sundays, each with a mug full of brew. A problem developed with Grisha Sablin, a village troublemaker, who had lost half of his ear in a fight sometime in the past. On that second Sunday after we enjoyed the brew, he started to pick a fight. The other guys started to laugh at his pranks so he thought he would scare everyone into submission by brandishing his jackknife. Grisha came at me while I was standing at the stove with crossed arms and hit me on the shoulder with the handle end of the knife. It bounced and he accidentally cut my wrist. The others rushed over to subdue him and he spent the night with tied up hands and legs, begging for forgiveness. On the following Sunday he didn't get any brew, which hurt his feelings.

The first batch was such a success we decided to brew a second batch and like the first, buried it under some sawdust. Chef's son had come home for summer vacation and he and some of his friends, along with the dachshund, decided to play hide and seek in the barn. Meanwhile, the contents of the barrel were fermenting and the whistle of escaping air attracted the dog and then the boys. They dug out the barrel and reported it to Chef. When the barrel was down on the ground Chef wanted to know what was going on and Grisha took the opportunity to get back at us.

The control officer was called and while everyone waited for his arrival Cybulya took the barrel to his room. Grisha was taken to a separate room next to the guard's for questioning. In addition to squealing about the brew, he also divulged that we had held back wheat seeds for spring sowing and used them to bake bread. I had experimented with grinding the seeds and was able to process about twenty kilograms. Of course, when the bread was baked Grisha had enjoyed it like the rest of us but now he was intent on doing what he could to bury us.

The control officer came with an interpreter from the sugar refinery, a man who knew me. I had conducted some transactions with the prisoners from the refinery when I unloaded Chef's entire harvest of sugar beets. The driver, Nicolas Suchov, butchered a sheep early one morning and brought it to the refinery for the interpreter and his friends. In exchange, they smuggled out a fifty-kilogram bag of sugar for us. Grisha reported about the sugar but he didn't know how we got it.

The interpreter told the control officer that I understood German well enough, that I didn't need an interpreter and the interrogation would proceed more quickly without him. The control officer interrogated me, poking his pistol into my temple a few times for intimidation. I interpreted for Nicolas and Jacob when they were being interrogated and tried to smooth over any controversial answers. In the end the officer promised to send our whole gang to a concentration camp and left. Good thing Grisha didn't stay in our barracks that night. Otherwise, he would have probably been dead by morning.

We were let out for work the next morning without seeing Chef. At noon we saw the control officer ride in on his bicycle. Nobody lay down for a rest and nobody spoke a word. We just waited for the sky to fall on us. Cybulya appeared at the usual time that afternoon and ordered us out to work. This time he let us walk with the girls. We still didn't know what to expect and walked in silence like in a funeral procession. Later we learned that the control officer had come to take us to the concentration camp but Chef decided against it. We knew his farm operation like it was our own and to exchange us for half skeletons from the camp wasn't in his best interest. Life went on. The barrel with the brew was still in Cybulya's possession. We decided to forget about it and not to aggravate anybody. Grisha was returned to our barracks. He tried to get friendly with a couple guys but everybody ignored him. He was a lonely person.

Cybulya had a friend from his hometown, who came for a visit every Saturday. He and his friend decided to remove the wooden choke from the barrel and got sprayed with a fountain of the contents. That made them mad at us. Most likely they tasted enough of the product to get a little tipsy. They came to our barracks late that night, woke us up and started to turn over mattresses searching for anything that might cause us a problem. Michael, the youngest in the gang, had new pants and a pair of new wooden shoes under his pillow. Cybulya slapped him a couple of times and yelled at us; obviously to make Chef aware that he was keeping us in line.

The next morning, Cybulya stormed into the barracks and jumped on Michael again and slapped him a few times. Michael ripped his shirt open and started to yell, "Shoot, you SOB!" Cybulya dragged Michael outside and ordered him to walk to the field, poking him in the ribs with his rifle. We waited anxiously to see what would happen next. A short time later, Cybulya came running in and ordered me to walk with him, telling me on the way what happened. He said he just wanted to scare Michael but he got away by jumping between the tall rape plants. Cybulya wanted me to persuade Michel to come out and promised not to touch him anymore. I shouted to Michael to get to the stables and wait there. Cybulya didn't lock the barracks and didn't show up until late evening. He came in the evening, looked at Michael, and locked the barracks for the night without saying a word. A few days later, while Chef was within hearing distance, Cybulya started yelling some nonsense at me. He swung at me with a bayonet in his hand barely touching my collar bone. Somehow, he dropped it on the floor, but I was the first to grab it. It was clear that he didn't want to hurt me. I handed the bayonet back to him handle first saying that I understood what he was trying to prove.

Like any German, Cybulya was afraid of being sent to the Russian front but eventually he received his summons. During dinnertime on that day, we saw Cybulya standing and staring at the sheet of paper. He disappeared into his room and a short time later came out with all his gear and walked by without glancing at us. One of our group whistled and someone else yelled goodbye and Cybulya was gone. Before he left, he went to say goodbye to the girls. Barbara, the tomboy, said in Ukrainian that she wished that the first bullet he encountered would hit him in the forehead. Cybulya didn't understand what she said so he took it to mean well wishes and said, "Thank you."

In mid-December of 1943 we waited in front of our barracks for Chef's orders. By this time, he had stopped running, yelling, and swinging his arms at us. Instead, every morning he greeted us with "Guten Morgen" and proceeded to tell us our orders for the day. This time he detained five of us and declared that we would be working in the bush until springtime. We left for the railroad station, got on the train and in one hour we were settled in our new place. The building had been someone's cottage with an all-glass front as well as part of the roof. Our sleeping room had a large window and five bunk beds. We were joined by an additional five people from other farms. Our guard was a sixty-year-old soldier with missing front teeth. Meals were prepared in a real kitchen by a heavy-set woman. Our food was strictly rationed as it was for any working person in Germany at that time but compared with our barracks at Chef's farm this place looked like sanatorium.

Our foreman was a seventy-five-year-old forester, who spent his whole life managing forests. He could have been the twin brother of Kraviec, with his broad shoulders and grizzly bear posture. He sharpened bucksaws and axes during lunch break. He had us work in pairs felling trees and cutting meter-long logs. Then we carried them out to the trail on our shoulders and placed them in a pile. Carrying single logs was time consuming. The foreman wanted us to speed up the process by carrying the whole trunk to the pile and cut it into logs once we were there. We protested saying that was impossible for a man to carry a whole trunk. The old man was a show off and to prove that we were wrong he carried out a few trees himself. All we had to do was lift it on his shoulders. Some days I cajoled him into carrying out three logs.

Occasionally we were allowed to build a bonfire. The guard was bored because he had very little to do so he would walk from one pair of us to the next telling the same story over and over. The foreman didn't like him interrupting our work but couldn't do much about it. The guard was as hungry as we were and saliva would run from the corner of his mouth as he retold the story about eating thick pea soup with pork every day while he lived on the farm, just before he came there. He also talked about his only son who was at the Russian front. One morning, just before we left the bush camp, he came to me with tears running down his cheeks and said, " My son is dead." He showed me the telegram slip which said that he died a hero's death. In that moment I thought about my parents and wondered if they had gotten any notification about me.

In four months, I learned everything there was to learn about the lumberjack trade. In spite of our meager diet the time flew by. We were much skinnier than when we came but were not starving and only worked eight hours per day. We had a considerable amount of reading material to pass the time. There was a weekly Russian newspaper edited by the newly organized Russian Liberation Army. It was a collaborationist army organized by a group of imprisoned Russian generals. The newspaper contained articles that were critical toward the Soviet Union, and in particular, its leader Joseph Stalin. They were true but the idea of collaboration with Hitler wasn't digestible at that time.

We talked about not going back to Chef's farm if we could exchange places with the other five but our idea wasn't accepted. We returned to face Chef skinnier than when we left. It was particularly noticeable on Ivan, who had lost his protruding belly and rosy cheeks. That was the first thing Chef noticed and he laughed until he turned blue. Ivan lost any future opportunities to milk cows and drink their milk. He had been replaced by the Tatar boy.

Every spring five additional prisoners arrived from the camp. Usually, they were very skinny but one year all of them could barely walk. They came in midsummer in the year that I worked as a cook. Chef instructed me to feed them a porridge-like concoction consisting of skimmed milk and potato starch for several days until their stomachs got used to regular food. The first day they stayed in the barracks eating what I had prepared for them. However, one of them couldn't resist temptation and ate potatoes. He got very sick and moaned and screamed in pain the entire night. A good thing for us was that they were in a separate room. The sick one had to be washed. He couldn't control his bowels and the contents in his stomach ended up in his pants.

On the second day only the sick one was left in the barracks. He begged me to cook him some borsch, the cabbage soup favored in Russia and Ukraine. He was sure that soup would make him well instantly. I returned to the barracks intermittently to see if he was still alive and as soon I tiptoed into the barracks he would start begging me again for borsch. I stole a small cabbage from the field and boiled it for him. While it was boiling, he delighted in the smell of the cooking cabbage with moans and groans. "If you die after your meal, don't blame me," I said, handing him the cabbage soup. He ate it all and slept through the night without a sound. In the morning he got out of bed and went to work with the rest of us.

In one of those groups, I met two boys from Chuvashia, my birth place. Late in the fall they returned to the camp to be sent to Denmark to build fortifications. Later we heard rumors that the boat carrying the prisoners was sunk by a Russian torpedo.

Every group that came to the farm included a unique character. For example, there was one man who came from Moscow and he couldn't tell which end of the cow milk came from. He didn't believe what collectivization did to the Russian peasants and how poor they were most of the time. He bragged about his job as a taxi driver in Moscow and how much money he used to earn driving vacationers from the far north to illegal girly establishments.

The following year another interesting character came in the group of five. From the first day he didn't hide his distaste for physical work. As a matter of fact, he introduced himself as a pickpocket, an armed robber, and a blackjack wizard. We nicknamed him Wizard. On Sundays, the boys would play blackjack for cigarettes, which they had earned from Chef for extra work. Wizard would decline invitations to play with a patronizing expression on his face. On one occasion he agreed to play and won all the cigarettes in twenty minutes. He returned the cigarettes to the losers and repeated the game with the same results.

The guard, who enjoyed tormenting Wizard all the time, watched the game. Wizard asked the guard if he was interested in seeing a real miracle. He put two spoons on the floor, covered them with his coat, and then lifted his coat to show that the spoons were still in place. He covered the spoons with his coat once again and waved his hands over the coat. When he lifted the coat this time they were gone. The guard grabbed the coat and shook it but there were no spoons. Then Wizard turned to me and said, "Tell the SOB to leave me alone. If he hits me once more, I will disappear like those spoons and he will be at the Russian front." The trick worked and the guard never touched him again.

In the summer of 1943, we watched bombers from the Allied forces flying high over Germany toward the Baltic Sea and a few times we saw dogfights between Allied and German fighter planes. In the spring of 1944, Allied bombers flew unhindered all over Germany. They dumped ribbons of aluminum foil by the ton to confuse the Germans' radar system. At that time, we prisoners didn't have any idea about radar and could only speculate about the possible meaning of their action. The bombers flew toward the Baltic Sea every day, wave after wave, and we could hear the roaring thunder of explosions a hundred kilometers away. German women, with children in their arms, stood looking at the planes and exclaiming, "What will happen to us now!"

Occasionally we saw silver-colored dots falling from the plane. They were empty containers for spare fuel discarded by the bombers. Once, when we were walking across the open field, two American planes flew by over Chef's property. A shiny barrel separated from the plane and came down directly over our heads. Everyone stopped to look at it, but Chef took off like a rabbit to the nearest ditch and hit the bottom on his stomach. He was dressed to go to town for the weekend and when he came out of the ditch with mud running down his belly, we roared with laughter. Without paying attention to us he ran home.

The only sound of German airplanes that we heard came from a farmer's barn about one kilometer from us. Factories had been levelled by Allied bombers and Germans were testing their remaining motors in farmers' barns. One night we woke up to the howling sound of an airplane flying overhead. We ran to the window hoping to see what was happening outside. The third time it flew over so close to the barracks, we hit the floor. Before we got up there was a tremendous explosion behind the stables. The guard came running and ordered us to stay calm. The next day we were locked in the barracks all day. A truck arrived carrying some soldiers. It left late that afternoon and we were let outside. Only a black circle was left in the spot where the plane fell and burned. The soldiers did a really good job cleaning up.

At noontime on June 6, 1944, the French prisoners reported that the Allied forces had landed in Normandy. The Germans, including Cybulya, didn't know about the Allied invasion until the next day and after they knew they didn't talk about it. Old Kraviec admitted that things at the front were very bad. A Polish girl, who had been brought to the farm, told us about the Warsaw Uprising. When the Russian forces reached the Bug River, the Polish Resistance rebelled against the Germans. Later studies showed that the Russian forces stopped advancing on the pretext they were reorganizing, but in reality, it was to allow the Germans to exterminate the Polish Nationalists. Stalin had his own puppet Polish government and didn't need the Nationalists. The Germans brutally suppressed the uprising and brought lots of Polish youth to Germany as slave labor.

One of these was a girl by the name Sophia (Zosia). She was a big girl with a mezzo-soprano voice. One day we were weeding sugar beets when Sophia started to sing a song called *Mother's Tears*. Everyone was captivated by the song. The girls started to cry and the guys swallowed the lump in their throat trying to hide their emotions. Even old Kraviec wiped away tears a few times.

One day Chef left the farm in a hurry and stayed away for two days. The next morning Kraviec told us about the unsuccessful attempt on Hitler's life. A short time later we heard about the execution of the conspirators. Allied forces were advancing from all sides and the end of war was in sight. This news bolstered our nerve and gave us encouragement. Though we prisoners were banned from singing on Sundays we kept on singing.

One day, Chef walked next to me, looking very sad. "We lost the war," he said, looking at me to see my reaction. The comment was completely unexpected and caught me off guard. After a slight hesitation I said, "What about the miracle weapon that is supposed to be ready soon? That may change the situation." He repeated that Germany lost the war and asked, "What do you think? Who will get here first, the Russians or the British?"

"Judging by the present situation probably the Russians," I said.

"What you suggest I do if the Russians come here?" he wanted to know.

"They may arrest you at first, and then let you out to do what you are doing now. You are a good administrator and a good farmer. You probably you won't be the burger master but will manage your own farm. But if it were me and I had a choice, I wouldn't stay here," I said. That was the first and the last man-to-man talk I had with Chef.

At nights I frequently lay awake staring at the ceiling as random memories of my life came to mind and for the first time realized how many close calls I had. Most of them were beyond my control and just happened unexpectedly. The last one happened two years previously. The tractor brought a trailer loaded with sugar beets and we pushed it into the barn for the night. Instead sitting on the trailer and using the brake lever I walked backwards in the front of the trailer attempting to guide it. I backed into a support beam behind me and tripped as the trailer kept on moving and started to roll over me. I felt the trailer bounce off my chest and roll back. Drifting in and out of consciousness I thought how strong the human rib cage must be to endure that much weight.

On the second day after the accident, I opened my eyes and for the first time felt real pain. The German doctor came from town to see me the same evening and left rubbing alcohol that had to be applied with a cotton swab on a stick. It made my skin burn but my ribs were less painful. Eventually the injured skin peeled off like from a sunburn. Two weeks after it happened, Chef visited me in the barracks and told me to get up and do some easy work. "To lie in bed is no good for you," he said. The first thing I did was to go to the barn where the accident occurred. There by the post lay a boulder that caused the trailer to roll back before it could flatten my chest completely.

Another time, I was in the process of lubricating the axle of a cultivator, when horses moved the machine. My middle finger got caught in the gears and was twisted right around. Skin and finger nail were ripped off. The tractor driver ran to me with a can of gasoline and poured it on my injured finger to stop the bleeding. That hurt more than from the injury.

The guard took me to see the doctor the next morning. He recognized me and asked how I felt after the tractor accident He was a gentleman in his sixties and spoke Russian better than I did. He told me he got his medical education in St. Petersburg before the Revolution. He wasn't in favor of Hitler or his politics and was sure that he would lose everything in the end. I came out of his office feeling more human than I had in a long time.

A ROA (Russian Liberation Army) propagandist was our regular visitor on Sundays. He also brought some reading material in addition to the propaganda. We were kept informed about the front and the Liberation Army's possible future. At that time the ROA had one fully equipped division, composed of collaborating units that were in the German army. A second division was in the process of being formed. On November 14, 1944, our usual work schedule was interrupted so we could listen to an important broadcast from Prague. After a short introduction, General Andrey Vlasov read the Liberation Committee Manifesto. Soviet citizens abroad were invited to volunteer for the Liberation Army.

For me it was an extremely confusing and soul-searching time. At a time when Germany's defeat was in sight, it seemed like an insane blunder to join their forces. The idea of collaborating with the enemy wasn't appealing to me either. On the other hand, all the Russian prisoners were considered traitors to the Fatherland by Joseph Stalin and returning home would be insanity. Either way we were doomed. After surviving so far, I didn't want to perish in the camps of the Fatherland but didn't see any solution.

Waking up during the night I spent many hours trying to picture what my future might be. After surviving so many odds I couldn't walk into a Soviet concentration camp voluntarily. I firmly believed that my fate was not in my hands and asked God not let me make a decision that I might later regret. Eventually my inner voice brought me clarity as to what I should do. If I had to face punishment, I would rather face it for my conscious action. Volunteering to join ROA would give me freedom of movement and I would have less of a chance of being a sitting duck in any circumstance, I reasoned. With the end of the war being so close there would be no time left to organize an army but we would be an organized group of people refusing to return to the USSR. The gang was shocked when they heard what I was going to do but no one criticized my decision. The only comment I got was from a school teacher from the Ukraine, who said, "I envy your courage and wish that I could do the same. We wish you all the best."

Shortly before I left, we were in the field harvesting the last of the turnips. Frequent rain made the ground muddy and difficult to walk with wooden shoes. Our bare hands were freezing in the muddy mess. We worked in pairs lifting full bushel baskets onto the trailer and receiving empty ones in exchange from the two guys on the trailer. It was almost dark and everybody was exhausted. Grisha, the one who betrayed us before, hit his partner over the head with his empty basket claiming that the guy grabbed his basket. They both came from same the district and the victim was the most peace-loving character, who wouldn't hurt the fly. Without saying a word, he started to cry like a child.

I felt something explode inside me. "It's time to smarten you up," I said to Grisha, and gave him two quick punches on both cheeks. The guard played dumb and walked to opposite side of the trailer so I took it as a signal. Grisha tried to play dead but I pulled him up by the collar and hit him again. He fell again and I kicked him hard in the ribs. Grisha pretended that he couldn't get up and moaned and coughed for two nights. On the second day the guard ordered Grisha to get up and go to work. He kept sniveling and coughing constantly but nobody sympathized with him.

Chapter 13

Stepping Into the Unknown

A week after the incident we came out for work as usual. Chef approached me with a smile, shook my hand and said, "You will be a soldier. Go to see Frau Ostrovsky, she prepared something for you." Frau gave me a loaf of bread and a stick of smoked sausage for the road. I had time to kill until the trailer that would take me to the station was loaded and ready to go so Frau told me not to leave without saying goodbye. I walked to her house and she gave me another sausage. As I was leaving, I thought wryly about her, the obedient citizen of Germany being not that obedient when it concerned their bread and butter. And even with the strict control of rationing and distribution they managed to have extra sausage.

At the railroad station I was handed over to a strange guard who boarded the train with me. Riding in a passenger car with civilians evoked strange feelings like crawling out from a dark pit into the daylight. The POW camp in Parchim looked different than the main Stalag II in Neubrandenburg. The barracks were not crowded: each man had his own bunk bed with a straw mattress. There was a barber shop, drama guild and musical instruments, including a few accordions. The shower and laundry facilities had hot water and were available on certain days. There were no visible guards on the towers or at the gate. Inside the compound inhabitants were free to move around and visit each other.

The idea of fighting against one's own people wasn't easy to digest for anybody, especially for those who were constantly being influenced by a crowd. They waited to be liberated by their own "Eagles." For the time being they were content with their improved living conditions even if they came with strings attached, namely joining the organizing ROA. The camp library had only pro German propaganda material. Glossy magazines depicted the Cossacks as villains fighting against the

Bolsheviks. According to our history books the Cossacks, or White Guards, were annihilated by the Red Army. We didn't know how many of them managed to escape. There were also pictures of the Uzbek Division in their down time, dancing with girls. I knew it was all hollow propaganda because the German forces were retreating on all fronts.

After we were individually interviewed by high-ranking officers we were loaded onto boxcars with a German escort in each car. For entertainment, an accordion was provided for each boxcar with the request that we take good care of them, because they were expensive. Our German escorts would take the instruments back to the camp. By the end of our journey not a single accordion was left to take back. They were exchanged for booze along the way.

Nearly every city along our route was destroyed by bombers. Occasionally a few bombs were dropped on the railroad stations. Some stations got hit the day before our arrival and trains couldn't continue. In several places we had to wait a whole day before the lines were cleared of debris. Hundreds of *Ostarbeiters* were engaged for such works. These were slave laborers brought to Germany by force. They wore an OST insignia on their chest, white letters on a blue background, to identify who they were. All the males were very young boys. They were waiting for their "Eagles" to liberate them and declined invitations to hop on the cars and go with us.

Looting was punishable by being shot on the spot but guys from our train couldn't pass up the opportunity when we passed through the bombed-out stations. On one occasion we got so much Swiss cheese there was enough to share with the boys working on the tracks.

And jumping ahead a little, there was another occasion where three ROA soldiers got in a jam for stealing cheese. They were arrested by the field gendarmes, the German military police and lined up to be shot on the slope of the railroad embankment, each holding a round of ill-gotten cheese. Someone reported the incident to a Russian colonel, who appeared immediately at the scene and ordered the German MPs to release the looters, threatening to shoot the MPs on the spot. He appeared to be absolutely fearless as he rode up on horseback with a machine gun mounted on the saddle horn. The fact that his left arm had been rendered useless from an earlier injury did not diminish his imposing presence. The Colonel said that the detainees were soldiers in German uniform and would be court marshalled in military courts. Then he ordered the detainees to drop the cheese and, using some choice profanity, told them to return to their details. The round cheeses rolled down the embankment and the detainees ran for their lives.

We traveled through Uelzen, Hanover, Kassel, Würzburg, Ulm and disembarked in Münsingen, a little town in the province of Württemberg in the Swabian Alps. During the entire journey, Würzburg was the only city not damaged by bombs but four months later there wasn't a single building left intact.

Münsingen was a picturesque little town nestled between the mountains. From the station we marched up the steep hill to a plateau where the military camp was located. It was formerly a German military compound but was now filled with recent inhabitants of POW camps, who didn't care for anything except their own day-to-day survival. It was large enough to accommodate thousands of people and was surrounded by a high fence to separate two clearly different worlds from each other, especially given the current situation.

We were temporarily housed in the attic of a horse stable that had been converted to barracks. Compared with the condition of the previous camp, the attic was a much brighter and cleaner place with enough straw to sleep on. As is the case in any overcrowded place, the atmosphere was sometimes tense and arguments erupted often. On one occasion, one of our party swore a Russian profanity when an officer was on the stairway. The officer was a highly decorated lieutenant with several medals and an iron cross on his heck, indicating that he was a German. The iron cross was not given to non-Germans. In flawless Russian he demanded that the culprit step forward. "I will teach you some manners," he said, and ordered the offender to run the length of the attic (that was at least forty meters long) twenty times. The officer stood there yelling, "Faster! Faster! Next time remember how to behave!" It was a clear illustration of how we non-Aryans would be treated in accordance with Hitler's politics.

Soon after that incident another officer visited our attic. He introduced himself as a special duty officer (sonder furer). He needed someone whose handwriting was legible in Russian and German. I volunteered and became the regiment's secretary. Ironically, our artillery regiment had as its commander, the one-handed Colonel I described earlier. At the time, the regiment's armament consisted of one 120mm cannon and several teams of horses with carts to haul whatever load we had. For the first two weeks I registered newcomers. After registration was complete my job got easier. In addition to translating a few orders each day, I wrote reports for the regiment commander, which were signed by the special duty officer. A few weeks after that I was transferred to the Division's office as a secretary. Because of my duties I was exempt from the training routine and considered myself very lucky.

One unforgettable occasion was the sending off ceremony of a battalion to the Eastern Front. The personnel of the entire camp stood in formation while two priests in black vestments performed religious rites for the battalion. Generals Vlasov and Truchin were there and gave short speeches, telling the troops what a historical mission they would be performing. It was a surreal feeling watching those men marching off to a certain death. Soviet forces were fighting on German soil, rapidly advancing to Berlin and Allied forces were taking their time, moving toward the east without meeting any resistance. The remaining German forces were moving to the Eastern Front to face the Soviets.

Allied planes attacked anything moving on the roads so the troops could only move during the night. Travel by train was especially dangerous. The first party of our regiment was loaded onto a train and was attacked by an Allied plane. Twenty-four soldiers and over twenty horses were killed. On the 14th of April we were loaded onto a train and safely reached the city of Munich, where we disembarked. The whole contingency of horse transport camped in a well-groomed park, in what seemed to be the outskirts of the city. I fashioned a tent from willow branches and slept in it all day. From then on, we marched during the night and camped during the day. We kept marching night after night singing songs to help keep us awake. A few times I fell asleep on my feet, still marching without losing step. A year later, I happened to be in the English Garden of Munich and recognized the spot where I made my tent by the shape of the tree whose branches I chopped off.

During our first morning on Austrian soil, we stopped at a farm. Our hosts were two sisters about sixty years old. They were friendly people. While we slept on the floor in the vacant half of the house, they baked bread. After we woke up, they gave us a whole loaf to share. For me, it was like being in a fairy tale to see a whole loaf of white bread offered by a granny in a farmhouse. We carefully sliced the loaf into ten equal pieces, and then had a blindfolded man draw each person's name to claim his "prize." The two sisters stood at the door wiping tears from their eyes as they watched us go through this ritual before eating the bread. They couldn't understand who we were and where we came from. Hitler's propaganda had taught them that Russians were savages who pillaged and raped every woman they encountered but they realized they were told lies. We were ordinary humans. They weren't up to date on current news either. When I told them that Hitler shot himself, they were surprised. The first words one of the sisters uttered were, "Who will give us ration cards now?"

We started to march again in the late afternoon and at dusk came to a large village. I approached a young man chopping wood on the street and started a conversation with him by asking how he was. Hearing my poor German, he asked who we were. When I said that we were Russian the axe slid out of his hand onto the ground. Through heavy stuttering he managed to ask, "Russians from Moscow?" I assured him that we were not those Russians but that he shouldn't be afraid of them either.

The next morning, we camped at another farm. One of our group sniffed out where a farmer was storing apples in his barn and found a way to get in through the ceiling. In a short time, everyone was munching the well-preserved apples. The farmer saw us enjoying his fruit and opened the storage room to find it half empty. He reported the trespass to the first officer he met. Our one-handed Russian Colonel arrived a short time later and after a stern lecture, ordered that the whole battery be marched off under guard to another location. A German sergeant, who appeared to be a deserter, asserted his opinion to the Colonel saying that in the German army the whole gang would have been shot on the spot for such an offence. In our military his speaking out of turn was considered to be reprimanding a senior officer. Further, his arrogant behavior indicated his attitude toward us or toward non-Germans in general. The Colonel reminded him that he was in uniform and spoke without asking permission. He continued by saying that while he could think of several reasons to shoot the Sergeant on the spot, he would let him live out of respect for his parents. The sergeant's face turned gray, he snapped to attention and apologized several times.

The following morning, we stopped at a large farm on top of a hill. We were met by two Polish fellows and a Ukrainian girl. All three had been brought to Germany as forced laborers and had worked together for three years. They told us that the Bürgermeister (Mayor) of the district had been hanged by some foreign workers. Farmers, who treated the laborers poorly, were now at their mercy. Several farmers had been beaten badly and some were even killed. Those three decided to stay at that particular farm and work till the end of the war. The girl was eager to return home as soon as possible but the Poles were hesitant to return to Soviet rule.

In the visible distance ahead of us was the Czechoslovakian border. We were ordered to cross the border in smaller units on a foggy and very dark night. We were met by a group of Slovenian speaking people. The march that started in Munich, Germany continued past Simbach, and

Braunau, through Linz, Austria, to Kaplice, Czechoslovakia, where we spent a whole week. The Czech people had rebelled against the Germans and had liberated most of that part of the territory. Although we didn't know it initially, we came to find out that Prague had been liberated from the German SS forces by Vlasov's army tank battalion. Although he was supposed to be fighting for the Germans, he had defected to support the Czechs in their uprising. Early the next morning someone saw a train that had been abandoned at the entrance of a tunnel and several men were dispatched to investigate. They found hundreds of people from some concentration camp in the sealed boxcars. According to witnesses there were more corpses than live people. We left them to the care of the village people.

There was a warehouse near the location where we were stationed that was being looted by the local population. Our boys rushed there and loaded bags of flour, macaroni, and a couple of barrels of apple schnapps onto their horse carts. The addition to our dwindling supplies cheered everybody up. In addition to being fed three times a day, one of our staff sergeants, who was a professional baker before the war, baked us fresh bread using the oven in a farmer's kitchen. It was a rare treat to actually have real, home-baked bread.

After a time, some of the men determined that the amount of flour being used up did not equal the amount of bread that was being distributed. They calculated that there should be forty percent more flour and wanted to know where it had gone. After listening patiently to the complaints, the baker went inside the farmer's house. Someone shouted a challenge for the baker to come outside and answer the question. Meanwhile a crowd of curious onlookers gathered outside the gate to see what was going on. The baker appeared at the door with a rifle in hand and asked, "Which one of you wants the answer first?" Everyone froze on the spot. He slowly pulled the bolt of the rifle asking again who wanted it first. In the blink of an eye his accusers vaulted over the fence and disappeared into the crowd. Spectators roared with laughter and the baker walked back into the house.

A group of civilian performers traveled with us and entertained the troops on the move. The most popular entertainer was a fellow who called himself Uncle Vanya. He did card tricks and sang Russian folk songs accompanied by a balalaika. Two years after the war ended, I saw him performing in a circus doing disappearing acts and sawing a girl in half. Another popular entertainer was a young, attractive lady with an extremely well-developed body, who performed acrobatic numbers with a young man who was much smaller than her. Her elderly mother travelled with them. Shortly after the war she married an American officer and immigrated to the United States with her mother. There was also an older lady in her 50s, who sang romantic gypsy songs. She was from Moldova and had real gypsy features. She passed as our regiment commander's wife and sang songs we had never heard before. I don't know what happened to them after the war ended but it wouldn't surprise me if they survived the forced deportation to the Soviet Union. In my eyes he was a hero and had a devil-may-care kind of personality.

By week's end we began to retreat in the wake of the approaching Soviet Army. Every afternoon we would hear the "Hurray" of the Soviet soldiers as they advanced from one village to the next and we would vacate a location as quickly as we could before they moved in. While we were traveling through Austria one fellow appropriated a farmer's bicycle but he couldn't use it. He gave it to me and I became the messenger, travelling between our units when they were located in different places. We spent two days in the last village, where most of the division was gathered in one location. That final afternoon, after listening to intensive "Hurray" for hours we got orders to vacate the village. I was commanded to deliver the orders to the last unit in the column but by the time I got there they were gone. I quickly returned only to find the place deserted.

The woman of the house where we were stationed came out to me and said, "I prepared scrambled eggs for the mayor but he left in a hurry. Here, sit down and eat them." I couldn't remember the last time I ate scrambled eggs. Not being able to resist that temptation, I sat down and ate the eggs in a hurry. As I was eating the woman expressed her confusion as to what was happening. After all, the long-expected Russians were coming so why were we (Russians) running away from them? "What's going on?" she asked me. I didn't respond to her question. I thanked her for the meal, got on the bike and left.

The house was situated at the top of a steep hill and as I started toward the street, I nearly hit a Soviet soldier walking on the street. He was as startled as I was. Fortunately, he took me for a civilian. He asked if there were any soldiers around to which I replied, "They were here this morning but I haven't seen them lately." Suddenly he changed his voice to a more official tone and asked if I would like to have a shot of vodka. Automatically, I said, "Yes, it's better if it's the *Moscovskaya* kind." He poured the vodka from his flask and handed it to me. I downed it and said thanks. I resumed pedaling down the hill as fast as I could and continued past our retreating column for several kilometers. The combination of vodka and adrenaline had its effect and when I finally stopped, I was exhausted. I got off the road and lay down in a rye field to rest. The sky was full of stars and bright lights were burning in farmhouses around me. The war was over and nobody was afraid of being bombed any more. I felt jubilant as I quickly fell asleep.

I woke up feeling rested. It was still dark and I heard the murmur of low voices on the road. The column had caught up with me and was standing still, apparently waiting for some decision. I pedaled my bike to the head of the column and was told that a delegation had gone ahead to meet with American forces. The wait seemed endless and while we waited there was nothing to talk about except rumors. One of them was that General Vlasov had been captured by Soviet forces during the night.

The sun that came up on the horizon promised a hot day. It was past noon when our delegation returned. After a short officers' meeting, we were told that our delegates would meet the American military brass the next day. Meanwhile we would make camp in a neutral zone, close to the American checkpoint. Everything was pulled off the road into the dense forest and we set up camp as usual. Most field kitchens had enough provisions from recently looted Germans supplies.

Waiting around created a lot of tension and everyone handled it differently. For example, my division commander got drunk and retreated to the bush determined to shoot himself, but his wife pleaded with him not to do it, and somehow he changed his mind. The monotony of waiting was interrupted by American patrols driving back and forth on the road and the occasional appearance of Soviet soldiers in their horse and buggy. They usually sat in the horse cart like mummies and didn't engage us in conversation. They were still wearing their winter hats and felt boots and their uniforms were caked with dried sweat under their armpits. Soon, another type of military personnel started to visit us, sent for propaganda purposes. They were very friendly fellows telling us that we should return home without hesitation. They said that we had won the war and Fascism had been destroyed. They told us not to worry about what Stalin had said about POWs. Everyone had been forgiven and we could return to our families.

One heavily intoxicated lieutenant came to tell us a different story. He had been captured by the Germans and liberated by the Soviet Army. After a lengthy interrogation by SMERSH (an organization founded by Joseph Stalin for three counterintelligence agencies; KGB being one of them) he was sentenced to ten years imprisonment and send to the front line to redeem himself through heroic action. The war came to an end before he had a chance to redeem himself and he said was expecting to be imprisoned for ten years upon his return. It was clear that he was searching for a more favorable solution.

We remained in that spot longer than was originally planned and our supplies were running out. Eventually only one field kitchen was left with provisions. The petty officer of that unit was resourceful and, without waiting for permission, had traded two horses for food supplies with a farmer. He saw me standing in line in his kitchen and asked who I was. That is how I met Simon Osatchook for the very first time.

Our wait finally came to an end. The delegation returned from the American zone and officers were called to a meeting. Everyone was on their feet waiting to hear the answer to our fate. Officers returned to their units and announced that everyone was free to decide his own future. We had permission to enter the American zone and trust our fate to them. All we had to do was march there in an organized fashion and leave our weapons in a designated spot. Those who wished to return to Russia could leave immediately and walk back to where we had come from.

One young fellow from Belarus came to me and asked what he should do. His mother had arranged a marriage for him hoping that by doing so he would not be conscripted and sent to Germany. He wasn't in the army but ended up in Germany as forced labor. I knew that he was homesick. I told him that I couldn't be responsible for his future by telling him what to do, but if I were in his place, I would take a chance. We hugged each other and he walked away to meet his fate in Russia.

It looked like at least a third of the people walked toward the Russians. Some were homesick, hoping to see families. Some hoped the Soviet government would be lenient and they would be sentenced to only a few years of forced labor. The most noticeable figure among them was a lieutenant on horseback wearing a full German uniform. I met him again later and heard how he was received by the Russians. He was dragged off his horse, slapped across the face, spit on, and called all kinds of dirty names. He said that they were marched to the railroad station without food and water, where a train of boxcars was waiting for them. Signs were painted on the door, *Traitors of the Fatherland*.

Eventually trainloads of returning prisoners were delivered to uranium mines in Siberia and worked without any safety protection. All died in a short time. After the war, Siberia was covered with concentration camps or *gulags*. Some survivors got their freedom after ten years while others served up to twenty years. Either way there were no winners.

Chapter 14

POW: The Second Time

With all our possessions on our shoulders we started to walk toward the unknown one-by-one. More people joined us on the road followed by those in horse buggies and on horseback. I felt some relief thinking that at least, for now, we were going in the right direction, to the American Zone. There was a barricade at the entrance to the zone, with a black and white guard off to one side. Two American soldiers stood watching us walk by. Occasionally they would ask one of our guys for the time and would then confiscate the watches of those who showed that they had one. In that respect they acted no differently than the Russian soldiers. Officers were permitted to keep their side arms but the rest of us piled our firearms in a designated space. While the column moved, another two American soldiers drove back and forth in a Jeep. After several hours of marching, we stopped in a large cattle pasture at the top of a hill. In the visible distance, on the opposite side of the pasture, loomed a castle-like structure without any signs of life.

The hungry crowd immediately started to butcher some horses and cook horse meat over bonfires. Two or three pails hung over every fire. The horse meat took a long time to cook and the fires burned all night and the following day. Eventually the problem that started off as hunger became the problem of upset digestive systems either because of improper cooking or overeating. Not a pretty sight or smell.

The next day armed soldiers appeared to organize us into groups. First, all non-military people were ordered to separate into a group, including officers' wives, and girlfriends. They were not supposed to cross an indicated line, which caused lots of crying and wailing amongst the women; some of whom had babies with them. A soldier, who was posted to guard the dividing line, stood yelling at those who attempted to cross the line for a last hug. Finally, he resolved the problem by shooting at an offender's foot.

We were divided into groups of fifty men with one elected leader for each group. We were instructed to take only personal belongings. Everything else remained behind. A line of trucks pulled up on the road and we climbed aboard, fifty people on each truck, packed like sardines in a can. The truck made its way through the mountainous region around Passau, Germany (a city on the border of Austria), swaying from side to side with every bend of the road. When making sharp turns on the slopes of the mountain, the truck's tires lifted off the road several times causing a violent reaction for some passengers prone to motion sickness. The stench was unbearable but the driver and his helper were in good spirits, literally, as they enjoyed a bottle of wine with their lunch. Everyone breathed a sigh of relief as we left the mountains behind. Before us spread level land as far as the eye could see. We were unloaded on the left bank of the Isar River, within view of the town of Landau. This would be our permanent location.

A detachment of military police met us there. Each group was given a spade, axe and rolled-up tent and was led to the spot where they should be put up. In a couple of hours, we had created a tent city surrounded by a row of barbed wire and a watchtower at the gate entrance, all erected by us. In a few days the whole place looked like a tourist town with graded streets, flower beds at each tent's entrance, and an open-air stage on the "town square." Every day we got three meals prepared in American field kitchens. We were told to keep army discipline and await further development. General Meandrov, the commander of the Second Division, was still with us. American orders were delivered through his office. The atmosphere at the camp suggested that the resolution of our fate was not far off.

Soviet officials came to the camp to try to persuade us to return home. According to them everything in the past was forgiven and forgotten and we should not worry. Their spokesman was the former Commissar of the Red Army. One of the officers in the camp left with the Soviet representatives and returned a few days later to tell us how well he was received. The men in the camp surrounded the Soviet delegation in a tight circle and someone stabbed the spokesman from behind with an awl. He started to scream for help. Two American MPs rushed in and led him out through the gate. That was his first and last visit as a propagandist to our camp.

Musicians and performing artists staged concerts every Sunday. A trumpet player in the brass quintet was a fellow, Nikita, whom I knew from home. One day he came to me to say goodbye. He was dressed in civilian clothes. "Watch me walk out of the gate among the civilian visitors," he said and away he went. I met him a year later in a refugee camp. He was married to a Ukrainian girl who had a baby. He said that after German doctors had conducted medical experiments on him when he was in one of their POW camps; he was not able have children. He said he avoided further damage to his health, even possible death, by joining the orchestra in the Russian Liberation Army.

In 1993, during my first visit to Chuvashia, someone from his village phoned me, anxious to verify that I met Nikita after the war. He was searching for him through the international Red Cross. He wrote an article in the local newspaper, where he speculated that Nikita might be playing his trumpet on the street corners of some city, for change. During my second visit a few years later, he wrote another article saying that his curiosity had been satisfied by an answer he received from the Red Cross, which stated that Nikita died in Hamburg, Germany, at the age of 80. I believe that Nikita lived a happy life. His family requested they not be bothered in the future.

The days of waiting were long and monotonous. My division commander organized a course to study internal combustion engines. The Americans provided an engine, which had been cut in half to make all the cylinders and valves visible. Most people spent time on the river bank that was loosely guarded by two soldiers. Some people walked out of the camp to enjoy temporary freedom and to work on the farms nearby. Simon Osatchook, who met me at his field kitchen a few weeks before, was among them.

Waiting for the unknown was nerve-wracking at first but eventually we got used to it. For close to two months, we had a peaceful life with good food and lots of free time. It came to an end in the middle of August. We were separated from the officers and driven to another location. It looked bad but the rolled-up tents were loaded with us and we were assured that we were not destined for the Russian Zone.

We passed the city of Passau again and turned to the west. Women working in the fields waved to us likely thinking that we were German soldiers returning home. After a two-hour drive we came to a place that was similar to the place we just left but had more permanent structures. This camp had about six wooden barracks and was surrounded by a row of barbed wire, just like the place we just left. The tower at the gate was equipped with a powerful searchlight. We occupied the wooden barracks and put up the tents for the next arrivals. This place did not feel right and I felt the urge to split from there as soon as I could. I talked to my three friends about it and they were willing to follow me. The wire fence was ten meters behind the barracks and looked easy to crawl through. I remained back there to wait until dark and see how the searchlight on the tower would operate. It started to rain and with it came early darkness. The beam followed the fence around the perimeter of the camp and took twenty minutes to make a full circle. We made a plan based on that information and made sure that everyone remembered it and followed it exactly.

Everyone in the barracks was asleep when we left. We stood behind the barracks and waited for the searchlight beam to pass by. As soon as it passed, I ran to the fence, braced the wire with two pieces of board and slipped through. I ran a few steps when the ground disappeared from under my feet and I rolled down a steep embankment that wasn't visible when we first surveilled the area. The rest followed suit and rolled down the embankment one after the other but we were not injured and we were free! We ran until we were out of breath. We were beyond the range of the searchlight but continued walking briskly.

Our goal was to reach the forested foot of the mountain that ended up being much farther away than it looked. Drizzle turned to pouring rain and we were soaking wet. Once we reached the wooded area, we took a short rest and then resumed walking. We lost all track of time as we followed a trail leading up the mountain. Eventually, the smell of manure told us we were close to a farm. We slowed down and listened for dogs barking but didn't hear any noise so we decided it was safe to look for shelter. Suddenly a farmhouse loomed before us on the steep slope of the mountain. We walked past the house and attached long building. At the back of the building stood an empty woodshed, where it was quiet and warm. We sat down on the floor leaning our backs to the wall. We could hear cows chewing the cud on the other side of the wall as we dozed off.

I was awakened by the sound of a man's low voice talking to the cows. I got up and walked to the cattle shed. The man sat on a low stool milking the cow with his back to the entrance. "Good morning," I said in a low voice, trying not to startle him but he jumped on his feet and froze forgetting the pail under the cow. I told him not to worry, that I wouldn't hurt him. I told him who we were and what we needed. He led us to the attic over the shed where we could sleep. We dug into the straw and fell asleep instantly. Later he brought us a large wooden bowl full of hot milk with pieces of bread floating in it. We ate it and fell asleep again. It was past noon when we were ready to get up. We ate bread in milk again and said good bye to the hospitable farmer and his daughter.

According to our host we shouldn't get lost even though some places were no more than a foot path. We continued walking up the mountain past a pasture with a herd of cows. One of the cows had a bell around her neck made from a tin can. The road made a turn and we began walking down the mountain. We could see the main road many kilometers ahead but had to overcome some obstacles before reaching it. One of them was a swift running creek. We followed it until we found a place where we could cross and had to undress up to the waist before doing so. The water was ice cold but felt refreshing.

We came to a barn beside the narrow road. It was too early to stop for the night, so we decided to take a short rest there and then continue on until we reached another farm or some kind of settlement where we might be able to get our next meal. Suddenly we heard sounds behind the bend and a team of horses appeared pulling a load of hay. The driver of the team didn't seem surprised to see us and calmly asked, in Polish, where we were heading. After we explained our situation, he suggested that we follow him to the estate where he worked. "At the very least you will get a good meal," he said.

The estate looked like a medieval castle with a courtyard shaped like a horseshoe. We walked in through a wide door to a large room, which happened to be the mess hall. There were about thirty men having supper, served by uniformed waitresses. We sat down at the table closest to the door and soon were served by one of the waitresses with no questions asked. I felt like I was in a fairy tale. Each one of us got a large plate loaded with mashed potatoes and peas with lots of gravy, and a mug with a drink.

After we finished our meal, I called the waitress over and explained that I wanted to see the *Chef.* Soon she returned and invited me to follow her. I walked in through a leather-covered door and was introduced to an impressive looking man dressed as though for a parade. He wore a black leather glove on his left hand, which he rested on the table. I realized it was artificial. His right hand held the leash of a Doberman lying at his feet. I was invited to sit across from him and state my case. After explaining our situation, I asked him if it was possible to work there, even for a short time and get some kind of identification. I could tell he was sympathetic to our position as he said, "I'm sorry but yesterday American MPs registered the foreign workers here and I cannot add new names to the list." That was it. He said something to the dog and stretched out his arm to shake my hand. At the time he was the most civilized individual I ever met.

It was dark already and we decided to return to the barn for the night. When we woke up the next day, the sun was up over the tall trees. We crossed a large plateau of harvested fields and walked through a dense forest without seeing any signs of life. In late afternoon we came out on the crest of the mountain. Deep in the valley we saw a roof with smoke coming out of the chimney and we headed down the path toward it. As we came closer, our noses detected the smell of freshly baked bread. The building was a watermill with living quarters attached to it. I walked inside and met a man in his fifties, who did not seem to be surprised to see strangers. I told him who we were and asked if we could have some bread. He handed me a half loaf of slightly warm bread and I went back outside to share it with my friends. We sat in the grass near the building enjoying our meal.

The miller came out several times just to chat. According to him we were about four kilometers from the city of Passau, through which we had passed twice already. He said there were control booths at the bridges but the MPs didn't pay attention to people who crossed them. That was good news but we knew we couldn't be too careful. The miller sent his thirteen-year-old daughter with us to show us the short cut to Passau. She walked up the mountain with us chattering like a bird and we parted like long-time friends. I think back to that time and wonder, "Who would send a young girl to walk in the dense forest with four complete strangers?

We passed a dozen small houses with white fences and gazed down on Passau, spread before us like a picture. Two long bridges spanned over two rivers. Black-and-white-striped booths on each end of the bridges sharpened our situational awareness, but the MPs on duty didn't stop anybody. It looked as though people were just strolling back and forth enjoying their long-awaited freedom from fear. We blended in well with the population and walked across casually before realizing that we had crossed the wrong bridge. We retraced our steps until we reached the other bridge and crossed over once. Everything was going so smoothly I felt jubilant and was ready to sing and shout.

We turned at a side road leading to a solitary white house. An elderly woman sat outside by the well peeling potatoes. We were thirsty and asked her for drink. "Unfortunately, I cannot offer you anything to drink," she said, looking concerned. Pointing her finger toward a larger house in the distance, she said, "Go there." We didn't argue with her, although she was sitting next to the well, and went on. We knocked on the door at the next house. A heavy-set man with a large goiter under his chin opened the door. After I told him who we were and what we wanted he invited us in. The man said the people in this valley don't drink water to quench their thirst and led us to three oval shaped oak barrels, with wooden faucets, which stood against one wall. He handed me a whole liter of foaming liquid. It was three-year-old apple cider. He told us that because of his thyroid disorder he could not serve in the military and he was happy about that. Before we left, he suggested that the next farm would be a good place to ask for food and stay overnight. "I don't have a wife to cook," he said.

At the next farm we were met by a ten-year-old boy, Rudy, who was anxious to tell us everything at once. The boy's father was killed in the war and his mother managed the farm alone. He knew a few Ukrainian phrases that he learned from two girls, who had been assigned there as forced labor during the war. The girls returned home after the war and only a local girl and Polish fellow remained on the farm. The Polish fellow was hesitant to go home because of what he might face under Soviet occupation.

We were fed the typical potatoes with buttermilk and then spent the night in the barn. Rudy was permitted to sleep with us, which made him very happy. Sometime between our arrival and settling in for the night, Rudy saw Paul's lighter and wanted to have it. He was willing to ask the kitchen maid to provide sexual favors in exchange for the lighter. Telling him that it was dangerous to play with a lighter didn't help. The next morning, after breakfast, we continued on our journey. Rudy followed us for a long distance, begging for the *feuerzeug*. I told him he could accidently burn down his house and then would have to live with the guilt the rest of his life. That seemed to be what he needed to hear and he ran home without turning around.

As we were walking, we passed two women loading sheaves by the side of the road. We stopped to chat and helped them load their cart just for the fun of it. During our conversation they offered us a deal. They said that since they were both widows any two of us could remain with them as husbands. We declined their offer politely by telling them that anything in the world was possible and miraculously, their husbands might return home.

After walking for a couple of weeks, we passed road signs that indicated we were approaching the town of Adelsdorf (about 254 kilometers north northwest of Passau), the residence of Baron Von Adelsdorf. We approached the town using side roads to see what was going on there. From the crest of a hill, we saw American soldiers gathered at a village pub. Across the street from the pub, at the entrance to the baron's estate, stood a guard post without a guard. Behind the pub was a typical farm courtyard, where a young man was chopping wood near the woodshed. From a distance we recognized him as one of us, which meant we would not be walking into danger. One by one we walked down to him and learned that we were in the right place for the time being. He said that several of our boys were working on the surrounding farms and there was no problem finding work. He pointed across the street and said there might be opportunities for one or two people.

I walked over to ask if they need laborers and was received like a long lost relative. Paul and I joined the family for supper. We were introduced to the family, which consisted of a grandmother, daughter, two granddaughters and a grandson, at the supper table. We wanted to fit in so we watched everyone closely and did as they did. Before the meal everyone knelt down while Grandma said grace. After the meal she said a shorter prayer standing up. Grandma was the head of the household but her daughter and grandchildren were in charge of the daily operation of the farm. We learned that during the war they had several forced laborers from the Ukraine, whom the grandson supervised. He tried to assume that authority over us a few times but I would remind him that the war was over and times had changed, and he would simmer down.

After the late harvest was completed, I helped several neighbors with their threshing. The community threshing machine was operated by an old steam engine and made its tour from one farm to the next. It took two to three days to finish the threshing at each farm. The work was hard but its conclusion culminated in a huge celebration with lots of rejoicing and good food. The next-door neighbor was the town's mayor. He issued us backdated IDs as long-time residents.

On Sundays I hung around at the *gasthaus* (inn or pub), where the soldiers were served real beer and played dice on the sidewalk. Occasionally some soldier would drink too much and get rowdy. The guards on duty would come and take the offender away to the cooler. I met several Russian-speaking American soldiers, whose parents were old immigrants from Russia. One of them asked me if it was true that Russian people ate salted herring and drank vodka for breakfast. He said that since his father did, he assumed that it must be a Russian custom. I replied, "If Russians had herring, they would probably eat them for breakfast, but there are no herrings freely available." That was hard for him to understand. Then he asked if I would be interested in washing dishes in their kitchen. I told him I was and he told me to bring all my belongings to the gasthaus, where I would stay.

The next morning, I came to work and was introduced to a Polish fellow, who cleaned and recharged the gas hotplates for the kitchen. He showed me what my duties were and then led me to the mess hall. The chef and his assistant met us at the door. I was led to a table and sat in a soft chair. The table was filled with leftovers from breakfast. The Polish fellow ceremoniously explained what each item was, saying "Those are pancakes and this is syrup for the pancakes. This cream is for the porridge and this is for the coffee." The chef and his assistant stood at the door speaking to each other in low voices. I didn't understand what they were saying but figured they were commenting on my reactions to the food. After all, this was the first time in my life I would be eating an American soldier's breakfast that included oatmeal, pancakes (made with powdered eggs) with syrup, fried bacon, and coffee with canned milk. I watched as a soldier took half a cup of black coffee and sipped it slowly. I tried to do the same but couldn't swallow the first mouth full. The Polish fellow suggested I use sugar and cream to make it more palatable.

After breakfast, I started work. All the utensils were aluminum and they had to shine like new after every meal. Everything on the menu was boiled in large aluminum pots including coffee, which left the pot black. I had to scrub those pots vigorously with steel wool to make them shine.

One day the staff sergeant showed me a pile of utensils that had been used during the war. They were as black as charcoal. I was given a rubber apron and gloves and a blue chemical that looked like unprocessed salt. I was told several times to be extremely careful not to spill or splash myself with the solution. First, I put the utensils in the sink and filled it with cold water until everything was immersed. Then I added the indicated amount of blue chemical. Almost instantly the water started to boil. After five minutes I removed the utensils and loaded the next batch. In a short time, everything was shiny. After I rinsed all the cleaned items in hot water several times my task was complete. As a reward for a dangerous job well done, I was rewarded with a week's issue of canteen goodies consisting of chocolate bars and cigarettes.

There was a tank battalion close by, whose tanks were stationed at the edge of the park. Periodically the detachment cleaned and did maintenance work on the tanks. On one occasion half the detachment went partridge hunting and returned with a pile of partridges. They asked me if I would clean them and I agreed to although I had never cleaned partridges before and didn't know the first thing about it. I soon discovered that skinning them was the fastest method. The chef's assistant prepared the partridges that evening and the soldiers had a feast. Again, I was rewarded with cigarettes and chocolate for doing a good job.

In addition to washing pots, one of my duties was to get rid of the leftovers. The Polish fellow told me to dump them in the garbage and they would be picked up later by one of the farmers. There were several refuge families in town that lived on ration cards. They came with pails and stood behind the garage begging for leftovers. Anything they could get was like treasure for them. I persuaded the Polish fellow that it would be nobler to let me give it to those families to feed their hungry children instead of leaving it for the farmer's pigs. I knew he had a reason to hate the Germans but these refugees were victims as well.

After the talk he didn't object to my giving away the leftovers and he stopped kicking the cleaning girls. The girls hated him as much as he hated Germans. One of the girls was from the eastern part of Germany. Her family kept several forced laborers at their farm before the Soviet Front advanced and forced them to flee. Now she was a cleaning woman in the employ of the enemy. She was a good-looking girl but I didn't like her attitude. "You are a proud person and looked down at the *undemenshen* (non-Aryans were considered sub human). The hardship you are experiencing now will make you a better person," I told her. Several times she asked me to walk her home through the park. It was the shortest way home for her but she was afraid that something bad might happen to her if she was on her own. Her sister was working for a farmer who owned the village pub. Later on, I had several occasions to stop there for a beer.

Every day boys from the village would sneak to the garbage to collect cigarette butts and every day the Polish fellow watched what they were up to. One day he called me to watch what he planned to do to scare them away. He poured a ring of gasoline around the garbage ahead of time and when the boys were gathered on the garbage pile, he ignited the gasoline and watched them run. Much to his disappointment the boys were back the very next morning so he gave up.

The Polish fellow didn't spend his allowance in the pub playing dice. Instead, he often counted and recounted what he had saved. He was also counting the days to his demobilization and often acted like a homesick kid. One evening he invited me to the upper floor where they slept to show me how ready he was to go home. He put on a civilian suit, striped shirt and necktie, and a straw hat. "Every Sunday I go to bed dressed like this," he told me.

The entire time I worked in the kitchen, the chef had an outstanding request for schnapps. I told the Polish fellow that if he could get me enough sugar, I would make schnapps for them. He gave me a cup of sugar every now and then but at that rate it would take months before I would have enough to be able to brew anything. I saw all kinds of old keys lying on window sills in the garage so I collected a few and tried them on the lock for the supply room. Every key I tried opened the lock, so one evening I went into the room and took a ten-pound bag of sugar. I kept the brew in the locker in my room and one night I distilled it. The result was five liters of pure vodka; my gift to the chef. The chef, Polish fellow and the doctor began a ritual of having a shot of vodka before their meal. The Polish fellow would pour a full glass and cross himself as he looked at a picture of Virgin Mary hanging on the wall. Then he would drain the contents of the glass and say, "I am a good Catholic!"

The doctor was a bald-headed fellow who spoke fluent Ukrainian. He traveled to Czechoslovakia twice to meet with Soviet representatives and understood our situation. He and I talked politics several times and agreed on most things. He told me that they would be relocating in the near future and tried to help me by asking the Battalion Commander to take me with them, but was refused. His advance warning gave me time to prepare. I put aside two new blankets, a pair of pants and a pair of shoes that had been discarded in the garage. My friend Simon had suggested some time back that I start drying the used coffee grounds from the kitchen. For the locals, real coffee was a rare commodity so even what the Americans discarded could be reused. Over time I dried a sizable amount of coffee grounds, which Simon exchanged for bacon and eggs. He traded regularly with the farmers and townspeople and got to know them fairly well so when the time came to clear out; Simon found a place for me to stay with his neighbors.

I was getting ready to move out of the gasthaus that evening and two boys came by to pick up some things that I didn't need. I saw two MPs on the street talking to the owner but didn't think anything of it. I continued packing the rest of my belongings when they appeared at the door and ordered us to follow them. They put us in their vehicle and delivered us to the Landau jail. The place was clean and warm and we were fed three meals a day. We would look through the window every now and then, beyond the fenced yard, and watch the outside world. I thought a lot about the owner of the gasthaus and his treatment of us. I could understand that he was anxious for us to vacate the premises but the way he went about it enraged me to the point that I fantasized about torching his property. We spent four days in jail not knowing what to expect. For us the worst-case scenario was that we could be delivered directly to the Soviet repatriation camp, located less than a kilometer from the jail.

An American sergeant finally came by to interrogate us but he didn't have any information about us. He asked each of us the same question in broken German: "Warum bist do im gefangen haus?" (Why are you in jail?). We said the only thing we knew was how we got there but not why. "What were our plans for the future?" was his second question. I had to answer what he wanted to hear and replied, "We are returning home." I knew that by answering that way I was taking a big chance because he could have driven us right to the door of the Soviet camp, but he let us go. We walked back to the same village and rejoined our friends.

Simon and Paul lived and worked on different farms. Mishka Yermak lived with a woman whose husband was a POW in Russia. We made her home our meeting place in case of emergency. She wasn't concerned how her husband would react to her keeping a younger border. He wrote that he was treated well by the Russians and hoped to return home soon. He had just finished painting a huge portrait of Stalin and the camp officials liked it. She had a big laugh telling us the story because her husband was a staunch follower of Hitler and hated Stalin.

Simon brought me to his neighbor, where I would be staying, and after introductions were made, he left. I was invited for supper. The whole household was at the table. The head of the family was a man past his seventies. With him were three women, who I thought could be his daughters and granddaughter. I came to find out that the older woman was his sister. She did all the cooking and baking. One of the others was his daughter (and our landlady), and the youngest was a hired hand. She was about seventeen years old and lot taller than the other two. There were also the daughter's five-year-old son and a young man from west Belorussia, who worked there all summer. He became my roommate.

The buildings on this farm, as was the case with all surrounding farms, were very old. The living quarters consisted of a two-story stone structure. A large room on the first floor served as the kitchen, dining and living room, and contained a large brick stove with a hot plate. A wide bench occupied the entire length of one wall and there was a radio receiver on a shelf. Adjacent to the kitchen were two rooms that served as rented living quarters. At that time, they were occupied by a young mother and her baby. A large porch entrance separated the living part of the building from the horse stable. Family bedrooms were on the second floor. Our sleeping area was directly over the horse stable and had a separate entrance with a narrow stairway leading to the room. It was not heated like the other bedrooms but we slept under down-filled covers and felt comfortable even on the coldest nights, which were never below freezing.

There were four horses and about thirty cows to take care of. First thing in the morning we would feed them and wash up for breakfast. After breakfast I would clean the stable and brush the horses while the Byelorussian and young girl tended to the cows. I saw the old man only in the evenings. He rarely talked at the table and after supper he would sit silently until we left the room. Once, I asked him if I could listen to the radio but he didn't respond. I got the impression that he hated me for some reason. I rarely saw him outside but once, while I was plowing the field that stretched from the barn towards his neighbor, I observed him sneaking out to measure the depth of the furrows. Then I noticed him checking the stable and horses. I knew that I did everything to the best of my abilities so I didn't worry about what the old man thought. I knew what was expected of me and worked in such a way that the women treated me as a member of the family.

By that time, I knew that the real boss was the old man's widowed daughter, whose husband had been killed in the war. I thought her to be around twenty-five years old but with her youthful looks she could pass for a teenager. She had a boyfriend that she kept secret from the old man. Her boyfriend was the owner of the neighboring farm. He used to come late in the evening and wait in the cowshed until the old man retired. Then he would sneak into the house.

One day my Belarus buddy told me that he had a personal problem and didn't know what to do about it. Reluctantly, he showed me his badly bruised privates. I convinced him to ask the landlady to take him to see the doctor. As a result the doctor decided to keep him in the hospital overnight. The same evening she asked me to go with her to look for a lost duck that hadn't returned with the flock. I sensed that she had something up her sleeve but went along out of curiosity. She clung to my arm with both hands and kept trying to get physically close to me. As we walked, she asked me what I thought about my friend's injury and told me that the doctor thought it was caused by excessive intercourse.

I kept listening to her babbling and was noncommittal when answering her questions; and I did not react to any overtures she made. We returned without the lost duck and parted at the door. In the morning the young girl told me what she overheard. The landlady was testing me to find out if I may have had intimate relations with the young girl but concluded that I was just a backward young man, who didn't know about sex. I passed the test with flying colors.

The young woman who lived in the spare rooms generally kept to herself but after I had been there awhile, she approached me with a request. She was a refugee from East Germany. She said she didn't know if her husband was alive, but if he survived the war, he would be in contact with some relatives in Hamburg. She was apprehensive about travelling alone and asked me to accompany her at least part of the way. I had to tell her I wasn't in a position to travel and explained why but reassured her that she and her baby would not be alone on the train and would be safe.

In post-war Germany and in particular where we were staying, any type of new clothing was difficult to find. I met a German fellow who worked the night shift at the dye-works and asked if he would be able to dye the army blankets and the slacks I procured, when I worked in the American kitchen, black. He was happy to oblige. Then, I found a tailor, who sewed me both a winter coat and a jacket from the blankets. In few weeks I was the best dressed fellow in the community.

Simon would come over in the evenings after work for short visits. I couldn't return the favor because his landlord didn't like strangers at his farm. He had enough problems making sure Simon behaved with his three daughters. On Sundays we met at the town pub to rehash current gossip. Sometimes we would visit with Michael and his landlady and have a little party. In spite of what we did outwardly, our main thought was always, "How long will our freedom last?"

It was well-known how the Cossacks were handed over to Soviet authorities in the Austrian city of Linz and in the Italian coastal city of Taranto. In Italy they were loaded onto the Soviet steamship, N. Gogol (named after Nikolai Golgol, a popular Russian novelist of the early to mid-1800s, who among his extensive writings, wrote a book, *Dead Souls*, in 1842). Another category of repatriates willingly returned to the Soviet Union from France on the ship, F. Dostoyevsky (named after Fyodor Dostoyevsky, a popular Russian author of roughly the same time period, who wrote a book, *Idiot*, in 1867). A saying became popular that the Gogol came after the dead souls and the Dostoyevsky came after the idiots. But it looked like forcible repatriation was far from being over. There were still several thousands of Russians interned in camps and we knew we could be added to them by a simple action of the American army. That thought kept us on our toes day and night.

That autumn, the old man caught pneumonia and was put to bed, where he stayed for several days. Meanwhile, one morning, one of the young bulls broke out of his stall and started wreaking havoc in the barn. The landlady hated the young bulls because they were a lot of trouble. She said the only thing they were interested in was breeding and creating lots of problems for her. She wanted to get rid of them but her father wouldn't allow it. It took some time to restore order but with the help of the women we got the job done. Later, as I was returning to the house, I met the old man standing at the threshold. His appearance left me with the impression that he wouldn't last another day. The two older women took him back to bed lecturing that he was not allowed to leave his room. First thing the next morning, the landlady asked me to harness the horse and drive her to the undertaker. The old man was dead.

We returned with the undertaker and a coffin. I didn't know how else I could help so I stayed out of the way. The undertaker hung a black curtain over the entrance to the door and people came by throughout the day to offer their condolences. The next morning the undertaker came with a hearse and took the coffin to town. The young girl and I stayed home. She had chores to do in the kitchen and I decided to chop wood in the woodshed. As I was working, I saw a German policeman walking toward the farm and thought that his visit might be connected with the funeral. He went in the house and left soon after. I ran to find out what was his visit about.

He left a message that I should report to the mayor's office at nine o'clock the next morning. I knew that meant we would be sent back to a camp and eventually handed over to Soviet authorities. I put all my belongings in a packsack and told the girl to keep it until I returned. I ran over to Simon's and to Mishka's to tell them that we had to leave that day.

The landlady returned from the funeral with some relatives. I startled her as we met face-to-face at the threshold. I told her about our situation and she said, "You are such a good person and I'm so sorry to lose you." She wished us well and we said good bye. We walked on the backroads to the Landau railroad station. Half of the bombed-out station building had been restored but the other half was only standing walls without a roof. The stationmaster told us that the train would be there at seven in the morning. The problem for us was that the building would be closed from eleven that evening until six the next morning. At eleven o'clock, the stationmaster apologetically asked us to vacate the building. We didn't blame the fellow for putting us out. "Befel is befell" (Order is order) was the German motto during the war and they followed it the rest of their lives. That may have been good for them but didn't apply to us in our current situation. We would only survive if we followed our instincts.

A Ukrainian fellow joined our company. He had come from Munich to barter some merchandise for farm products and turned out to be the link in a chain of events for us. Without him we would have been lost in Munich. We stood outside the station looking at gently floating snow-flakes that melted when they hit the wet ground. In the roofless part of the station, we found several sheets of plywood leaning against the wall and placed half of them on the ground to protect us from the dampness. Then, we lay down, and covered ourselves with the remaining sheets. We got as close as we could to each other on our makeshift bed so we could share body heat and fell asleep. The next morning, we woke up feeling the weight of wet snow on us. Soon the station building opened and we enjoyed a cup of boiled water free of charge.

The train came in on time and we left Landau at exactly at seven o'clock. As we got closer to Munich, two policemen would board the train at every stop looking for suspicious luggage. Their presence made us sit on pins and needles because none of us had a valid ID. Thankfully, the police weren't checking travelling papers. They were looking for large bags loaded with farm products.

We reached our destination without any problem and followed the Ukrainian to his place of employment. He lived in a new barracks occupied by thirty men. They worked for a construction firm removing the ruins of bombed buildings. They were paid a low wage, fed one hot meal per day, and had a place to sleep. For the time being it would not be a bad place to start but for us it turned out to be impossible. The office manager said he needed extra room and extra bedding for us and neither was available. He phoned several places to no avail and apologized for not being able to accommodate us. Then he recommended that we try the United Nations Relief Camp located in the Deutsches Museum.

We reached the Deutsches Museum at nine o'clock in the evening, past closing time. After a long period of persistent knocking the guard finally opened the door and told us to come back in the morning. He was not sympathetic to our pleas and the fact that we had no place to sleep so we pushed past him and told him we were staying. The three of us lay down on the cement floor near the heating radiator and fell asleep. We woke up to the shuffling sound of many footsteps. A new guard showed us where to get breakfast and told us to return to the same spot after we ate.

Before long the offices opened up. A gentleman from the nearest office approached us and introduced himself as Count Putylin. He asked how we could be helped and we explained our situation to him. He asked us to remain where we were and wait for him. He returned a short time later and explained which office we needed to go to, to be processed. "Be calm," he said. "The officer will ask your name, date and the place of birth, and the country you were living in before 1939. Your surname name shouldn't sound Russian, and the country you came from should not be the Soviet Union. Good luck!" he said.

Chapter 15

The International Relief Organization

Walking into the office, I met an elderly gentleman behind a desk, who asked me to sit down. I answered all four of his questions without hesitation and got a wallet-size ID card that stated: Buz Ilja, born in Dvinsk, Latvia on July 27, 1921. Now I was, more or less, a legitimate displaced person (DP). The same afternoon Count Putylin called me into his office for a "chat." He told me he had left Russia during the civil war and had lived in Paris driving a taxi for over twenty years. Now he was a transit and supply officer at this camp and he said he needed eight strong men with a good work ethic. Could I find such a crew? The next morning, I introduced him to our work gang of eight men. Our job was mainly loading and unloading. We worked hard but it was a rewarding job.

Two trucks, driven by African-American soldiers, ran back and forth all day delivering supplies and clothing to the camp. Included with the used clothing were used shoes that were often in poor shape. Count Putylin set up a shoe repair shop and Simon started to work there. Eventually he got to know a real shoemaker outside the camp and we were able to buy made-to measure shoes.

Used clothing in large bundles came from the United States. The loose clothing probably belonged to concentration camp victims. The clothes were distributed to the needy people who passed through the camp. There were different categories of people. Some were returning to their country while others were refusing to return. One time over a hundred Jewish girls were brought to the camp. They were former Polish and Rumanian citizens but had been kept in orphanages in Kazakhstan. Their behavior was that of rebellious youth. They swore like delinquent street kids, deliberately crowded the hallways, and sang patriotic songs of the Soviet Union. Their destination, like that of all Jews there who had survived the holocaust, was to go to Israel (which did not exist as a nation until 1948) to establish their own state.

There was a Ukrainian fellow who worked for the camp using his own truck to haul whatever was needed. In 1941, he lived the nightmarish experience of Babyn Yar. This is a ravine in the Ukrainian capital of Kiev, where German forces massacred tens of thousands of Jews in an effort to eradicate them from the city. He was one of the men forced to dispose of the bodies in a mass grave and those memories haunted him continually. At the end of the war, he managed to reach Germany with his whole family, including his grandmother.

The Ukrainian's truck was a former German military vehicle that used wood for fuel. The compartments that carried the wood were located toward the rear part of the truck bed making it narrower in the back. Once, our gang was tasked with loading gasoline cans on the truck. The soldier guarding the depot counted the row of cans lengthwise and multiplied by the cans on the back row. He didn't realize that front half was wider than the back. We ended up with twenty-four extra cans of gasoline, which we managed to hide in the woodshed. We got rid of them gradually by selling them on the black market for 250 German marks per can. I exchanged one can for a piece of fabric and got my first made-to-measure suit.

The incident with the gasoline inspired us to be on the lookout for more such opportunities. For example, every morning we brought hundreds of loaves of bread from the bakery so we knew we could "pinch" a few extra loaves of bread when the need arose. One time, we loaded several sacks of sugar for the camp. The driver of that truck, an African-American soldier, wanted some sugar for his German girlfriend but didn't know how to get any. We helped him out by using a pencil to create a hole in one of the sacks and letting the sugar spill out into a paper bag. Then we fixed the hole by arranging the threads back into place. The solder was happy and rewarded us with packs of cigarettes.

One day I met Sasha, who lived in the main DP camp that was located in a former military barracks. His female friend was an actress. She had organized a theater guild and wanted me to join them but I wasn't inclined to move into the camp. Regardless, we remained friends. Gradually he told me a few things about his past. He was a specialist at forging documents. He said that during the purge of the military brass in 1937 he was arrested in Moscow and kept in the infamous Lubyanka prison for two years. Then he was released for no particular reason and returned to his former position. From the beginning of the war, he worked for German intelligence printing forged Soviet passports. Later he worked in ROA headquarters and knew General Meandrov personally. After General Vlasov was captured by the KGB, Meandrov took over leadership of the ROA to negotiate its fate with American Forces. Meandrov was currently interned at the prison camp in Plattling, 135 kilometers away, and Sasha wanted to see him. He asked me to put together a small package and accompany him.

The visit was not what Sasha hoped it would be. Packages were not permitted at the camp and internees were only allowed to talk with visitors through the fence at a prescribed distance. The general had wanted a capsule of cyanide in the event that he was forcibly handed over to Soviet authorities. Evidently, Sasha couldn't find any. Later, I heard stories about the general's unsuccessful attempt to commit suicide by cutting his wrists with broken glass. Eventually he was handed over to the Soviets and was hanged in Moscow. In the summer of 1946, Sasha was arrested, handed over to the KGB, and perished there as well. His "wife" married another man and moved to Belgium.

One evening in February, Count Putylin told us that he was sending us to the bush for a week. He told us we would be supplied with canned food and coffee and the rest would be delivered daily. The next day we set off for our destination about an hour's drive away. We came to an area of full-grown, felled spruce trees that crisscrossed each other. I thought that this had probably been a German defense line. We were equipped with six axes and a chain saw. First, we chopped some wood and built a bonfire for cooking and staying warm. Then, the driver fired up the chainsaw and cut a truckload of wood in no time. We dispatched ten truckloads of wood per day for the next six days and then returned to the camp. The next morning, the Count told us why he decided to send us to the forest in a hurry. The same day we left, the Soviet Repatriation Committee was expected at our camp to identify and remove Soviet citizens. For some reason it didn't happen but to spare us from unnecessary worry he decided to keep quiet until the danger had passed.

The following month detainees from the camp in Plattling were handed over to the Soviets. The whole procedure was similar to what transpired in Linz with the Cossacks. The clergy, dressed in black, held services in an improvised church to mourn for those being taken away. Nobody went willingly to the waiting train. When American soldiers (many of them intoxicated) barged into the barracks and started to beat the inmates with clubs so that they would leave, people tried to commit suicide by hanging and cutting themselves with whatever instruments they had prepared ahead of time. Stories were told that over three hundred dead bodies were loaded onto the boxcars. How many of those wretched souls committed suicide before they reached the Soviet zone and what happened to those that didn't kill themselves? Nobody but the KGB will ever know.

After the train pulled out, the intoxicated soldiers started to sober up and realized what they had been forced to do. Some of them fell on the inmates' bunk beds and cried. The story was told about the commanding officer, who said, "I know that many of them are innocent but for the sake of peace I would shoot them one by one myself." That was the saddest blunder of the Allied command. The peace between them and Stalin didn't last long and that was the last mass delivery of Soviet citizens to their homeland by Allied forces. Hunting after individuals continued, but ordinary law-abiding people were safe.

Our living quarters in the Deutsches Museum housed forty people. Twenty bunk beds stood alongside the walls with a long table in the middle of the room. Some guys played cards all night. Some got drunk on raw alcohol and got into fights. The alcohol was boiled with coffee, allegedly to eliminate the poison, but close calls occurred regardless. One time, one of the men, Pasha, went berserk after drinking the mixture and went around picking a fight with everyone who crossed his path. He could not be persuaded to settle down and I was forced to slap him hard on the face, which seemed to do the trick. Eventually Pasha lost his life because of excessive drinking. A few years later, in Belgium, he was found dead on the street stabbed to death. The police even didn't try to find out who did it. There were all kinds of foreigners working in the mines and they were expendable.

Simon eventually rented a room in a private house and invited me to move in with him. It was only a hundred meters from the main entrance to the camp. The house had been badly damaged by bombs but the owners, an elderly couple, managed to restore it to a livable condition. The old man was digging in the ruins and piling up everything he found. There were doors, window frames, iron beds and kitchen utensils in separate piles. Bedroom doors were still missing in the house and the sewer system was not working. At night the owners used an old pail for their bathroom functions and we got to hear all the sounds that went with it. After couple nights of biting our lips to avoid laughing out loud we got used to it.

Another old gentleman, Grandpa Gromov, lived in what remained of the shell of the building next door. This is also where he kept his mule. He came from the Don River district, where he endured persecution during collectivization. He personally knew the renowned Soviet writer, Sholokhov, and some of the people described in his novels. He didn't talk much about himself except that he traveled from the Don River to Munich in a horse cart pulled by a mule and lost his wife on the way. When asked a question he would often answer with the words, "It is written," followed by a long recitation from the Bible. Those citations made me feel some kind of conviction but I couldn't gather the courage to ask him about the Bible.

Grandpa Gromov tried to be a good influence on two fourteen-year-old boys, Nick and Peter, who were brought to Germany as slaves. Nick said he spent his childhood on the streets of a mining town in Ukraine. Growing up in labor camps they became tough characters. Nick knew all the places of prostitution and even at that age was in and out of the hospital for venereal infection. He didn't know the feeling of shame and didn't care whom he hurt.

He made up a story telling Gromov that MPs were on the street watching a crowd of Cossacks that were going to be sent to back to Russia. They were hungry and asking for bread. The old man wanted to do something to help these people and went with Nick, who brought him to the gathering place of prostitutes and left him there, surrounded by women, each offering their service. While Nick was giggling like an idiot and telling the story, Grandpa came in with tears in his eyes. He was hurt and humiliated beyond measure. That was the end of Gromov's relationship with Nick and Peter.

Nick continuously bragged about robberies he committed and how the victims reacted as he pointed a gun at them. He even told a story about how he shot a priest in his rectory. Not believing his tales, I told him he would be wise to shut up and never blabber such things in public. He pulled the pistol from his pocket and said, "You don't know how powerful this thing is." Four years later I met Peter in Belgium. He told me that Nick was caught after committing an armed robbery, sentenced to death by military tribunal and shot. Many young men lost their lives after the war because of their foolishness.

The right bank of the Izar River, opposite the Deutsches Museum, was always crowded. It was the site of the main black market in Munich, where one could find plenty of American cigarettes and real coffee, which attracted even ordinary working German people. It was also a place I avoided because it invited Military Police scrutiny. Periodically MPs surrounded the market square with armored cars and checked everyone's IDs. Younger females were taken to the hospital by the truckload for medical examination. Those who were found infected with venereal disease were kept in the hospital until they were cured. People who looked suspicious were detained for interrogation and handed over to the Soviet's repatriation committee never to be seen again.

Simon was always out somewhere making connections with all kinds of people. He was an expert in the black market and knew where to buy and where to sell. With all his networking, he soon found a better place to live and moved out, leaving me with the elderly couple. His landlady was a widow about the same age as Simon and she recommended a room for me at her friend's place. On the following Sunday we went to see the room. It was the storage room in a one-bedroom apartment, occupied by a woman fifty-five years of age and her eighty- four-year-old mother, who was blind. The woman introduced herself as Frau Anna Figel and apologized for the small room before showing it, saying that I could use the rest of the apartment as a member of the family. She didn't hide how anxious she was to rent out the room, which contained a single bed, a night table and an upright clothes closet. It also had a small window looking out onto a courtyard. The next day, after work, I moved into a new environment.

After living in primitive conditions and crowded barracks for so many years the private little room looked like paradise. One day I brought home a loaf of white bread and a small block of butter. I sat on the edge of the bed looking at the bread and felt hot tears running down my cheeks. I stifled the sobbing but let the tears flow freely until they ran out. I couldn't tell why I was crying. It may have been partly from overwhelming happiness and partly from thinking about my parents, and how much harder their hard life must be, if they were still alive.

Most evenings I stayed home and got to know the women. Frau Figel was a long-time divorcee. Sometime in the past, her husband gave her an ultimatum to choose between him and her mother and she chose to take care of her mother. She had one married sister living in town. They were two of the few, fortunate Germans, who spent the whole war in their home without being bombed out. The hardest thing they had to endure was running to the bomb shelter during alarms so they couldn't imagine the hardships of evacuees or homeless people. They didn't like Hitler and preferred to be called Bavarians instead of Germans. They lived on the meagre diet provided by ration coupons. I often watched the blind lady search her already empty plate with her fingers hoping to find a remaining morsel of food. If she found even a missed pea, she would make a funny joke. She never complained and was always in a good mood.

A few weeks after I moved there a picture of a young lady appeared on the buffet door and the following Sunday, the young lady appeared in person. Frau Figel introduced her as her niece, Fraulein Edna. After having tea together, the older ladies retired to the bedroom, leaving us alone. Edna probably knew what Aunty was up to and told me that she was engaged to a soldier she met one year ago, when he was on furlough in Munich. She said he wrote often during the war but she hadn't heard from him since the war ended. She said he might be dead but she promised she would wait for him and could not break her promise until she knew for certain where he was. I got the impression that she was honest and practical, as were the majority of Germans, and even though they preferred to be called Bavarians, they were German to the core. Frau Figel had asked me to walk her niece to the street car but I walked her all the way home. Edna talked the whole time and I came away thinking she was a mature, self-sufficient young lady who was waiting to get married and have a family. For me it wasn't the time to think about a serious relationship and marriage. We were in agreement that she wasn't ready to endure the hardships and uncertainty that would come from getting involved with someone in my position.

On Sunday Frau Figel invited me to visit Edna's parents with her. I conducted myself as gentlemanly as was expected, mainly to please the Frau. This time I had to do the talking. They were fascinated to hear the stories of war from the other side of the fence. Frau Figel was pleased to tell me that I made a good impression.

One day I came home to find that another woman had come to live with Frau Figel. She was the Frau's childhood friend and had been evicted from her apartment because she was the wife of a high-ranking SS officer. She was a heavy smoker but since tobacco was a rare commodity, she smoked some unknown mixture that raised her blood pressure to dangerous levels. She lived literally waiting for word of her husband every single minute of the day. When she heard rumors that he might be liberated, she asked if I would help her retrieve her husband's overcoat from the apartment. She was an extremely nervous woman who was afraid of everything. She wasn't sure if her old neighbors would object to her being there of if she might get robbed. We went to the apartment without incident. I put on the coat, which was made from good material, and we walked home without any problems.

While I was boarding with Frau Figel, I found temporary employment at a warehouse that carried sporting goods. The "warehouse" was actually just several huge tents. The sporting goods came by the trainload and our job was to unload the merchandise and organize it for distribution to military units. Included in the merchandise were some musical instruments, including expensive looking accordions. A very healthy-looking German fellow worked with us. One day we were joking around with him, saying that he must be eating a lot to look that good. He responded that he ate well but not a lot. The next day he didn't show up for work. We found out that during the night he was caught trying to cart off two accordions and had been arrested.

Rumors started going around that Belgium was taking coal miners on a two-year contract. The only thing I knew about coal mines was what I heard from miners; that it was hot and dirty work. Initially I thought that I might not be able to endure that much hardship but given my present circumstance I knew I had nothing to lose. I started to prepare myself mentally to become a miner. Simon and I registered with the Belgian consulate, passed the medical and signed the contract, all in one day. I often compared the efficiency of different offices with Soviet autocracy before the war. As far as I could remember the only agency in the Soviet Union to move quickly was the KGB. They knew how to arrest and exile people efficiently.

On weekends Simon traveled to a refugee camp out of the city to see friends. One day, just before we left for Belgium, he came up to me with a young woman and introduced her as his wife. "We just registered our marriage at city hall one hour ago," he said, showing me the rings and giggling like a kid.

Before long, the day came for us to leave Germany. Frau Figel and her friend walked me as far as the streetcar and there we said, "*Wiedersehen* (see you again)." The long freight train bound for Belgium stood in an open field a visible distance from the refugee camp. A steady stream of people from the camp and streetcar stop moved toward it, loaded with backpacks and suitcases. There were mothers with babies in their arms following their husbands to say a last goodbye. Children were crying and mothers were secretly wiping away unwanted tears. There were also extended families, with several children and grandparents surrounding the only breadwinner of the family, who was leaving them. According to the contract, families would be reunited with their bread winners after three months.

Loading didn't take long. The train started to move slowly and gave two short whistles. Everybody waved goodbye to family and friends. We were heading toward the unknown but were excited to leave behind our aimless life in post-war Germany and the underlying threat of the Soviet repatriation committees. People who knew each other kept together in groups hoping to work in the same mine. I saw Valentin Zarubin and another guy from Latvia who worked in the mess hall at the camp. They invited me to join their group. Their leader was an older fellow by the name of Novak. He was one of the White Guard immigrants, who lived in Belgium before the war. He knew the mines and promised to get us into the safest one.

The train passed by distinctly rebuilt cities as it rolled along. In two short years ruined cities had noticeably changed their appearance. In every city we passed, streetcars were running. After I got tired of watching the scenery pass by, I stretched out on the floor and fell asleep. In my sleep I had the same nightmare, German soldiers playing soccer with human heads. I was awakened by a loud voice shouting orders. I tried to process what I was hearing and realized I was I listening to someone speaking French. I opened my eyes and saw a crowd standing by the wide, open door of the train car and laughing at someone. The train itself was not moving and a few fellows had gotten off, out of curiosity, to see what was going on. They were ordered to get back on the train by Belgians in uniform. "Hurray!" I thought. "We are on Belgian soil!"

After establishing myself in Belgium, I wrote to Frau Figel. She wrote back that her friend's husband was released from prison, but he didn't come home to his wife. He had a younger girlfriend and went to live with her. The abandoned wife lost interest in living and soon died from heart failure.

Chapter 16

Belgium

The train started to move again at a slow speed, leaving behind herds of cows grazing among apple trees. I thought back to my first impression of Germany, when I looked upon it through the barred windows of a boxcar five years previously. Even the windblown old barns looked tidy then. Nearly every barn had the same *Salamander* and *Shell* sign painted on one side, in black letters on a bright yellow background. I didn't know what it meant at first but found out it was advertising for heaters and a gasoline company. The Belgians also painted advertising on the sides of barns. One of them was a picture of three bottles with a caption, "Dubo - Dubon - Dubonette." It was advertising for a popular French wine. As the train rolled along slowly, it crossed the narrow rails of street cars in the most unexpected places. Later we discovered that in Belgium, one could reach every village by streetcar.

At that time, I didn't know much about any foreign country, including Belgium. In Grade Seven we had new geography books that provided a half-page description for every country. What I learned about Belgium was long forgotten, including the fact that it had a king. When I signed the contract to work in the coal mine for two years, I was thinking only of material wellbeing, a peaceful existence, and trusting that by the grace of God, I made the right decision.

The train finally stopped and several cars were detached from the train. Mine representatives were waiting on the platform. Novak told us to wait for him and disappeared into the crowd. He returned shortly with a representative and our group followed him to a waiting truck. The truck climbed a steep hill covered with lush forest and continued on past different villages. Before we reached our destination, we passed several mines with smoky slag pyramids that spread the obnoxious stench of sulfur.

Novak explained that the mine where we would be working didn't have that stench at all and was only 120 meters deep. For me, personally, that didn't say much. The only thing that stuck in my mind was what I heard from someone else saying that coal mining was next to living in hell and I was apprehensive about finding out. The only thing that gave me any sense of calm was that I wasn't in it alone.

It wasn't long before we reached our destination, a small town called Battice. Our boarding house was a two-story building attached to neighboring buildings on both sides. The first floor had two large rooms that contained several bunk beds, mess hall, and a kitchen. The rooms on the second floor were furnished with bunk beds and metal lockers. The backyard was surrounded by a green hedge with an outhouse in the back corner.

A young girl in a sleeveless dress was gawking at us as though we were strange creatures. Novak went over to talk to her to explain that the bicycle he brought with him needed some air. She brought him a bicycle pump and soon he took off to see his wife. Now we knew why he was so anxious to come to this mine. The visit was a short one and, upon returning, he settled in with us in one of the rooms. Although he didn't say anything, we sensed that something must be wrong. We were right. The next morning two gendarmes took Novak away. From the point of view of the Belgian government, he was a German collaborator. He was later released and eventually became the camp cook.

On the day that we were to report for work, someone from the mine came to fetch us and we were led to the mine office. We were issued badges and work clothing, the cost of which would be deducted from our wages. I was fortunate in that I already had the appropriate clothing and needed only a miner's helmet. The mine operated on three shifts. We were posted to our jobs two of the three shifts. A small crew of miners worked the night shift preparing for us for the next day. Day shift was from 6:00 a.m. to 2:00 p.m. and the afternoon shift was from 2:00 p.m. to 10:00 p.m. Almost everybody favored the day shift so I opted for afternoons because it was easier to find a posted job on the afternoon shift. That became my regular schedule.

We left the office and walked together to the gate, where each of us showed his badge to the guard. We were told that was just a formality for the first day. After changing into work clothing, we each received a heavy lamp with a corresponding number on a badge. After the shift, lamps were returned to be recharged and exchanged for the badge. This was a safety precaution to know the whereabouts of each person. We joined the other miners on the platform near the cage. There were three foremen and one shift boss, who instructed them by drawing the lines on the floor with chalk. He acted like a commander on the front line ordering his subordinates.

Looking at the old miners, I tried to imagine what I would look like after twenty years of mining coal. I pictured myself as a worn-out hunchback, walking like a gorilla, chewing tobacco, and constantly spitting on the ground. Chewing tobacco was supposed to prevent coal dust from passing into the lungs. Miners were supplied with respirators but some found it hard to breathe through them and preferred to chew tobacco instead. Fortunately, I didn't find it hard and used my respirator all the time.

We watched the old miners getting into the cage and squatting down along the wall, three on each side. Running, pushing, or horseplay was not tolerated anywhere near the cage or underground. We got in and the door closed. The cage started descending so rapidly, I felt a popping sensation in my ears. The cage stopped and we came out onto a brightly lit platform. Three tunnels with narrow rails led in separate directions. We were told to watch our step and follow each other closely. There was a lot of water underfoot and we had already heard about miners having to lay in the water while they worked. Such stories made my hair stand on end. I hoped that I would not have to work under those conditions or if I did, that I would get used to it without difficulty.

We reached the end of the tunnel and the older miners sat down on the logs and told us to do the same. We learned that sitting for a moment before starting to work, as if in silent prayer, was their ritual. We watched as the older miners hung their lunch from the ceiling to protect it from the rats and we did the same. However, it didn't work for us. We did not have metal lunch containers like the veteran miners and without them it wasn't possible to keep our lunch intact. Rats were everywhere but no miner would kill one underground. There, they were a miner's friend because their presence indicated a safe place to work. For example, we were told that rats would leave a dangerous place several days before a cave-in occurred. We left the rats alone and made sure to buy a metal lunch container as soon as we were paid.

Our boss rose to his feet and said, "Well, boys, follow me," and crawled through a hole near the ceiling. We crawled up after him, and moved forward on our knees, trying to avoid contact with the lumps of coal scattered on the ground. Most places were not even high enough to crawl through and that's where the belly crawl I learned during army training came in handy. When we finally stopped, we were in a passage two meters wide and a meter high between a row of posts and an undisturbed layer of coal. Next to the coal ran a metal chute and a two-inch pipe suspended to wooden posts on the other side. Sliding down the chute, the foreman marked off the length of coal he expected each miner to work.

Each newcomer was paired off with an experienced miner. We were told again and again to be observant and pay close attention to what was going on because our lives depended on it. Considering all the nationalities working side by side it wasn't possible to rely on the spoken word so, for most of us, the most effective way to learn was by watching. I was paired off with an older Dutch fellow, who spoke German. He showed me how to attach the air hose to the chipper and started to work. Chunks of coal fell and disappeared down the metal chute with a clattering sound. Then, similar chunks started to clatter by and the chute was filled with chunks of coal. My job was to push the coal down the chute when it piled up, as well as shovel up the dust and smaller pieces and place them in the chute. The dust in the air was so thick I could move it by waving my hand and wondered how people could breathe without a respirator.

That day I worked with my body in many positions but none of them was a standing position. After the coal was removed, the ceiling was secured with braces and wooden posts. We finished our quota and had an hour and a half before the shift ended so we were able to sit for a whole hour and share our experiences. Based on the first day's experience everyone concluded that it wasn't as bad as we imagined. We walked to the cage following the foreman in same order as we came in.

With the exception of the coal cutter, everyone was paid a daily wage of 126 francs, the equivalent of $ 2.50 US. For a single person it was enough to live on comfortably. After two weeks of work, we got our first pay, a little over 600 franks. Thereafter we received our pay every Saturday evening after the end of the shift. We showed our badge to the pay master, who sat in the guard cabin at the gate, and received payment in cash. During the six years I was there, we never heard about someone holding up the pay master of the mine. Those were different times.

One of my roommates, Pasha, was one of those characters that always liked to be the leader. One day, he came up with the idea that we should attend church on Sundays. The only one close by was a Catholic church, where service was conducted in Latin. We didn't understand what was said but it didn't matter. We would put on our new suits and solemnly walk to church. We sat on the bench in the back watching the worshipers and when the collection basket came by, we put some money in it. At the end of service, we would leave quickly because we felt self-conscious about being in a Catholic church when we weren't Catholic but the people were friendly and being there made me feel good.

After church we would walk to the store and purchase sausages, cheese, and a bottle of vodka. Pasha wanted to try a different beverage every Sunday. We would return to the boarding house with our purchases, set the table and have the first shot of vodka. In a short time almost everyone in our group would get drunk. Those who were waiting for families didn't spend their money foolishly like we were. I became convicted that it was utter nonsense to spend time and hard-earned money like that so after two or three weeks, I decided to disassociate from the group except for going to church. Pasha didn't like it but he had enough followers without me.

Sasha was a steady participant in Pasha's drinking parties. He got alcohol poisoning from excessive alcohol consumption and ended up in the hospital. His close friends visited him every weekend and would update us on his progress. One Sunday they returned to announce that Sasha would be released from the hospital. Sasha returned looking like a ghost, pale and extremely skinny.

Pasha organized a welcome party for Sasha, which included lots of drinking. The last thing Sasha needed at the moment was alcohol in his system but he took a drink. The same day an ambulance took him back to the hospital. I went to the hospital to see him. He was calm, probably because he was so weak, and accepted the fact that he was dying. He asked me to get a priest. The next day I returned with the priest and after confession Sasha received communion. Sasha died in his sleep and his remains were taken to the lab for research. After surviving the horrors of war every funeral left me sorrowful but wasting away like a homeless dog was beyond description.

Pasha had a friend, Michael, who had been hospitalized due to a minor injury he sustained at work. Michael was released from the hospital a few days after our arrival sporting a bandage over one eye. We shared the same bunk bed, with Michael taking the lower bunk. He was a very active and talkative person. On Sunday evening we went for a walk around the block and he told me about his injury. A small piece of falling coal had hit him on the bridge of his nose that had been fractured by a capo's club when he was interred at a concentration camp. He said it was not a big deal and the injury would heal soon. The next day he removed the bandage, leaving a small piece of tape on the wound, and rode around on Novak's bike. He ignored his friends' pleas begging him to slow down and take it easy. He just couldn't seem to relax. After spending a restless night, he was taken back to the hospital. We were told he needed surgery to remove a splinter of bone from the old wound. Shocking news hit us when we came off of our shift: Michael died on the operating table.

It was a hot day in July. Six pallbearers clothed in brand new miners' attire stood at the church entrance waiting for the hearse. A crowd of people lined up from the street to the entrance. Any funeral, especially when it involved a miner, was a community affair. This one had special significance. In a few weeks the families would be brought from Germany to reunite with their loved ones. Everyone was anxious to start a normal life, but one of us didn't make it. Personally, I felt so sorry for Michael and his family. After enduring so many years of suffering in the concentration camps, he had just started to build a decent life, and now he was dead. It didn't make a sense.

The church doors opened slowly as soon as the hearse showed up in the distance and the church bell started to toll. The hearse stopped at the steps and the casket was carried inside the church, followed by the crowd. We sat solemnly listening to the priest chant in a language that we couldn't understand. The whole procedure was new to us. After the funeral mass the service moved to the gravesite. Two young boys in long white robes walked at the head of the procession holding tall candles. They were followed by the priest, who was reading from an open book. The pall bearers came next, carrying the coffin on their shoulders. After a short service graveside service, the coffin was lowered and we threw a handful earth on the coffin, wiping away tears as we left.

Pasha organized a memorial feast, as was customary, where participants would drink for the soul of the deceased, wishing him into the heavenly realms. I felt like it was committing a sacrilege against heaven and the deceased because to me the heavens represented holiness and that didn't fit in with getting drunk. It didn't do any good for the deceased either.

When we first arrived at the camp, the company cook was a Polish fellow, who had owned a movie theater and restaurant before the war. He was a good cook and knew how to prepare delicious meals for large groups of people. We were fed very well for a reasonable price. Unfortunately, Novak, after he had been released from prison, wanted his position. Novak knew how to manipulate people and started by enlisting Pasha's help. He made it look like it was Pasha's idea to convince the others about the need for a new cook who would be able to prepare real borsch and other familiar Russian dishes. Sensing that something was going on behind his back the Polish guy resigned his position and went underground as a miner. Novak took over the kitchen with a new helper, a guy named Nemlik, who followed Novak's orders to the letter. From then on for breakfast we had coffee and fresh white bread with margarine and molasses. Dinner always was borsch and fried pork with potatoes.

Pasha knew Michael's wife and in-laws from Nuremberg and acted like he was the only one entitled to meet her. Two days after the funeral, Michael's wife, Tamara, arrived with her fifteen-month-old daughter, Irene. It was a name I had not heard in sometime and hearing it took me back to a memory of a lifetime ago when, as a boy, I was riding a horse and nearly ran over the little girl next door. Tamara was given a room next to the mine offices and a position as a helper in our kitchen. She was also offered a position as a domestic worker by a lawyer's family but Pasha was against it. He persuaded Tamara not to accept the offer, saying she should stay close to her own kind of people. She was young and on her own in a strange country so she trusted Pasha and remained in the kitchen.

Tamara started work at seven in the morning. She walked from her residence with the baby carriage and, for the first few days, left Irene with us. Before going to work on the afternoon shift, most of us had nothing to do so there was no shortage of babysitters. Then, at the recommendation of the mine director, she temporarily placed her daughter in an orphanage, where she knew Irene would be safe.

Shortly after Novak took over as camp cook, he began to complain that he was falling apart trying to please everybody and nobody appreciated his efforts. He also took out his frustration on the kitchen staff. During meal times Tamara worked on the run but nothing she did seemed to please Novak. He decided to deduct the cost of meals from her earnings, which left her with so little money she found it difficult to pay for her daughter's stay at the orphanage. Tamara quit her job in the kitchen and started to work in a factory making tin cans. It was dangerous work and many workers lost their fingers under the cutting machine. Eventually she found safer work making spools in a textile factory.

At the camp there was a secret rivalry going on among several men for Tamara's attention, but everyone was too shy to reveal his intention as she had been tragically widowed for such a short time. I watched and listened to the men talk about her and, after three weeks, I made eye contact with her and exchanged a phrase. I wanted to let her know about Michael's last days but didn't want to put salt on a fresh wound. I knew if I said anything it would have to be sometime later. Then I caught myself thinking of her more often and would get up early just to see her coming to work. That started up the process of thinking about the future.

Before the war, workers in the Soviet Union never knew when they would get paid. Now, I was paid a decent salary every Saturday and, in spite of the hard work, my living standards were better than I could have imagined. I knew that I would not be able to return to my past life. In my given situation the idea of moving forward and perhaps starting a family didn't seem that strange so I decided to test the waters.

I wrote her a note hinting at my intentions without putting myself in an embarrassing position. It said, "It is obvious that there are many suitors waiting for the proper time to ask you to marry them. I wonder what my chances would be if I joined the group?" The next morning, she handed me a note asking, "Are you serious?" That was enough of an answer for me. I knew we would need to get to know each other better before we made any commitments.

I asked her to go to the movies and she accepted the offer. Suddenly we had six or seven chaperones following us. By the end of the movie everyone understood that we were a couple and walked ahead so we could have some privacy. Everybody took it in a stride except for Pasha. He acted as though he was responsible for her future and said that my "untimely intrusion" might have an adverse effect on her wellbeing. After a strained conversation with him, he backed off and turned his attention completely to his drinking buddies.

Tamara and I wanted to get married as soon as possible but Belgian laws prevented that. According to the law, a widowed person was not allowed to remarry for a year. I talked to the mine director about our situation and his reaction surprised me. "This is not a problem," he said, "and there is a simple solution. We will provide a place and you can live there like any married couple. The law is one thing and real life is the other. Nobody is forced to follow the law to the letter." That comment awakened uncomfortable feelings that deeply bothered me and nagged at my conscience. Since the time that I was forced to give false data at the refugee camp (or face Soviet repatriation or worse), being a liar bothered me but I didn't how I could change anything. At the time I decided to come to terms with what I could not change and not think about it anymore.

On two different occasions I was asked if Ilja Buz was my real name and if I was really born in Latvia. I wasn't told the reason why those questions were asked but it became clear later, when the same question exploded worldwide. A well-known Soviet writer immigrated to the USA under the assumed name, Rodion Berezov. Eventually he became a Christian by accepting Jesus Christ as his Savior and he confessed his assumed name to both the church congregation and the Immigration authorities. This put him in the status of an illegal immigrant. His case reached the US Senate under the title, *Berezov's sickness*. It allowed refugees to correct their data without penalty. It bothered me for a long time. I spent sleepless nights thinking about what might happen if I tried to correct my information and what advantage it would bring. After a lot of soul-searching,

I finally decided not to worry about it anymore and remained Ilja Buz for the rest of my life.

We moved into a large room on the second floor of an old building. The lower floor was occupied by a Polish family with a grown daughter. Shortly after we moved there, we were invited to celebrate the daughter's birthday. There were five couples sitting tightly around the table. I sat between Tamara and the birthday girl. After a few drinks, I felt the girl's hand stroking my leg, but I totally ignored her and didn't react. The next morning, she and I happened to get on the same streetcar along with several other Polish women. They were being flirtatious and one of them asked who the handsome man was, referring to me. The birthday girl, who was probably angry at being rejected, commented loudly that in her opinion I was not a man but a #$### (crude expletive). I didn't show any reaction but thought, "God help the man who marries her."

Tamara and I got married in the town hall as soon as the Belgian government would allow. All the paper work was done ahead of time and on the appointed day we came with two witnesses. One of the officials met us at the entrance and led us into the hall. The mayor, dressed in impressive regalia, sat with two officials on each side. We were seated facing them. Our vows were read in French and translated into Russian by Madame Paramonov. After the short ceremony and congratulations, we left the office and came out, followed by our two witnesses.

The stairs to the old building were made of limestone, whose sharp edges had been worn down by countless footsteps over many years. I was excited about finally being married and was not paying attention to where I was going. I placed my heel on the edge of the top step and slid down the entire length, just hitting each step with my heels. It happened so fast, as old saying goes, in a blink of an eye. I looked up to see my bride's astonished expression and thought, "I could have hit the edge of the stairs with my head and died right there but I didn't even lose my balance. It was one more close call. I guess God wants to keep me around for a long time." I was a happy man and exceedingly thankful to the Creator.

We moved shortly after we got married. In literally two months' time a little village grew up across the street from the mine's entrance. Thirty-two living quarters were built just for our party of refugees. Four low buildings formed a rhombus-shaped complex. They were constructed from cinder blocks and plastered on the inside and outside. The ground around the buildings was covered with crushed slag. The white buildings on pitch black ground stood like toy houses. Our two-room apartment faced away from the courtyard and looked onto huge piles of logs with brush growing sporadically between the piles. We built a flower bed along the wall and planted nasturtium seeds. They happened to be the climbing variety so I put up strings from the boxes to the eaves. Our window was covered with a green curtain from the outside and it was the talk of the village. Our second daughter, Ludmila, was born there and was baptized in the Orthodox Church in Liege by the priest, Valentine Romensky.

In the autumn we went to the city of Verviers to buy a winter coat for Tamara. She saw a fur coat in the display window of a store and instantly fell in love with it. It cost 7,000 francs but we only had 3,000. The coat suited her perfectly and we asked if we could put it on layaway for a week because we didn't have enough money. The store owner asked where I worked and asked a few more questions. I told him our story and he insisted that we take it right then and there. He trusted us and said we could pay the rest when we had the money. It took some time to save up 4,000 francs but we eventually paid it off.

We were a community of Slavic people getting to know each other and forming small circles of friends. Walter Paramonov, Nickolas Plitchko, and I studied mathematics by correspondence and became friends. We subscribed to a weekly, Russian newspaper from Paris and a magazine, *GRANY*, that was printed by the White Guard organization, NTS. Both papers were anti-Soviet and anti-Communist and for us they were the only dependable source of world news.

One couple was receiving a newspaper printed by the Soviet Repatriation Committee. It was the usual Soviet propaganda paper, calling refugees to return home where they would be met with open arms. Their neighbors kept a distance from the couple to the point that they would not allow their children to play with each other. Occasionally I asked to read the paper for curiosity's sake and the man would give it to me without comment. He never asked about my opinion or tried to discuss any politics with me. He probably felt that I was the least prejudiced of all the neighbors and didn't want to stir up any ill will. Eventually the couple immigrated to the USA in the same group as Nick Plitchko, who wrote to me and said that the immigration officials kept this couple on Ellis Island for a long time before deciding they were eligible to be admitted onto American soil.

Tamara's parents and family were sponsored by an American family and immigrated to the USA in 1950. We soon received an invitation to join them along with the necessary papers to fill out for the Embassy but we never did.

The mining contract expired after two years and some people were no longer working. We heard rumors that they were being detained in a jail. We were called to a meeting with a representative from the International Relief Organization so he could provide information and we could voice our concerns. After he listened to a few of us, we were asked to be tolerant and wait for an orderly resolution to our fate. As we waited life went on. Except for having to renew our work permit every six months, nothing changed. Every family was comfortably settled in their little nests. We were familiar with the local culture and store owners knew us by name. People from different countries lived side by side and trusted each other. Every household had a bicycle for local transportation. Bicycles were left unlocked I don't remember anybody losing one either at work or on the street.

I worked one more year in the same mine. Some of the people who refused to work after the contract expired immigrated to Argentina and Australia, and some returned to refugee camps in Germany. One couple from our settlement left for the USA. He was born in the USA but his parents returned to Poland before the war started. During the war he was in a labor camp in Germany. He stayed there as a refugee and got married to a girl from the Soviet Ukraine after the war.

Polish people who served in the armed forces during the war immigrated to Canada on contract to work in the lumber industry. The Canadian embassy started to receive applications from those who had enough money to pay their way. One of them was my friend, Simon. He worked in another province where the mines were larger and had saved enough money. He was refused a visa, which put him in a panic. He knew that his neighbor wrote to the Canadian embassy telling them about Simon's collaboration with the Germans during the war.

In an attempt to improve his reputation, he decided to baptize his two sons in the Orthodox church and asked me to stand as their godfather. I took a train and was met in the station by a ten-year-old girl leading the small boys by the hand. When Simon got married in Germany, he neglected to tell me the women had a child. I didn't like the fact that he kept this secret from me but let it pass, thinking that everybody has his secrets. The Orthodox Priest referred him to see Pastor Krigman who was from Latvia and was the pastor of a Baptist church in Brussels. At that time, I didn't' know much about Baptists but apparently Pastor Krigman was an influential person worldwide.

Two weeks after meeting with the pastor, Simon immigrated to Canada. He was met by members of a Baptist congregation in Sudbury. After a few months I got a letter from Simon. He wrote, "Here, there is no brother or father; only the dollar rules. Starting out is difficult and steady work is hard to find. I am working part-time and hope eventually to get a steady job." He suggested that regardless of the difficulties I should put every effort into coming to Canada; that somehow it would work out.

Now I had a clear direction to follow. First, I would have to move to a larger mine where I could make better money. One day I toured all the mines in the city of Liege without success. On the way home, I decided to make a three-kilometer detour to a mine that had a bad reputation. The man at security directed me to the director's office. I told him what I was looking for and why. I wanted a job where could earn more so I could pay my way to Canada. I was told I could start the next day on the afternoon shift. I came home and went to see the director of the mine where I was currently employed. He didn't object and let me go.

The next day I pedaled my bicycle eighteen miles to work. The drift foreman, an older Polish fellow, led me to the end of the drift and left me there by myself. He told me to stay there and be on the lookout for areas that might need to be reinforced to keep the ceiling from settling down. I sat there for the whole shift until he came to fetch me. After sitting there for three shifts I was told to join rest of the gang.

The same foreman led us to a different spot. He told us the area we would be mining was wet but we wouldn't be there for more than two shifts. We crawled on our knees for about thirty meters to clear out a remaining corner of coal. Water ran from the ceiling in a steady stream and washed away dust and small pieces of coal. We lay flat on our backs in the running water cursing the whole universe. I kept thinking about what I would do if we had to work like this every day. At the end of the shift, we walked to the cage feeling the water run down from our head to our toes. We left our wet clothing hanging in the dry, hoping it would be dry by the next day. After two weeks I received my first paycheck. It was about twice as much as I earned before.

Meanwhile I had to find a place to live that was closer to work. The only places available were new buildings, with amenities such as indoor toilets and showers. They were intended for large families and even though we only had two children at the time we had to pay the full rental price, which took all the money we were supposed to be saving. The street and sidewalks were made from cement slabs. Our daughter, Irene, had a couple of accidents involving the cement slabs. She had picked one up and dropped it on her foot, breaking her toe. We lived there for six months and finally found an affordable place.

This next place was an old two-story house with a small garden and a chicken coop. The occupants were immigrating to Canada and wanted us to buy their chickens and rabbits. We moved in at the beginning of the summer when a couple of hens were sitting on their eggs, hatching little chicks. By fall we had a yard full of chickens and half a dozen rabbits. The next summer I put two hens in the chicken coop to brood and had another two whose nests were hidden in the weeds. After the chicks were big enough to perch there was not enough room in the chicken coop so the young chicks started roosting in the trees. Some chickens didn't return to the coop and ended up living in the bushes. One night we woke up to the sound of cackling chickens. Chickens were running around and bumping into each other in a panic. The following morning, I found a couple of mangled chickens. It was clear a skunk had been there.

Our old house didn't have any modern conveniences. Water was brought in from an outside well, heated on the kitchen stove and dirty water carried outside and dumped in a ditch. Disposable diapers didn't exist then. They were washed and reused until a child became potty-trained. This was one of the jobs I got to help with. In addition to carrying water in and out I washed diapers. It was an unpleasant task at first but like anything else, something I got used to.

All in all, we were enjoying life here. Tamara kept herself busy cooking meals and taking care of our two daughters. She knitted and sewed all the girls' clothes. We bought milk and Limburger cheese from the farm located a hundred meters down a steep hill, at the bottom of the valley. We liked the cheese in spite of its strong taste and peculiar smell. When fruit was in season, we didn't have to buy any. Fruit trees grew all over this farmer's pastures and he kept telling us to help ourselves to as many pears and apples as we needed. Our neighbor was equally as generous in allowing us to pick cherries from his tree, and our yard had a plum tree. In the summer, Tamara planted a garden so we ate our own vegetables. Chickens lay eggs year around and we had plenty of eggs to eat and sell. Every little bit of income was added to the money we were saving for the road.

If we could be faulted for anything it was for being too hospitable to visitors. Friends and neighbors from the first place came for a visit, unannounced, nearly every Sunday. The wife of one of the frequent visitors once said, "My husband said, 'Let's go to Ilja and Tamara's, to have a drink and good food.'" We knew they were using us but couldn't say anything without feeling ungracious. We met them again in Canada twenty years later and they were still the same stingy, calculating people.

Eventually my earnings improved beyond my expectations. The Polish foreman and I were transferred to new drift. The first week would be spent testing what we would be able to extract. The bed of coal was four feet thick with a layer of slag, a foot thick, in between. The hardest part was removing the top layer. The slag came out in big solid chunks, which was pushed to an empty space and used to build a wall to support the ceiling. On the second day, I was able to extract a six-meter length of coal with two hours left before the end of the shift. The foreman told me to continue at that pace until we got our first paycheck so we would know what the rate was. The rate turned out to be sixty francs per meter.

I was consistently earning more than the others and one day the Director came down to watch me. The foreman told me to work as though no one was watching. If I worked faster because the Director was there our rate might be cut. The Director didn't stay long. After two hours of watching me work, he wished me well and left. The rate remained the same and the foreman told me to remain at same rate of production. 360 francs per shift was good money and everyone was happy.

I worked there for over one year earning exactly the same amount every week. Then the foreman tasked me with cutting a passage from one level to the next. My partner was an Italian, a good worker. We had to cut a 2.5-meter-wide passage through a 1.5-meter-thick bed. From the very first shift we didn't like the place. We had to work at the very end of the drift where methane gas accumulated easily so we had to carry a carbide lamp to detect the presence of methane. Two large pipes hung from the ceiling. One blew fresh air in and the other sucked stagnant air out. The pump motors were noisy. The work was much harder than what we left but nobody was standing over us so we could work at our own speed. Half way through the project we discovered, quite by accident, a risky but easier way to extract the coal. We finished the project in two months' time and returned to the old place.

Shortly after we returned another Italian, who worked next to me, got killed. That was the only fatality I witnessed during my six years working underground. This man enjoyed cursing heaven and earth and everything in between on a regular basis and would conclude his tirade by blaspheming the Virgin Mary. One day, at the end of the shift, I was sliding down to a lower drift when I heard the foreman's voice calling me, "Russky! Russky! Come back here fast!" I crawled up as fast as I could, sensing something out of the ordinary had happened. He met me with the words: "The Italian got killed and the rest of them just ran away." I looked at the Italian lying on his back, arms spread out on each side. A cone shaped boulder about the size of a fist lay next to his head. It looked like he was putting up the last support to hold the ceiling when the boulder dropped from a seamless, perfectly solid ceiling and landed on his forehead leaving a visible bruise on the bridge of his nose. I got a strange feeling as I looked at his lifeless body and thought about his constant cursing. Why was he there in that particular spot at that particular time? It was hard to believe that it was real.

We were expecting our third child to be born in February. Tamara decided to give birth at home. The doctor referred her to a midwife, who visited Tamara at home for physical check-ups. She also gave me some instructions, including when I should come to fetch her. She lived about two kilometers away from us and there was no easy way to reach her. On the day in question, I walked up a steep hill half of the way and rode my bicycle the other half. I knocked on her door and immediately the light came on and the window opened. She told me she would hurry, then opened the door and asked me to come inside and take a seat while she fried some eggs. She offered me some as well but I was sitting on pins and needles and silently wishing she would hurry up. We walked all the way back.

Once we were at the house, the midwife told me to stay in the next room while she tended to Tamara and the delivery. I stood at the window looking out into the dark night and listening to the noises coming from the other room. Suddenly I heard the baby cry and the door swung open. The midwife handed me a little bundle, saying, "Here is your little daughter." The baby was quiet and Tamara was very pale and weak. The midwife came the following day for a checkup and left without saying much. Tamara was very tired and weak. She was hemorrhaging and we didn't realize how dangerous her situation was. The next visit was the same. I slaughtered a rooster and made her some chicken soup. It helped somewhat, but it took a long time for her to regain all her strength.

Among the things I bought from the former occupants was a Blaupunkt radio receiver. We couldn't hear the Voice of America before the war because it was jammed by the Soviets to keep the people from hearing the truth. I enjoyed listening to it here. The one thing that I could count on hearing when I listened to the Moscow news was the same propaganda inviting its former citizens to return home. Even after the war had been over for so many years, they would spout the same refrain: "We destroyed fascism, the most evil enemy of humanity, and now the Fatherland needs you to restore your country."

In early 1953, I tuned to the Moscow channel and heard mournful music. It was a solemn march that was played at government officials' funerals. Stalin was dead and it was good news to my ears even though I knew that evil would remain for a long time, and I wasn't thinking of returning. Our immigration papers were at the Canadian Embassy and we would be in Canada that summer. We managed to save close to 33,000 Belgian francs, the equivalent of $660 US dollars. That was enough for the tickets and I had at least another. six months to work and save even more.

A couple of months before we were scheduled to leave, I awoke one night with a sharp pain in my abdomen. Thinking it was just ordinary stomach pain I pushed my fist against the sore spot and fell back to sleep. When I awoke the next morning, the pain was gone but I went to see the doctor "just in case." He sent me for X-rays and found that I had an acutely inflamed appendix. The doctor said that I was very fortunate he found it when he did. The next day I had my appendix removed.

The surgery was a more complicated procedure than it is today. I was kept on my back for five days and was not allowed to eat solid food. Having to lie flat on my back without moving was very tiresome and somewhat aggravating. I managed to turn over on my belly and instantly fell asleep Soon I was awakened by a nurse, and the first thing I saw was her fist waving in front of my face. She whispered sternly that I was not to move. When I was finally allowed to get up, I couldn't stand on my feet without assistance. I felt like I was standing on broken glass. I walked up and down the corridor a few times with a nurse on either side of me and slowly got the feeling back into my legs. I returned home after ten days and stayed on sick leave for a whole month. After staying out of work for that long, I was able to clear the coal dust from my lungs and was able to smell the sweet aroma of the blooming fruit trees.

I hated the thought of breathing coal dust again and planned to return to work two weeks before our departure but an unexpected event changed my plan. Tamara had washed diapers in a large tub and I was carrying the tub of dirty water outside when the health inspector from the mine walked in. He asked when I would be returning to work and I automatically blurted that I would be there the following Monday. We exchanged pleasantries and he left. I worked underground for another five weeks and quit one week before our departure.

We sold what we could and gave away what we couldn't take with us. Everything we were taking was packed into two trunks and a couple of suit cases. We send the luggage to Brussels ahead of us, by train, and followed a little later. By the time we arrived in the late afternoon we found the luggage room closed but I saw our things on the loading platform. It wasn't long before the busses arrived that would take us to the port of Le

Havre. A caravan of several busses, loaded with passengers and luggage, left before dark. They drove all night, with one stop, and by sunrise we were at our destination. With passports in hand family after family walked on board the *Arosa Kulm*, a steamship sailing under the Panama flag with a German crew. By the time everyone was on board our luggage had been loaded by a crane.

There were six hundred passengers and a crew of forty men. The men were assigned to the bottom part of the ship, next to engine room. I didn't notice when the ship cast off from the wharf until a man's voice started to sing in German and English. Clearly the song was composed by an American soldier leaving Germany and his sweetheart. The lyrics went something like, "Goodbye my sweetheart, if love is true I will come back to you, Goodbye sweetheart." That was the first time I heard that song but it brought tears to my eyes. We were saying goodbye too and would probably never see Europe again.

I was awakened from my daydream by Tamara's voice calling me and asking where our children were. Instantly the world turned upside down. I was sure that they were with their mother. I ran through every hallway on the ship calling their names. All kinds of crazy thoughts ran through my mind. I was sure they had not been left behind on the shore, but where could they disappear so suddenly? I ran up to a deserted upper deck for the third time and saw a crowd gathered. Then I heard Irene's voice calling, "Dad! Dad! Come here! Look, look!" Irene and Ludmila had joined the crowd on the hull of the ship, and were clapping their hands and jumping up and down.

We had a similar experience once before we left Belgium. We were invited to someone's birthday party. The Irene and Ludmila were playing on the lawn and suddenly they disappeared along with an older, mentally challenged girl. It was clear the older girl led them away, but where? I jumped on my bicycle and checked the road for kilometers in all directions but nobody saw the children. While everyone was wracking their brains about where to look a car stopped and our children came out. The older girl had taken them for a walk and got lost. A woman saw them walking by themselves and took them to her place. They couldn't tell her more than their names so the woman called a taxi and took them for a ride. The children recognized the little store where we bought household necessities and finally found their home.

For the first three days we spent most of the time lying on the upper deck and reading magazines. The ship had a library and a buffet, where alcoholic beverages were sold. Everything on the ship was duty free. A bottle of beer only cost ten cents but except for an occasional bottle of beer nobody spent money on drinks. The first evening on the ship we watched a movie. On the second evening a group of American students gave a concert. They had gone to Germany to entertain the American soldiers and were returning home. On the fourth day people started to feel sea sick and the deck looked empty. Tamara got really sick and didn't eat supper. The next morning her face turned green. One crew member suggested she try a pickle and rye bread. I bought a pickle and half a slice of bread from the cafeteria for $1.00 US. At that price it was probably black-market stuff, but I was glad that Tamara was able to eat it and hold it down, and she didn't suffer from nausea after eating it. The days started to get boring so to break the monotony I would take Irene and Ludmila by the hand and walk them around the ship several times a day. Every time we made a round, I stopped at the captain's cabin to look at the map and see how much progress the ship had made. It was moving slowly but one third of the passage was behind us.

On the seventh day, the passengers were told that a storm was approaching but to remain calm and not worry. During the night the ship rolled and pitched on the waves. In the morning I found all the doors locked. I took the children for breakfast and found the mess hall empty. A few oranges had fallen off the table and were rolling to and fro from wall to wall. The crew was rushing around with worried expressions pasted on their faces. Darkness fell early that afternoon and the waves got really rough. Without holding on to a railing, it was difficult to move at all. I went to bed thinking, "Thy will be done."

In spite of the rolling of the ship I was able to sleep intermittently, waking up every time the noise from the engines stopped. When the ship was on the crest of the wave its propellers were out of the water and I couldn't hear their humming sound. When it was at the bottom and started to climb the next wave, the propellers engaged the water and I felt the pulling force jerk the ship forward. Every time that happened, I kept thinking, "Thank you Lord, we are still afloat. By Your grace we will get to shore sometime."

After four days and nights we woke up to face an unbelievably calm sea. By noon everything was normal. Crew members were smiling, dinner was served and half of the passengers left their beds to come out on the deck. I brought Tamara out on the deck too, where she felt better instantly. In the past four days the ship covered approximately one day's distance. Now it was moving at full speed. Someone saw a school of dolphins following the ship, which meant that we would see land soon and we did the next day.

The ship reduced its speed and before long a motor boat appeared alongside. Six men in uniform boarded the ship and started to process our landing papers. They were finished by the next morning and another motor boat took them away. Our ship drifted down the St. Lawrence River. We could see the houses on the shore with their white picket fences. There was a white church building with couple of cars parked in the front. As I watched the cars travelling on the road, I thought that maybe one day I would return to this place and drive though these villages as a tourist.

Fourteen days after we left Le Havre the ship dropped anchor a few meters from the dock in Quebec City. In the morning we would step on Canadian soil to start a new life. How it would turn out, only God knew. We were told that we would not be able to take any food or drinks off the ship with us so people started to feast on European style meat products and free drinks. I preferred a good night's sleep and retired early so I could step on Canadian soil with a clear head.

Chapter 17

Canada

After disembarking we picked up our suitcases and walked to the waiting train. We were the only family to change trains in Montreal and travel to Sudbury. In Montreal we had to wait several hours for the train to depart. I decided to walk around the block just to see what a Canadian city looked like. Passing by a store I saw two men inside so I opened the door and asked if I could buy a soft drink. "We are closed," one of them said, in unfriendly tone, so I returned to station.

The train left the station at 6:00 p.m. We put the children to bed and settled down for a long trip. Besides us there were about a dozen passengers in the car. The conductor came by to check tickets. He was a friendly fellow and suggested that we stretch our legs on the empty seats. I don't know if the train made any stops during the night but the next morning I woke up as soon as the train slowed down. One talkative passenger came to sit next to me. He was excited to see newcomers like us and, according to him, we made a smart choice in deciding to move to Sudbury. He said it was a good place where it was easy to find a good job. This contradicted what Simon wrote to me but it was encouraging to hear a different opinion. He was a local man and saw things from a different perspective.

The sun came up on the horizon as the train began to slow down and we looked out at the passing landscape. As far as the eye could see was bare, black rock with not a single tree or blade of grass in sight. Two tall smoke stacks appeared on the left side of the railroad next to huge black buildings. A heavy stench of sulphur filled the car. I looked at Tamara. She was crying. Scraggy little bushes appeared on the slopes of huge rocks. We continued on past a lake and a short time later the train let out two short whistles and came to a stop. This was Sudbury, where we would live.

We got off the train and saw Simon with his wife, Fridele, walking towards us. We shook hands and walked to our future living quarters. They had already been in Canada for two years and we corresponded regularly. On the way to the apartment, Simon explained that the house belonged to the church. The man who was responsible for the house would come by to meet us and would explain the rest. There was some furniture left by the former occupant who had moved to Toronto. When we reached the apartment, Simon said our luggage would be brought from the station later. He also told us there was a store just around the corner if we needed to buy anything for the first night. Then they left, promising to return in the evening. He was not the Simon I remembered but a Canadian, where no father or brother existed.

After they left, I started to look around the rooms. A rusted kitchen sink was surrounded by a worn-out linoleum counter top. The toilet was a small cubicle without a sink or bathtub. Everything was old, neglected, and ready to fall apart. In the evening two Ukrainian speaking men came to see us. They expected us to pay $40 a month for rent and buy the furniture. After the first night we discovered that our apartment was infested with cockroaches and bedbugs. Mike Tatarin, one of the Ukrainians, brought some chemicals to exterminate them.

Simon and Fridele also came to visit. Fridele wanted to make a goose down cover and had asked us to bring the down from Belgium. It was not heavy but occupied lots of space in the luggage but we brought it anyway. We also bought similar outfits for the two boys as a present from me, their Godfather. Instead of saying thank you, she said: "Oh, you shouldn't have." I should have known better. After all, Simon did write that in Canada there is no brother or father; only the dollar rules.

Simon told me that he and his wife had been baptized and attended church regularly. They cleaned the church building every Saturday and got paid $50 a month. The pastor helped him to get a job in the smelter. He said, "If you attend church and get baptized, they will find you a job too." Then he really shocked me when he said, "Who cares what they are preaching? I will listen as long as I need them." I didn't say anything to him or to anybody else.

The first morning I walked down the street and stood on the corner of Durham and Elm Streets hoping to hear a familiar Slavic language. I didn't have any success but I returned to the same spot that afternoon wondering if what I was doing made any sense. Suddenly two men walked by speaking Ukrainian. I stopped them and introduced myself explaining my situation. They were genuinely concerned and decided to take me to see another person who might be able to figure out what to do.

The man was sleeping after working the night shift in the mine. They woke him up and explained my situation. The man's surname was Popov and, in many ways, his past corresponded with mine. Mr. Popov got dressed and said, "Let's go to a bar and have some beer. He ordered beer for all of us and said, "Don't be shy. I won't go broke." He told me where to meet him the next day and we parted. The next day he took me to see another fellow by the name of Ivan, who worked as a house painter for a contractor. That evening Ivan told me that I could go to work with him the next day.

I met the contractor, Mirko Milanov, a Serbian guy who was married to a British woman. I was hired on a temporary basis for $1.00 an hour. I worked for him for four weeks and acquired some knowledge painting. In Copper Cliff I painted the church steeple myself because nobody wanted to climb that high. One morning, while I was on my knees sanding baseboards, Mirko's wife walked in. I looked up at her and said, "Good Morning." At the end of the day Mirko told me not to come back the next day. He didn't need me anymore. Ivan figured that I got fired because Mirko's wife probably complained that I didn't get up on my feet to greet her. Mirko owed me $10.00 for a day's work and I went to see him on the usual pay day but he refused to pay me. I bugged him for several weeks but he still didn't give me my honestly-earned money. We ran into each other every now and again and he always acted like he was happy to see me. Later on, I heard that Mirko got divorced and died at an early age.

My second job was unloading railroad ties from box cars. The ties were soaking wet and very heavy. This job needed strength that I didn't have. A man with experience could unload one and a half cars per day. I spent two days unloading one car. I got $10 and was told not to come back the next day; that I wasn't cut out for this type of work. I walked away with bloody blisters on both hands.

On Sundays we went to church with Simon and Fridele. Our children asked Tamara to take them to church because they liked the singing. Reverend J.R. Boyd was preaching in a low voice. I didn't understand a single word and his monotone voice made me sleepy. Tamara suggested that we should look for an Orthodox Church. There was a Ukrainian Orthodox church on Baker Street and one Sunday I decided to check it out. I came in while the service was already in progress. Several faces turned around to look at me, and on every face, I saw the question, "Who could that stranger be?" I knew that the majority of the congregation were collaborators with the Germans and each one of them was afraid of Soviet spies searching for traitors. Nobody, including the priest, showed any interest in who I was. I came home and told Tamara that I wouldn't go there even if it was the last church in town.

There were friendly people who came to see us but they were Baptists. The only thing I knew about that denomination was what I remembered from childhood and a short experience when we were in Belgium. Any talk about religion made me feel uncomfortable. I was ignorant.

Two families lived on the second floor of our apartment building. When they flushed their toilet, the water spilled over into our toilet bowl. Even my experience working in the pig stall on the German farm didn't help to endure that filth and Tamara was in tears. About the same time two Polish men came to visit us. One was called Skovronek and he had a problem. His wife ran off to Toronto with her boyfriend leaving him with three small children. He needed someone to look after his children in exchange for a place to live. Three weeks after we moved into his house, the wife returned. He didn't want her but she threatened to burn down the house so to avoid further problems he allowed her to stay and we had to pay rent.

I found temporary work on Pine Street building forms and pouring cement for the addition of Nickel District Collegiate. In those days even the largest building contractor in the city didn't have cement mixing trucks. The mixer was run by an electric motor and the mixed cement was transported by wheelbarrow. We built forms by nailing boards to 2x4's and finished pouring the cement in four weeks. The foreman let me work another four days puling the nails from the boards and putting the boards in a neat pile. It was on that job that I met Nicolas Siborow, who was married to a German girl, Hilda. Nicolas had arrived in Canada four years earlier and had worked in a logging camp for one year. After the construction job was completed, I was without work again and during the winter it was impossible to find work. INCO (International Nickel Company) only hired men who knew English but my English was not good enough.

I went to the immigration office for help. All they had available was a position as a janitor in a Catholic church but I wasn't Catholic so I wasn't a suitable candidate. I was asked if I was willing to work out of town. I replied that if no other options were available, I would go anywhere to find a job. The officer called someone on the phone and talked for a long time. When he hung up, he told me I had a job at a bush camp in Devon. It was six hours by train and the pay was ninety cents an hour. I bought rubber boots with a felt lining and a hat with flaps to cover my face. Mr. Kuc donated his used woolen jacket and I was ready. Mike Tatarin came to tell me that they would watch closely to see when Falconbridge would be hiring miners and when I got a call from home I should come without delay. That was encouraging moral support and gave me hope for the future.

I walked to the railroad station under a light snow. I bought a ticket for six dollars and boarded the train at 4:00 p.m. The train made numerous stops to take on and let off passengers. Most were Native Americans. They would get on at one stop and get off one or two stops later. At one of the stations, a passenger carrying a heavy backpack boarded the train. Two rifle butts stuck out from his bag. I helped him get the bag off his back and he sat down facing me. He asked me where I was going and when I told him he said that we would be getting off together. Our conversation consisted of a few words in English, a few words in French and lots of hand gestures. I understood that he was a trapper and that he was going to live in the wilderness for three months. His journey was a long one and he would have to sleep in the open for several days before reaching his final destination. He said it was something he had been doing every winter since he was a teenager.

Just before we were to get off, the trapper stood up and started to put on his jacket. He told me we were getting off at the next station. He had just finished getting the backpack on when the train stopped. He said, "I am going to jump first and will call you when it's time for you to jump." Then he disappeared into the dark. The snow swirled in my face and I couldn't see a thing when he called for me to jump. I was expecting to stumble and fall but landed in snow up to my waist. He called again and I followed his silhouette, often losing sight of him. We soon came to a small shack. He heaved his backpack onto the back of a waiting truck. As soon as we climbed in, the truck motor came to life with a roar and we careened down the snow-covered road at a fast speed until we came to a log building, where we got off.

I followed my companion into the building. We removed our heavy outerwear and then went to get something to eat. We picked up a tray and walked to the kitchen pass through where we were each handed a plate filled with fried potatoes, several slices of bacon and thin sausages. After supper he pointed me toward a row of bunk beds and told me to pick one. We lay down and slept soundly through the night. The next morning, we were fed the same thing for breakfast. The trapper put on all his gear and told me to wait until the office opened up so I could pick up the camp mail. "I will walk slowly and you will catch up," he said and left.

When I walked into the office a young man greeted me in French. I detected a German accent so I said, "Guten Morgen." He didn't speak French well so he was glad to hear my response and acted like we were brothers. He gave me a bundle of newspapers and envelopes to carry to the camp. I asked how far away the camp was and was startled to hear him say it was a five-hour walk. He said there were no roads, only a foot path. He told me I shouldn't get lost if I followed a blue wire attached to the trees. He wished me good luck and I started off.

It wasn't long before I caught up with the trapper. He told me not to wait on him but to walk at my own pace. I walked in fluffy, knee-deep snow all the way and after five hours, came to a road. I heard voices and as I turned the bend, saw two men standing beside a heavy truck. In the background were two log cabins, a small shed, and endless piles of logs along the lakeshore. The men knew I was coming and were waiting to take me to camp. The driver was a talkative young man of Native American origin, who had been born in that area. His father was the foreman of the camp and his mother was the cook at the main camp, where I spent the night. His sister worked with his mother as a helper. He let me out near a log building and drove away.

The building smelled of fresh lumber so it had probably been erected recently. There were bunkbeds along one wall, lockers for each bed and a table. There were fourteen men at the camp, three teams of horses and two dogs. Six of the loggers were young Germans between the ages of twenty-two and twenty-five. They worked in pairs. During the winter the men worked in the forest. In the summer they worked at the sawmill. Soon after I arrived the crew returned from a day's work. After supper they sharpened their chain saws and went to bed.

Everybody was up at six o'clock the next morning. I met the foreman, a sturdy old man, at breakfast. He introduced me to his new assistant, a man about the same age as himself. The foreman's assistant was excited that I could converse in French fairly well. After breakfast, he and I headed out to our work site. I carried an ax and crosscut saw and he led a horse.

The two German shepherds followed us. Every now and then they would take off after a rabbit but in the deep snow they couldn't keep up with them. Once they chased after a wolf and almost caught it by the tail. I don't know that a wolf would be afraid of dogs, but there may be some truth to the old saying, "A wolf isn't afraid of dogs but doesn't like its bark."

We came to a frozen brook and the assistant explained what we had to do. There were about a dozen dead trees alongside the road. We would cut them down and haul them out onto the road. We felled the first tree and then felled another one and sawed it into three pieces, like the first. I sawed off the branches and used some of them to build a fire. The assistant rigged up a tripod and hung a pail of snow over the fire to make tea. When enough snow was melted, he brought it to a boil and threw in a handful of loose tea. After it had steeped to his satisfaction, he threw in another handful of snow to stop the boiling.

We ate lunch and sat drinking the tea for two hours. All the while the assistant was feeding blue jays and talking to them in French. I could see that the birds knew him and this was not the first time he was feeding them. After lunch we cut another tree and that was our day's work. He kept telling me not to be in a hurry, that for 90 cents an hour I was working hard enough. I worked on that job for five days. On Sunday I sat in the steam bath for a long time. The loggers prepared their equipment for the next week. Apart from eating three meals and looking at newspapers in a foreign language, I didn't have anything to do. Downtime was boring and I missed my family.

On Monday morning I was told to wait for the first truck loaded with logs and hitch a ride back to where I was picked up when I first arrived. I would be helping another old man on the dump. This old man, like the other two, had worked for the company his whole life. He was 73 years old. The lakeshore was full of logs on the ice. My job was to arrange the logs in a pile and make a skid row, fastening straight poles across the logs. The old man wanted me to build long skid rows. It wasn't hard work and he was content with my efforts.

We slept in a log hut under dozens of blankets. It was an old building without a ceiling. The roof was made from split logs and the gaps between the logs allowed me to see the stars through it. Every night before retiring we shoved two logs into a stove made from an oil drum, and watched it turn red hot. By morning most, if not all, of the heat had dissipated and we dressed quickly and built another fire. To start the fire cold the man poured gasoline on the logs in the stove. I tried doing the same thing once but made the mistake of using naphtha gas instead of gasoline. A ball of flame hit me in the face and burned off my eyebrows and eyelashes. Apart from that I was unhurt. Once the old man knew I was okay he had a good laugh.

Trucks were bringing up to eight loads per day and we kept rolling the logs further onto the ice. One morning, when the temperature was -35 degrees, I came out wearing only the felt lining from my boots because the logs were easier to walk on that way than in rubber boots. A lot of logs were piled up, waiting to be arranged at the end of the skid rows. I was standing half way up the pile when the ice broke with a loud bang and logs under my feet started to roll. I was running and jumping over the rolling logs while they passed under my feet like spilled matches. Luckily, I was able to keep my balance.

I made my way to the shore and looked around. All I could see was white steam coming from the water but no old man. He had disappeared into the lake with the logs. I ran to the cabin to call someone on the phone when a truck appeared with the first load of the day. The young driver guessed what had happened and ran with me to the phone. After the call we came out and saw the old man crawling to the shore spitting water and coughing. We half dragged, half carried him to the hut, took off his wet clothing and dressed him in spare underwear. Then we wrapped him in several blankets. Soon we heard the sound of a snowmobile approaching. We loaded the man onto the snowmobile and watched it take him away. I heard that he survived the incident but never saw him again.

With the old man gone, I was alone and had practically nothing to do. The logs disappeared under the ice and the lakeshore was clear. For several days the truckloads of logs were rolling into the water and sinking. On Christmas Eve the driver brought me some holiday treats. When he came with the last load, he told me to go back with him to the main camp, where I would be more comfortable. Everybody was off for two days and I was by myself. The loggers left for town. They made $20per day and could afford to pay for transportation out of there. After the two-day holiday, I returned to the dump and cut a few skid-row poles just to pass the time. During the night I heard a wolf sniffing around the area where I dumped old dish water so I rigged a trap in the empty shed using frozen baloney as bait. The following morning, I went to see if my trap worked. I cracked the door open a little bit and saw a wolf staring back at me. It lunged at the door with such force, the door swung open and wolf jumped between my legs and took off.

On December 27, I got a message to come home at once. That meant I had to leave at 2:00 a.m. for a five hour walk back to the office. I had to arrive there by 7:00 a.m. in order to catch the train at 8:00 a.m. It was a cold night. Trees were cracking constantly from the frost. I reached the paved road at exactly seven o'clock. Looking to the left I saw a school kid running my way. He caught up with me and the first thing he said was, "It's cold, -40 Celsius," in French. He had ice beads hanging on his upper lip.

The owner of the company was waiting for me in the office. He repeated the message that my wife phoned and needed me to come home right away. "I will pay off what you have earned. I don't think you'll be coming back but if you change your mind, you can come back without phoning. Just show up," he said. I thanked him and we parted. I boarded the train at 8: a.m. and by 3:00 p.m. I was at home. All the way home I hoped there would be good news when I got there. I was not disappointed.

Mike Tatarin left an application form I needed to become familiar with. He came over in the evening to help me practice how to fill it out. I filled out the application while Mike watched me. He was pleased that I did it without making any mistakes. He said that the next day Reverend J.R. Boyd would drive me to Falconbridge's employment office and I would have to fill out the application for real. When we arrived, we were told that Mr. Cook was busy and we were asked to wait. After a short wait, we were escorted into Mr. Cook's office and sat down. He called me to his desk and asked if I had the application that he sent to me the previous day. I pulled out the completed application and handed it to him. He looked at it and then asked where I was working.

"They don't pay much, do they?" he asked when I told him what I was paid. "Tomorrow you come here for a medical. If you pass the medical, we will pay you a little bit more than ninety cents an hour."

Mr. Boyd drove me home without a word. Later I heard that he thought I had blown my chance of getting a job because I gave Mr. Cook an application that had already been filled out. I returned the next day and was one of twenty men who passed their medical. We were told to return for work on January 7th, 1954. We were also told that for the first three months we would be on probation and during that period we were not eligible to be Labor Union Members. And finally, if we or any family members required medical attention, we could only use the company's medical service.

During our first year in Canada, Tamara needed minor surgery but without medical insurance it was a big financial burden. Our neighbor, a woman from Czechoslovakia, took Tamara to her doctor. He excised the boil from her shoulder for $40. The incision bled for a long time and took a long time to heal. After it healed that shoulder was lower than the other one. The doctor should have been sued for malpractice for botching the surgery but we were not familiar with the laws regarding such things. Later, our children got sick and Mike Tatarin called Dr. Piduty. He visited the children a few times free of charge. After I was eligible for insurance coverage, I delivered the necessary papers to his office. It was difficult to describe my appreciation for his compassion.

All the newcomers to Falconbridge Nickle Mines were called scrub men and were kept on clean-up jobs. On my first shift I was led to a place called the bumper in the smelter. There was a huge pile of hot slag on the floor that was scaled from the ladles used to carry molten metal. My job was to break it into smaller pieces with a sledge hammer and load it on a boat. After explaining how to handle the material the foreman left me. While I sprayed the slag with water a big man stepped on my boot and, looking me straight in my eye, asked, "Where did you come from?" He was the general foreman of the smelter, Baldy Pernue. I was told by the old timers that he was a heavy drinker and gambler. Every time I saw him after that I would greet him with a "Good morning," but never got a reaction from him. It was as though I wasn't there. Still, I continued greeting him for six years. Somewhere during that time, he must have gone to a leadership "charm school" and learned that a friendly attitude toward subordinates resulted in better productivity. Baldy Pernue started responding to my greetings and occasionally asked how I was doing.

After our three-month probation was up, we were permanent employees and became members of the Labor Union of Mine Mill and Smelter Workers. My foreman, Gordon Backnam, asked me if I wanted to ride with him to work. He would pick me up at the door and drop me off for the same price as the cost of a bus ride. I accepted without hesitation. During this time, our landlord, Skovronek, had been after us to find another place to live. His wife had managed to patch things up with him and she wanted us gone. We had been looking for another place but obviously not fast enough for our landlord. One time when I was waiting for my ride to work, I dozed off. Gordon came to the door and the landlord told him that I was gone. I woke up as the car left. Being a fairly new employee, I could have been in big trouble if I missed my shift. Thankfully, I was able to get there on time by taking a taxi.

I was angry at the landlord for being so low. He begged us to move into his house when he needed us, and now he couldn't wait for us to find another place to live. He knew how difficult finding a place was. People lived in crowded rooms, often two families together. In June of 1954, we moved into a four-room apartment on Eva Street. The landlord was Ivan Bowshar, a fellow from Belarus, married to a Ukrainian woman. Four rooms on the first floor were occupied by the landlord, his wife, their two children, his in-laws, and another family with one child. We took in one elderly Ukrainian from Oshawa as a boarder. He worked at the dry cleaners and served as a preacher of a small Pentecostal group. I thought it strange that he lived away from his family but he justified it by saying that God called him to preach even if it meant being away from them. Next to Baptists, Pentecostals were another group of peculiar people that I had met thus far.

During the winter, we attended night school to study English for beginners and that Christmas learned how the holiday was celebrated in Canada. Each family received a turkey from Falconbridge. After the New Year I received my statement of earnings. My earnings for the year 1954 were $ 3,505. After deducting for the Registered Pension Plan, Income Tax and Union Dues I had little over $3,000 left. After the second year, we were able to save a couple hundred dollars, and in 1956, I purchased a $500 Canada Saving Bond, which I was able to pay off in less than a year. During that time, we moved to Garson to save some money. A fellow worker, Joe Michalowiz, bought a house and asked me to move there for less money than we were paying at Bowshar's. We couldn't get along with Joe's wife and moved back to Bessie Street in the Donovan.

Our next landlord was Arcady Popescu, who came from Romania in the 1930s. He was a very polite, soft-spoken person. Seven families lived in his house. He drove a new car and was an active member of Berean Baptist Church. In the spring of 1956, he took me smelt fishing. I came home with a pail full of smelts, which I left overnight in the hallway. The next morning, I saw a strange creature crawling in the pail. That was the first time in my life I saw a salamander.

Arcady had been in Canada for a long time and seemed unaware of the current political situation in his country. Romania collaborated with

Germany during the war and was now under Soviet rule. What was actually going on there was just speculation. He probably remembered the Romania of his time and decided to travel there to see if his parents were still alive. I was shocked to hear that he died when he was there. The Romanian Embassy notified his family of his death, such a sad ending.

That same year I decided to write a letter to my parents, composing it as though I was someone else who knew me during the war and wanted to know if I was still alive. I wasn't sure where they were but addressed it to the village. After four anxious weeks I received a letter. The top edge of the envelope had been cut open and taped. I recognized my father's hand writing. He wrote that after receiving a notice in 1941 that I was missing in action they hadn't heard anything further. He added that my mother cried often and still hoped she might see me one day. I wrote again offering my condolences and received a response in a much shorter period of time.

My father wrote that after the first letter, government officials concluded that I was still alive and cancelled the pension my parents were receiving for their missing son. After fifteen years of silence, I caused them another blow by making them lose the small pension they were receiving to supplement their meager existence. I was sorry for writing the letter. We sent them a parcel, which they received intact and from then on, we sent three or four parcels a year to compensate for their lost pension.

In our search to find a church where we felt comfortable, we came across a small congregation of Russian speaking Baptists, who held church services at a house on Lansdowne Street. The house was owned by the Slavic Baptist Union of Canada and was occupied by the minister of the congregation, an elderly man named Mr. Gnilitsky, his wife, and his brother-in-law, Hoyenko. Additionally, two of the rooms were rented out to help pay the mortgage. Gnilitsky and Hoyenko visited families at their homes regularly. Hoyenko, who was a chorus leader in an Orthodox Church before becoming a Baptist, often came to sing hymns with Tamara. In 1956 she was baptized in Black Lake, near the City of Sudbury by a Russian speaking Baptist minister.

Tamara took the children with her to church every Sunday and when I was not working, I would join them. Listening to the preachers raised lots of questions. When we lived in Belgium, I read the Bible once from cover to cover but nothing was retained in my memory. My heart was telling me to be patient and continue listening, the answers would come. In the meantime, I continued going to church. Tamara had the gift of hospitality and we often hosted out of town visitors and helped people when they asked. Later we heard that Sudbury was the most hospitable place to visit.

In 1956, CKSO-TV started to broadcast. Television was a marvel that was out of this world. Godard Appliances on Durham Street put a set in their display window and every afternoon people gathered on the sidewalk to watch the news. Very few people in our blue-collar community could afford to buy a TV set. The price for a 17-inch screen was close to $700. I knew it would be a long time before we would be able to afford one but an opportunity opened up for me.

In September of 1956 our fourth child was born and we became a large family. Mothers received a monthly allowance for each child and our income tax deduction decreased accordingly. Our two-room apartment became more crowded. Irene and Ludmila changed schools four times in three years. We needed to find a permanent place to live but didn't have enough money for a down payment. We continued to save what we could, and in the summer of 1957, I found a place for sale that required a $900 down payment and a mortgage payment of thirty dollars a month. I bought it without bringing Tamara to see it first. She cried when she first saw it and they weren't tears of joy. In retrospect, if she had come with me to see the house, we most likely would not have bought it. A few days after we moved in my in-laws came for a visit. My father-in-law's comment regarding the house was, "I wouldn't have it if someone gave it to me."

The house was a frame structure sitting on top of a ten-foot-high wall made of concrete blocks and was divided into two separate living quarters. The stairs in the front of the house were mounted to a flimsy platform and provided the entrance to the smaller apartment. A similar set of stairs on the end of the building led to the entrance of the larger apartment, which we occupied. It consisted of four small rooms. The smaller apartment consisted of two rooms and was rented to the former owner, who had Native American women coming and going at all times of the day and night. Usually, they were drunk and abusive. On two occasions we had to call the police to evict them and ultimately had to ask the man to move out.

Small shrubs and blueberry bushes were growing under the living quarters. I wanted to clear out that area to provided additional living space but when I started to dig another unexpected problem appeared. Solid rock extended diagonally from one corner to the other. A Polish fellow, Louis Ledzwa had a similar problem in his basement. He worked as a powder man in the mine and knew how to blast rocks. I helped him clean out his basement and he helped me with mine. After it was cleared out I was able to poured a concrete foundation.

I bought an oil furnace and electric water heater from Goddard's Appliance on credit and installed them myself. One of my neighbors was an electrician and he helped me connect the water heater. So now we had a heated house with hot water. The next thing we needed was a bathtub but our street didn't have sewers at that time so I improvised drainage by running three rows of clay tiles under the garden. I helped in the demolition of a wooden structure on the Kingsway and out of that I acquired enough lumber for the roof. Our Baptist friend, Hoyenko, framed the roof free of charge and with the help of coworkers was able to finish roofing the house.

We lived literally counting pennies from payday to payday. Tamara's Sunday shoes had holes in them but we couldn't afford to buy her new ones. Things were so tight that at one point I couldn't pay city taxes for two years. When the City of Sudbury decided to install a sewer line on our street, we had the option of paying $400 all at once or we could pay by installment. We could only afford to pay by installment, and in the end, it cost us $800.

In September of 1958 a TV repair school opened up. The cost was eight dollar a week for three hour-long classes. I also had to buy a radio receiver kit. During the process of building the radio I learned how to read the schematics and how to locate the resistors and capacitors on the actual set. The first time I saw a TV chassis I felt helpless but after building the radio receiver it became much clearer. After one year I graduated and was able to look at the inside of a TV chassis with confidence.

Gradually people started to buy TV sets and my services were in demand on a fairly regular basis. TV sets were real headaches. Tubes burnt out often and customers were not happy to have to pay to replace the same tube over and over. On the plus side, I was able to retrieve and repair an old disposed TV set and keep it. Around 1960 TV sets improved. First, the heavy power transformer was replaced by a silicon rectifier. Next, tubes gradually became obsolete. By 1980 TVs became transistorized with printed circuits. They worked virtually without any problem for years. Trying to keep up with the rapidly advancing technology was a time-consuming process and I decided to quit repairing TVs.

Tamara found jobs where she could to help out. She worked in a boarding house for $15 per week and was later able to find a job as a short order cook at a small restaurant for one dollar an hour. Every dollar was a big help. By 1960 I was earning over two dollars an hour and with occasional part time work and Tamara's help we were able to keep up with the payments. The children were growing fast but they were dressed as well as their friends. Inside the house all the remodeling was complete. Only the doors were missing. The outside stairs were gone and indoor stairs connected the two stories. The kitchen, living room and dining room were now downstairs and the bathroom and all the bedrooms upstairs.

Remodeling the old house required upgrading the electrical wiring and it was an expensive job. I took a correspondence course for the Practical Electrician to help cut costs. My neighbor, who was an electrician for the school board, helped me occasionally, and when he needed an extra pair of hands, I was able to return the favor. My added skill set also helped me supplement my income. With the increase of electrical appliances, older houses with 60-amp service had to be upgraded to 100-amp service. People also started to build new houses and they were happy to have someone they trusted to provide service for a reasonable price. The city electrical department didn't care who did the wiring as long it passed inspection. The less sophisticated electrician job paid better than repairing TVs. As I came closer to retirement age, I didn't need to do any part time work so I took on fewer jobs and eventually stopped altogether. That in itself was a good pay-off.

Tamara decided to have another child before her biological clock ran out, this time hoping for a boy. On January 9, 1962, she went to the hospital to give birth to our fifth child. Our only phone was downstairs so I decided to sleep on the couch in our sparsely furnished living room (a couch and record player on a small stand) close to the phone. Its ringing woke me up at two in the morning. I heard Doctor Kosar's voice telling me, in Ukrainian, to buy cigars. "You have a fine baby boy. Son and Mother are doing fine. Now go to bed and have a good sleep," he said laughing. That was the end of my sleep for the night.

In the spring of 1964, Morris Martin, our carpool driver got transferred to working underground so he would no longer be a part of our shift. He put up his Volkswagen van for sale and I bought it for $1800. I figured that by transporting nine passengers it would pay for itself. It kept developing small problems and I soon realized that the van wasn't able to carry that heavy a load. On the evening of January 9th, 1965, I was working the night shift and drove to work in the pouring rain. The freezing rain continued throughout the night, and in the morning, roads were a sheet of black ice. Driving very slowly we made it to Garson. Road construction had been going on in that area that left an uneven second coat of asphalt across the road. As soon as the front wheels hit the two-inch elevation the van swerved sideways across the road and hit an oncoming car broadside.

I lost consciousness for a moment, and then remember being pulled out of the van and laid on the ground. My neighbor, who was seated on the passenger side, was moaning, and an Italian fellow was telling him to shut up because there were other passengers worse off than him and they were not making any noise. I heard the ambulance siren and someone's voice telling me to keep calm. The next thing I remember was hearing my own voice saying, "Oh my head! Oh my head!" I felt that I drifted in and out of consciousness for a long time. When I finally regained consciousness, I lifted my hand and touched my face. I could feel a long row of stitches above my right ear. My right cheek felt swollen and numb. Two nurses led me to the washroom and I got to look at my face in the mirror with one eye. My right cheek was black and swollen out of proportion. After two weeks I was strong enough to leave the hospital.

The insurance adjuster came to see me to let me know the van was a total wreck and had been written off. The good news was that after driving the van for eighteen months I received exactly what I had paid for the van, $1,800. The van had been towed to the Ford car lot on the Kingsway so I walked there to see the wreck. It was bent in a V-shape. For sale on the lot was a two-year- old Ford Econoline van, with low mileage, for $2000. I handed the insurance check to the salesman and drove the Ford van home. It was a good vehicle and I held onto it for seven years.

At the beginning of 1970 we decided to leave the Slavic Baptist Church and start attending an English church for the sake of our younger children. By this time, I had read a lot of Christian literature and listened to preachers on TV. The first time we went to All Nations Church we had a warm reception and soon felt at home. Pastor Kitchener Manhood was the founder of the church and he used to drop in unannounced every now and again. Sometimes he would bring visitors from Ireland, his home country. He was very easy to talk to. I was helping to rake leaves on the church property one Saturday and when it was completed Pastor Mahood and I sat resting on a pile of logs, chatting. Suddenly he asked me, "Brother, have you been baptized?"

"No," I said. "Why not?" he asked. He continued, "We will do it at the next baptismal service in November." So, I was baptized in November of 1976.

Despite the fact we stopped attending the Slavic Baptist Church, we didn't cut ties and remained a part of that community. The Baptist Union of Ontario bought an abandoned farm near the town of Fergus in early 1970. Their plan was to convert it to a children's camp and a retreat for the Slavic Churches of Canada. All the work was done by volunteers and eventually we got involved in helping them out. Tamara was asked to cook for children's camp for two summers in 1973 and 1974. At the same time, I volunteered to provide electricity to the cabins and help with whatever had to be done.

Converting a barn into a church building was not an easy job. The first floor was a former stable for cows and had cement troughs for their food and water. We dismantled them using sledge hammers and once all the debris was removed, we poured a cement floor. An open kitchen was installed on one end of the large hall and was furnished with wooden picnic tables. Half of the hall was reserved for church services and was furnished with long benches. The second floor was cleared of old hay, straw and farm implements and was converted to a dormitory for the campers. Eventually the barn was transformed into a modern building with a comfortable meeting hall, which included a podium, furnished bedrooms for fifty people, hot water, and showers. A large upgraded kitchen and mess hall completed the project.

In 1972, I traded in the Ford Econoline for a salesman-owned Chevy Impala station wagon. The cost with trade-in was $5,200, which I paid in cash. The station wagon served us well. We used it to go on our first long trip to Chicago. We also travelled to Pennsylvania several times to visit in-laws and even made a trip to Florida. In the summer time of 1978, we took our first long road trip to Florida together with Irene's family. It took about a week together and we camped along the way, sleeping in a tent. We spent the longest amount to time at Tania's place in New Smyrna Beach, within walking distance of the beach. From then on until retirement we traveled to Florida every winter for two or three weeks.

In the summer of 1983, Falconbridge offered an early retirement for workers of a certain age with so many years seniority. I qualified but couldn't decide what to do. We had returned from Florida a week before the offer expired but that wasn't enough time for me to weigh the pros and cons so I decided to remain at work and hoped the offer would come up again. The winter came early that year with heavy snowfalls. I had to constantly clean the snow from my parking space and leave early to be at work on time. I was sorry I had passed up the opportunity to retire.

One day I came to work earlier for the afternoon shift and met two top supervisors in the lunchroom. We had a short conversation. "Hi, Buz. How are you?" said one of them. "Everything is perfect" was my answer. "Repeat what you said" was his request.

"I said everything is perfect. Is anything wrong?" I asked.

"No," he responded, "but we never hear that kind of answer. Usually, people start complaining but you said 'perfect.' That is unusual."

"It could be better if I was retired but I missed the opportunity. One could be made to retire suddenly," I said, alluding to two workers, who expressed resentment at being forced to retire.

"One of those was overweight with a bad heart condition and the other's wife was in the hospital for a long time so we decided let them go out of compassion. You are healthy and a good worker and close to retirement any way." That ended the conversation.

A month after that conversation I was called to the supervisor's office. It was noontime and I was halfway through my shift. I was told to take a shower before seeing the supervisor and to go home after seeing him. I walked into the supervisor's office and sat down at the desk facing him. He asked if I remembered our talk and asked if I was joking or serious about retiring. I responded, "If all the incentives are paid, I'm serious. If not, then I will continue working." He said, "We discussed your case and decided to let you retire starting now as our appreciation for your good service. Good luck and enjoy your leisure," he said, shaking my hand.

Tamara was surprised to see me home so early and asked what happened. "You're looking at a new pensioner," I said. She congratulated me with a hug. The next day I received a call from work asking me what shift I would be working that day.

"No more shifts for me. I'm retired," I said.

"Who told you that?" asked the voice on the other end.

"Mr. MacCage," I replied.

"Oh no," said the voice. "Things are done differently in this office. You have to give two weeks' notice before you retire."

Good thing I didn't throw away my work clothes in my excitement. I returned to the afternoon shift but my position was already taken so I spent the rest of that shift week making coffee and reading books. The next two days were my scheduled days off and then I returned for the night shift. The lunchroom had been set up for my retirement dinner. The long table was covered with newspaper and set with disposable plates and lots of Chinese food. We ate a good meal and I got lots of memorabilia from work as a present. After the meal the shift boss told me to go home and remain at home the rest of the week. He said he would punch my card at the beginning and end of every shift. After thirty years of service, my retirement date was January 1, 1984.

I was never bored after retirement because there was always something to do. During our long winters there was generally lots of snow and I cleaned a few driveways on the street for disabled, elderly people. In 1986 we took a road trip across Canada to see the World's Fair in Vancouver. As we were travelling, Tamara and I were impressed to see endless prairies with rows of oil pumps extracting oil right in the middle of wheat fields. The Okanagan Valley in British Columbia was so scenic with apple orchards on the shores of a lake and vineyards on the mountain slopes, with modern wineries nearby. We stayed with friends who were transplants from Ontario and enjoyed their generous hospitality. We also enjoyed what we saw at the World Fair as we walked the exhibition grounds for three days.

I have always enjoyed learning, so after I retired, I took a class on Religious Studies at Laurentian University. It was taught by Dr. John Sahadat, whose family had immigrated to Canada from Trinidad. I first met John when he was a student at Laurentian University. He lived with Pastor Manhood's family and on Sundays he preached at All Nations Church when it was located on Churchill Street. After graduation he left town and I didn't see him for six years. He left to get his Doctorate degree in India and when he returned it was to inspire and motivate others.

A friend from post-war Europe, Don Hourtovenko, and his wife, Sophia, began attending All Nations church in the late 1970s. It struck me as being curious because he had been so active in the Pentecostal church. In fact, he had helped in the construction of their church building. He didn't offer an explanation and I didn't want to pry so I never found out why. In 1980, All Nations needed a larger facility to accommodate their growing membership and bought the Pentecostal Church building that the Hourtovenkos used to attend. When All Nations moved to that building, they left and joined the Slavic Baptist congregation on Lansdowne Street so I figured he must have some emotional connection with that place.

We still attended the Slavic Baptist church on special occasions but after my retirement, Don talked to us about rejoining that congregation. He said that the English-speaking people were okay without us and that we should stick together and help this smaller community. Tamara and I didn't like the idea of skipping from one church to another so I talked to Pastor Mahood about it and he approved the idea. He said that if we could be useful there than we should serve there.

Soon after we started attending church, we were visited by two members of the Slavic Baptist Union. Pastor Peter Kolybajev, the Chairperson of the Slavic Baptist Union asked me if I would teach Sunday school. I heard my inner voice saying I wasn't qualified and that I didn't know the Bible well enough to teach so I told him that I would think about it. They were back the next week and called a prayer meeting. They were persistent about me teaching and even though I found myself in a really shaky situation, I agreed, knowing that I would only succeed with God's help. Tamara was elected to be the secretary and bookkeeper at the same meeting. The former bookkeeper handed Tamara a scribbler with the first page missing and three months of data. There was no money to pay utilities and heating. We found out that Hoyenko has been paying the bills out of his own pocket. After a serious discussion Tamara ordered collection envelopes.

The members of this little church were somewhat stingy in their giving. Even a $10 bill in the collection plate would be a rarity. The Sunday after the meeting, Don whispered to me that he and I should put $20 in the plate and watch what happened. I followed his lead and we watched the reaction of the other members. In a few weeks every member was putting $20 into the offering. In a short while there was enough money to pay off the bills and we opened a savings account at the bank of Nova Scotia.

After I had been teaching Sunday school for a few months, the leader of the congregation, Ivan Krupp, asked me if I would consider changing positions with him. He wanted me to preach and he would lead Sunday school. He felt that I was better educated and better equipped to deliver God's word to the congregation than he was. Pastor Kolybajev was invited, a prayer meeting was called, and our positions switched. The following years were a time of great spiritual growth as I was constantly reading and studying to prepare a message for every Sunday.

Slowly the congregation began to get smaller and smaller. Some of the older members had passed away and many families had moved. In the early 1990s the congregation consisted of only a handful of people. They agreed that it was time to close down the church and join other congregations. Tamara and I went back to All Nations Church and remained there.

Chapter 18

Simon Kartaszow

My father-in-law, Simon Kartaszow, was born in 1900, in Temryuk, a Cossack settlement on the shore of the Azov Sea. He had two brothers and two sisters. Like many Cossacks, his father was a well-to-do member of the Cossack community. In 1917, the country was in a Civil War, with brothers literally fighting against brothers and sons against fathers. Being a peaceful man, Simon's father tried to keep his sons out of the war. The college Simon was attending was closed so Simon returned home to wait for the end of the war but as he watched the Red Guard terrorizing people and confiscating their property, his Cossack temper prompted him to join the White Guards as a volunteer. Eventually the White Guards lost the war and left Russia. The majority settled in Yugoslavia, and some moved to France.

After wandering among people with a strange culture and language, Simon and a dozen of his friends chose to settle in the eastern part of Poland. He found employment at a railroad station in Bluden. He eventually married, built a house, and lived peacefully. After his first child was born, his mother-in-law gave him a cow. Apart from being homesick, Simon was a happy man, content with what he had. He could have gotten a better job if he became a Polish citizen but his patriotic spirit would not allow him to abandon his country. He hoped that one day in the near future he would be able to return home, where the soil was rich and the climate was warm. As he waited for that day, the family grew to five children. They were taught German by a tutor. The two oldest children, Luba and Tamara, were taught to knit at an early age and were able to contribute to the family budget by knitting socks and sweaters for people.

Life was peaceful until Germany attacked western Poland, on September 1, 1939. People started to behave like ants in a disturbed ant colony and some Jewish families disappeared from the village. Two weeks later the Soviet Union occupied western Ukraine and Belorussia and on September 17, 1939, they invaded Poland from the east. Soviet propaganda was hard at work in that part of Poland trying to convince the people that they were being exploited by the Polish nobility and the Russian Amy was coming to liberate them from the oppression of the land owners. Some young men couldn't wait to be liberated by the Soviets and left the village one night to cross the border.

Some of Simon's friends joined a secret organization of Soviet patriots. They were distributing propaganda leaflets and waiting for liberation day. Simon saw a bundle of leaflets in his neighbor's house but kept quiet and saved him from going to prison, for his children's sake. His friend made a good salary. He and his wife had four daughters and one son. Two oldest girls studied German and were tutored by a Jewish lady. On weekends, they enjoyed get-togethers with friends, playing cards, playing stringed instruments, and singing Cossack folksongs.

When the Russians arrived at the village, the *Friends of the Soviet Union* met the "liberators" with red banners. Girls donned red kerchiefs and ran from house to house with the good news. They urged the parents to dress their children in their best clothing and come out to meet the liberators. Simon's neighbor and like-minded friends organized the people of the village to greet the Soviet soldiers with a loaf of bread and salt (an eastern European greeting ceremony).

Meanwhile, there was no news about the young men who had left earlier for Russia. After what they had lived through, Simon and his friends speculated that they could have been shot at the border as spies or they could have been sent to a concentration camp. People were quietly watching to see what this "liberation" would turn out to be. Simon also heard his neighbor predicting that soon members of the White Guard, like Simon, would be hanging on telephone poles.

The Soviet propaganda motto read, "We stretch out our arms for a brotherly handshake." At the same time the liberators whispered among themselves, "We will stretch out our arms but soon you will stretch your legs." That meant being starved to death. In two weeks' time privately owned stores were closed and owners disappeared. Shelves were empty in the remaining cooperatives. The last items left in the store were wash rags and brooms made from birch twigs. The church was closed down, the cross and bells removed, and the building was converted into a bakery. People lined up early every morning to purchase bread. On Sundays they worshiped at the small chapel at the cemetery.

Simon was ordered to work in a lumber camp for much less money and that put the family into financial hardship. His mother-in-law started to provide milk and vegetables for his family but that didn't last very long. The local priest had resigned and left the village a few months before the occupation, and his aged father-in-law took his position. Now the old man was working with Simon as a lumberjack.

The local garrison was located in an old school building but there wasn't enough room so some soldiers slept in private homes. Simon had to accommodate a dozen soldiers, but in a way, it was a helpful arrangement for his family. One time a petty officer observed that the family didn't have bread and ordered two loaves from the bakery. When the soldiers moved out, they left behind a sack full of dry biscuits and bales of hay in the stable. Politics aside, they were not the enemy.

By chance, or so it seemed at the time, Simon met a petty officer from his home town. The officer befriended Simon and talked about the hardships he encountered on the Finnish front because of a very cold winter. The reason for the mysterious chance encounter was answered a short time later when Simon was suddenly sent to Brest on business. His wife gathered all the money they had to purchase shoes for the girls, believing something had to be available in the city.

At the railroad station in Brest, he was met by two KGB agents in civilian clothing and was ordered to walk between them to the office. Their maneuver was clean and simple. He wasn't formally arrested but was locked up and detained for several days. During that time, he was interrogated and beaten in such a way so as not to leave distinctive marks on the outside but to damage organs on the inside. After signing a paper not divulge where he was or what had transpired, he was released with the parting words that he was a fortunate man to have a large family. "There is no room for scum like you, not even in Kamchatka," he was told. "You are going home now because of your five children, but we will get you soon.

Barely alive, Simon came home empty handed. He was in excruciating stomach pain and mentally in a dungeon. He couldn't share his experience with his wife, couldn't plan for the future, couldn't travel farther than his job and couldn't sell anything from his house. His wife didn't know what he went through and gave him a dressing down for being so incompetent. She said that other people travelled to Brest to go shopping and found what they needed in the open market, but he couldn't tell her anything. He was afraid that if she knew she might openly curse the occupiers and get the whole family into trouble. He felt shackled in body and soul. A couple of times he asked her to prepare dry biscuits, something his injured stomach would be able to tolerate, but she didn't get the hint. He also had to return to work without the proper winter clothing.

The children lived in their own world. They all studied diligently and participated in school activities. For New Years, the school staged a play ridiculing old customs and religion. Simon's son, Walter played a priest and used his mother's black dress as the costume. The children were always unsure about how to act around their mother because they were sometimes told to do something at school and were not sure what her reaction would be. For example, one time their mother slapped Luba for singing a song about Stalin. Another time, a teacher told Tamara to make a list of prospective Pioneer members (the Communist youth). When she returned the list without her name on it, the teacher asked why and she didn't have an answer. She knew her mother would slap her for putting her name on the list, but then she thought that if she didn't, it might have an adverse effect for her father. She decided to add her name but did not wear the red neck tie.

After some discussion with the family, Simon decided to write a letter to his brother in the Soviet Union. His daughters also wrote their uncle and received a response from their cousin. It was clear that they were not surprised by the letter. Simon's niece wrote that the KGB had been to visit them and knew about Simon and his family. Eventually Simon's brother wrote back to him saying his daughter was getting ready to start studying at the university and continued correspondence might damage her reputation. After that they stop writing.

During the winter, so-called untrustworthy people disappeared from the city. In early springtime, several cattle cars of people were shipped out. They were roused from their sleep during the night and loaded onto trains without proper clothing. Local activists, like Simon's neighbor, decided the fate of the families that were taken away and before train had even left the station their homes were looted by the same activists. "Rob what is robbed" was their slogan.

On June 20th, one of these trains appeared at a nearby station. By then people knew from experience what would come but Saturday passed without incident. Simon's family spent the night fully clothed, just waiting for the knock at the door during the night. On Sunday morning, the children went to chapel just to get out of the house and their mother told Luba and Tamara not to look for them if they were gone. It was a warm, quiet day. People left after the chapel service. Young people walked in groups chatting and laughing. Suddenly the sound of an explosion attracted everybody's attention toward the railroad station in Bereza. A German plane roared by firing at the train with a machine gun. People ran in a panic to hide behind buildings and some hit the ground. That was the beginning of countless suffering in the world, but for Simon's family it was salvation from Soviet exile.

Tamara and I visited Bluden, Poland, her birthplace, in 1993, after more than seventy years since the start of WWII. As we were walking along the street with her second cousin, we met two elderly men riding in a horse cart. The men stopped to ask if we came from Canada. Tamara explained who she was and how her family left the country in 1943. One man introduced himself as a retired school teacher and the other said he was a former chief of police in the village. He knew Simon Kartaszow and remembered his name being on the list of people identified for resettlement. This old man was still thinking in terms of resettlement but for people like my father-in-law it was exile and possible death along the way.

The first days after the Germans attacked were absolute chaos. The Soviet army retreated hastily and the local administration dissolved. Local people took turns guarding their villages at night. The German soldiers came and first started to look for stray Russian soldiers. Simon got captured, because his head was shaven like a typical soldier. His children ran after the column of prisoners, calling, "Papa!" A German soldier asked the girls to identify their father and let Simon go. That same day three stray solders were found hiding in a farmer's barn and were shot on the spot.

Simon's neighbor became a frequent guest at his house but now acted like he was ready to kiss Simon's feet instead of hanging him on a pole. The Germans put him to work in a steam engine repair shop at the railway station. Local guerrillas were sabotaging trains by hiding explosives in chunks of coal. When the doctored coal was shoveled into the furnace it would explode and destroy the engine. A local engine was eventually sabotaged and, in retaliation, the Germans shot the families of those who worked in the shop. Simon's neighbor perished with his whole family.

That first winter the Germans were jubilant. They ruled the occupied territories according their laws and forcibly took young people to Germany as slaves. People were obligated to work for daily rations and farmers were expected to deliver a certain quota of everything they produced. Despite the guerrilla activity against the German occupants the railroad functioned with little interruptions. Trains with military equipment travelled to the east and those with wounded soldiers to the west.

The Bauzug, a train belonging to a construction firm, arrived at the station with a labor gang of fifty people. Simon met the foreman of the gang by chance, an elderly German by the name of Muller, who was suffering from ulcers and wanted to know where he could get some milk. Simon said he would be able to provide a small amount of milk regularly and invited the German to his home for tea. Eventually they got to know each other and came to understand that they were not enemies. Muller gave Simon a job as a delivery man for the labor gang. Simon's wife, Maria, and his eldest daughter Luba, worked in the kitchen as cooks. Tamara was assigned to the grain depot as a bookkeeper. This arrangement saved the girls from being shipped to Germany as slave labor.

After Germany lost the battle of Stalingrad, the situation on the front was reversed and the German forces were in constant retreat. The Front Line moved close to the former Polish border. Almost all those who hated Soviet rule had already left. Simon knew that he couldn't wait for the Soviet KGB. The best he could expect from them was a bullet in the head. Muller told Simon that his train would be leaving soon. He knew about Simon's predicament and offered a boxcar to load his family and belongings and move out with them. "For your goodness to me in your country, I'll try to do good for you in my country," Muller said. The very next evening the train left the station with Simon's family in one car and his cow and chickens in the other.

To avoid enemy planes trains moved only at night. It took a whole week to reach the western border of Poland where the majority of the population were Germans. This area did not seem to have been affected by the war in that even though ration capons were in effect the stores were full of merchandise. People were friendly toward the evacuees and willing to help in whatever way they could. After a short stay the train continued toward the west until it reached the suburbs of Munich, in Bavaria. Workers were distributed among the remaining factories in the city and traveled to work on street cars while Allied planes flew over the city by the scores to bomb cities on the Baltic Sea.

Every time the air raid sirens went off the people ran to bunkers or to an open field. In the spring of 1945, a few months before the war ended, Tamara ran to a field when the sirens went off. She lay down on the green grass, fell asleep and caught pneumonia. She was kept in a hospital for *Ostarbeiters* (foreign slave workers from occupied Europe) until her condition became very grave. A German doctor transferred her to a hospital for Germans under the care of Catholic nuns and that saved her life. After spending six weeks in the hospital, her condition improved, but she wasn't ready to be discharged. Luba came to visit her with a message from her mother saying that she had to return home because rumors were going around that they would be relocated. Tamara was released after promising the doctor that she would take good care of herself.

While she was in the hospital, her brother, Walter, got into trouble by stealing something. Muller was able to smooth things over so he wouldn't have to face punishment, but he got a severe beating from his mother. That was too much for a fifteen-year-old boy to bear, so as soon as the war ended, he ran away. Some people said they had seen him in a Polish refugee camp and after a while he disappeared completely. The family accepted the fact that he had returned to Poland.

In April 1945, Munich fell to the Americans and, for the Kartaszow family, the war was over. The only Europeans that were not jubilant were the Russian White Guards, the Russian monarchists, who collaborated with Hitler's Germany. They were interned in a prisoner camp in the Austrian city of Linz and were soon handed over to Soviet Russia. Train loads of war prisoners were delivered to the Russian occupation zone. They were declared traitors of the fatherland by Stalin at the beginning of the war and eventually all of them perished in Soviet concentration camps. People, who lived outside of Russia before 1939 were allowed to stay in International Relief Organization camps so Simon's family was safe from being turned over the Soviets.

In 1946, a year after the war ended, a few rare individuals were eligible to immigrate to the countries of their birth. Simon moved his family to the City of Nurnberg and found work at an Army warehouse. In 1951, he and his family immigrated to the United States and they settled in Phoenixville, Pennsylvania. He found work in a lumberyard and soon gained a reputation as a trustworthy employee. In 1953 he was able to buy a home close to where he worked. He built a carpenter shop in his garage and eventually became a good cabinetmaker. After reaching retirement age, he continued working part time on a cash basis.

All Simon's daughters, Luba, Tamara, Vera, and Maria, did well. They all married, had children and grandchildren, and had careers. A few years before they died, Simon and his wife received a letter from the Soviet Union. After more than forty years they finally heard from their son, Walter. They began to send parcels, which was a tremendous help in those days.

In 1990, Walter and his wife were able to visit their sisters in Pennsylvania. He told them what happened to him after leaving the family behind in 1946. He returned to Poland, graduated from high school, and was drafted to the Polish army. He befriended some Soviet soldiers stationed in Poland and often participated in their drinking parties. This attracted the attention of the KGB and he was called in to chat with them. He denied his origins and who his parents were. He was let go, but after a short while was arrested by the KGB and interrogated. At that meeting the interrogator said, "Walter, let's stop playing games. You can't fool us. Your parents and sisters immigrated to the USA in 1951 and their current address is so and so." This was the first time he had heard where his family was, so he confessed his so-called guilt. He did not understand Soviet politics and lost the game because of his foolishness.

He was sentenced to ten years of hard labor just because of who his father was and was released when the Soviet government ceased to exist. He didn't say where or when he was beaten but he ended up losing a testicle. He was in poor health and a heavy drinker. Parcels from the United States only helped him buy more alcoholic beverages and cut his life short. After his wife passed away, he was left with one son and two daughters. It is not known when he died but it happened before he was old enough to retire.

As they reached their seventies, both Simon and his wife began to decline in health. At one point he agreed to have surgery hoping to regain enough strength to take care of his wife, but she ended up passing away two years before him. Those last years left him lonely and forlorn. He regretted having the surgery that extended his life. He lived to be seventy-eight years old. In my mind Simon's sore spot was that he never got to see his beloved homeland or his son again.

In Loving Memory

Written by Irene Aniol and reprinted with her permission

It is with deep sorrow that the Ilja Buz family siblings announce the death of their father, Sunday, November 29th, 2020. He left this earth to meet his God and to reunite with his precious wife, Tamara, predeceased May 2015.

Ilja was born in a village not far from Komsomoloskoye, state of Chuvasia, Russia, to Alexei and Daria Antonov, and is survived by his sister Vera Antonov, Chuvasia. He is survived by his children: Irene (George Aniol) of Sudbury; Ludmila of London, Ontario; Tatjana (Duncan Pitts) of Florida; Tamara (Peter Bolton) of Durham, Ontario; and Richard (Melissa) of California. Ilja is grandfather to Michael, Donna, Karen, Darrell, Jordan, Larra, Natasha, Rochelle, Natalia, Angelina, and Sophia; and great grandfather to Andrew, Matthew, Hannah, Joseph, Francis, Louis, and Helena.

After graduating from school in his village, Ilja continued his education in Cheboksary, Chuvasia, in Theater Arts. While living in that city, which sits on the Volga River, he also worked as a broadcaster for a radio station until such time as he was drafted into the Russian army to serve in the Second World War.

Ilja was captured by the Germans and was a prisoner of war from 1941–1945. Upon his release, he met up with the American army and worked in their kitchen as a dishwasher, then was moved to a Munich refugee camp until April 1947. Having escaped from this refugee camp, to avoid repatriation, Ilja made his way to Battice, Belgium, where he found work in a coal mine. It is here that Ilja met his wife, Tamara.

Ilja was determined to immigrate to Canada, a land of hope for his family. He worked hard in the coal mine for six years, saved his earnings, and finally saw his dream come true when he landed by ship in Quebec City in July, 1953. Travelling by train, he arrived in Sudbury with his wife and three daughters to a house arranged and prepared by a friend he had met in Germany. Ilja took odd jobs, including work in a lumber camp in Chapleau, until finally getting a job with Falconbridge in the smelter, where he worked for thirty years, retiring in 1984.

Over the years, Ilja took courses to enhance his communication skills and to provide him job opportunities on the side, fixing TVs and wiring homes. After retirement, at the age of sixty-four, he bought a computer, took computer courses, and typed his memoirs. He was also inspired to take a course in religion at Laurentian University. A very bright man, Ilja learned well and flourished in his abilities to pick up more than half a dozen languages, some of which he picked up in Europe. He loved communicating by computer with distant relatives and friends in Siberia, Chuvasia, Russia, Canada, and the USA. Another hobby he enjoyed was gardening, which made him proud of what he was able to reap at summer's end.

Ilja will be remembered for his love of family, his smile, sense of humor, wisdom, and his storytelling. His mind was sharp to the end of his time. He was a man of faith, and having experienced his war years at a young age, he realized he had nothing to fear about life and death. He knew his name was recorded in the Book of Life; God would share him with us and take him "home" at the appropriate time. He left a rich legacy and will be remembered and missed by all who knew him.